C000091536

OXFORD TEXTUAL PERSPECTIVES

Living Through Conquest

GENERAL EDITORS

Elaine Treharne   Greg Walker

Living Through Conquest

The Politics of Early English,
1020–1220

ELAINE TREHARNE

OXFORD
UNIVERSITY PRESS

OXFORD
UNIVERSITY PRESS

Great Clarendon Street, Oxford, OX2 6DP,
United Kingdom

Oxford University Press is a department of the University of Oxford.
It furthers the University's objective of excellence in research, scholarship,
and education by publishing worldwide. Oxford is a registered trade mark of
Oxford University Press in the UK and in certain other countries

British Library Cataloguing in Publication Data
Data available

Library of Congress Cataloging in Publication Data
Data available

ISBN 978–0–19–958525–0 (hbk.)
978–0–19–958526–7 (pbk.)

Printed in Great Britain by
MPG Books Group, Bodmin and King's Lynn

For A, J, I, and Mum

SERIES EDITORS' PREFACE

Oxford Textual Perspectives is a new series of informative and provocative studies focused upon texts (conceived of in the broadest sense of that term) and the technologies, cultures and communities that produce, inform, and receive them. It provides fresh interpretations of fundamental works, images and artefacts, and of the vital and challenging issues emerging in English literary studies. By engaging with the contexts and materiality of the text, its production, transmission, and reception history, and by frequently testing and exploring the boundaries of the notions of text and meaning themselves, the volumes in the series question conventional frameworks and provide innovative interpretations of both canonical and less well-known works. These books will offer new perspectives, and challenge familiar ones, both on and through texts and textual communities. While they focus on specific authors, periods, and issues, they nonetheless scan wider horizons, addressing themes and provoking questions that have a more general application to literary studies and cultural history as a whole. Each is designed to be as accessible to the non-specialist reader as it is fresh and rewarding for the specialist, combining an informative orientation in a landscape with detailed analysis of the territory and suggestions for further travel.

Elaine Treharne and Greg Walker

PREFACE

This book has been a long time coming. I have been publishing on eleventh- and twelfth-century English for years now, but what seems so familiar and obvious to me may yet surprise and interest readers. Much that is exciting about this period in the literary history of English has been under-represented in scholarly discussion, and, together with scholars such as Aidan Conti, Orietta Da Rold, Patrick W. Conner, Mark Faulkner, Susan Irvine, Kathryn Lowe, Stephen Pelle, Mary P. Richards, Don Scragg, Mary Swan, and George Younge, I have sought to show how significant the English vernacular materials produced in the later eleventh and twelfth centuries are for our understanding of the development of textual culture in England; how important English is as a political, intellectual, religious, and ideological tool through two conquests and beyond. I owe these scholars a large debt, and particularly so to Mary Swan and Orietta Da Rold, who, as Co-Directors of the AHRC-funded project, 'The Production and Use of English, 1060 to 1220', have played a major role in the development of my thinking over the years, and with whom I have shared long and productive conversations, and learned a great deal.

I am immensely grateful to the libraries and librarians who have facilitated my work and who have made my visits a great pleasure; I should especially like to thank Gill Cannell and Suzanne Paul at the Parker Library, and Sandy Paul at the Wren Library. Staff at the British Library, the librarians at the University of Leicester, and those at Florida State University have been immeasurably helpful (thank you especially to William Modrow, Ben Yadon, and Jane Pinzino). Thanks to Brepols Publishers for permission to include small extracts of 'Categorization, Periodization: The Silence of (the) English in the Twelfth Century' (*New Medieval Literatures* 8 [2006], pp. 248–75) into Chapter 7.

My colleagues while I was at Leicester were a source of inspiration and support: Gordon Campbell, Jo Story, Anne Marie D'Arcy, Jayne Carroll, and other members of the English Department—thank you. A number of friends in the profession have helped shape my ideas, including Pat Conner, Nick Doane, Rick Emmerson, Martin Foys, Jill Frederick, Joyce

Hill, Matt Hussey, David Johnson, Chris Jones, Catherine Karkov, Clare Lees, Roy Liuzza, Andrew McNeillie, Bella Millett, Gale Owen-Crocker, Caroline Palmer, Alex Rumble, Don Scragg, William Stoneman, Peter Stokes, Matt Townend, Elizabeth Tyler, and Jocelyn Wogan-Browne. My sincere thanks to Laura Ashe, Tom Bredehoft, Orietta Da Rold, Andrew Prescott, Greg Walker, and George Younge for reading parts or all of this book. I should especially like to remember with gratitude Derek Brewer, Steve Glosecki, Nick Howe, and Phillip Pulsiano. I thank them, and those who have listened to and commented upon my publications, conference papers, and lectures and have provided useful critical feedback. Thanks particularly to those who participated in the excellent Obermann Centre, Extreme Materialist Readings of Medieval Books Workshop organized by Jon Wilcox at the University of Iowa in 2008, which altered my research trajectory.

Of course, I didn't get where I am today without the assistance of Professor Greg Walker's supply of Extra Strong Mints, unstinting friendship and wise advice; and to my family, the Treharne-Fryetts, diolch i chi gyd am eich cariad mawr. This book is for them.

ET

Tallahassee,
St Neot's Feastday

CONTENTS

LIST OF ILLUSTRATIONS

ABBREVIATIONS

BL	British Library
Bod.	Oxford, Bodleian Library
Camb.	Cambridge
C'bury	Canterbury
CCCC	Cambridge, Corpus Christi College
Clemoes, *CHI*	P. Clemoes (ed.), *Ælfric's Catholic Homilies: The First Series: Text*, EETS s.s. 17 (London: Oxford University Press, 1997)
CUL	Cambridge University Library
Dictionary of Old English	Antonette diPaolo Healey, with John Price Wilkin and Xin Xiang (ed.), *Dictionary of Old English Web Corpus* (Toronto: University of Toronto Press, 2011) [http://tir.doe.utoronto.ca/index.html]
EETS	Early English Texts Society
EHD	Dorothy Whitelock (ed.), *English Historical Documents*, vol. i: *c. 500–1042* (London: Eyre and Spottiswoode, 1955
ex	(in relation to manuscript dating) end of
Gesta Pontificum Anglorum	M. Winterbottom (ed. and trans.), William of Malmesbury, *Gesta Pontificum Anglorum*, Oxford Medieval Texts, 2 vols. (Oxford: Clarendon Press, 2007)
Gesta Regum Anglorum	R. A. B. Mynors, R. M. Thomson, and M. Winterbottom (eds. and trans.), *William of Malmesbury, Gesta Regum Anglorum: The History of the English Kings*, Oxford Medieval Texts, 2 vols. (Oxford: Clarendon Press, 1998)
Godden, *CHII*	Malcolm Godden (ed.), *Ælfric's Catholic Homilies: The Second Series Text*, EETS s.s. 5 (London: Oxford University Press, 1979)
Ker, *Catalogue*	Neil R. Ker, *Catalogue of Manuscripts containing Anglo-Saxon* (Oxford: Clarendon Press, 1957; repr. with Supplement, 1990)

med.	(in relation to manuscript dating) middle of
MS	manuscript
n.s.	new series
o.s.	Original Series
ODNB	*Oxford Dictionary of National Biography*
RES	*Review of English Studies*
s. xi[in-2]	*saeculum* (century): beginning to the second half of the eleventh century
s.s.	Supplementary Series

Introduction

'Their dialect, proverbs, and songs'[1]
The Context of Conquest

In 1932, R. W. Chambers pointed out that 'today it is generally denied that there is any continuity in the history of English prose':[2]

> Of course the Conqueror did not land at Pevensey with any deliberate intention of destroying the English nationality and the English language; but it was an inevitable consequence of the Conquest that both were nearly destroyed.[3]

But there was nothing 'inevitable' about events after the Conquest, just as there had not been a mere fifty years earlier in 1016 following the conquest of Cnut. For a good many years after 1016 or 1066, the English presumably had no inkling that the conquerors were a permanent fixture; indeed, Cnut and his brief dynasty had not been. It could not have been obvious either that William's victory of 1066 was assured, or that English

---

[1] Rudyard Kipling, in C. J. Fletcher and Rudyard Kipling, *A History of England* (Oxford: Clarendon Press, 1911), pp. 51–3. All of the chapters in this book use quotations from Kipling's poetry to remind readers of the complexity and longevity of colonialism.

[2] R. W. Chambers (ed.), *On the Continuity of English Prose from Alfred to More and his School*, EETS o.s. 191A (London: Oxford University Press, 1932), p. lvi.

[3] Chambers, *Continuity of English Prose*, p. lxxxii.

would, apparently, lose its prestigious position as a major written language. Cnut's conquest, fifty years earlier, had not succeeded in supplanting English; nor had Cnut aimed to achieve anything of the kind, even though this was still a period of cultural trauma. A teleological interpretation like Chambers's, encouraged by the benefit of hindsight, tempts us to assume the virtual demise of the Old English literary tradition, and with it 'English nationality and the English language'. This is a misreading, but one that has been so often repeated that the supposed death of English literature after the Norman Conquest has become an accepted part of literary history recounted by most standard analyses of the period.[4] This perceived hiatus in the production of English texts has contributed to the notion that the 'Old' English period ended shortly after October 14th 1066, and it was not until the advent of Early Middle English that a new literary heritage was born, endowed with those qualities of originality and 'importance' that the majority of contemporary scholars seem most to value.[5]

Textual Separation: Chronologies

The division of literary history into ever more precise and specific periods and interests is a familiar, and perhaps inevitable consequence of the politicization of university curricula, professional associations and academic subject areas. Our need to mark out and 'defend' our teaching and research specialisms, coupled with the modern obsession with labelling and categorizing, make it unsurprising that literary-historical eras such as 'the medieval' are broken down yet further into 'Anglo-Saxon', 'Old' or 'Middle' English. These superficially imposed divisions of English literary and linguistic

---

[4] For example, David Wallace (ed.), *The Cambridge History of Medieval English Literature* (Cambridge: Cambridge University Press, 1999) begins in 1066. This presumes literature prior to 1066 should not be considered 'medieval'. A dozen years after the publication of this volume, Cambridge University Press has commissioned the *Cambridge History of Early Medieval English Literature*, to be edited by Professor Clare Lees. For other scholarship denying English literature exists from *c.*1066 to 1200 or so, see Chapter 5 below.

[5] On this, see Christopher Cannon, *The Grounds of English Literature* (Oxford: Oxford University Press, 2004), who, while decrying the neglect of early literature nevertheless perpetuates the same myth, treating only the *Anglo-Saxon Chronicle* from the pre-1100 period, and erroneously claiming *The Worcester Fragments* for the eleventh century. His first chapter is called 'The Loss of Literature 1066'.

development identify broad historical differences, but have resulted in the neglect of those texts that fall into the gap of c.1060–c.1200, a gap created because the majority of the surviving texts produced in the twelfth century are clearly not 'Old English' or 'Anglo-Saxon', since they fall without the chronology of that political state, and illustrate numerous, systematic changes in the language used, but they are so obviously not Middle English either, in terms of their dependency on earlier English materials, and their varying proximity to the literary Standard, late West Saxon.[6] There is a larger issue here, too, of what is retained and what is excluded in the formation of the cultural history of a modern nation state. One might argue that the emerging sense of English identity in the eighteenth and nineteenth centuries contributed to the creation of an understanding of 'England' that was essentially post-Conquest, and that everything that went before that landmark event in 1066 was something other, partly because the Norman government ceased to use English shortly after coming to power.[7] When English reappears as a dominant language, it is no longer 'Old', but 'Middle', even though the literature is often amalgamated into the 'Medieval'.

The chronological demarcation of English literature as 'Medieval' has been an issue for comment since at least 1930 when Kemp Malone published 'When did Middle English begin?'[8] Roger Lass's essay, 'Language

---

[6] This is with the obvious, and important, exception of the *Ormulum* and a number of other twelfth-century homiletic and devotional texts. In the nineteenth century, Richard Morris published his two volumes of late twelfth- and early thirteenth-century homilies under the titles *Old English Homilies and Homiletic Treatises of the Twelfth and Thirteenth Centuries*, Series I and II, EETS o.s. 29, 24, 53 (London: Oxford University Press, 1873; repr. as 2 vols., Woodbridge: Boydell and Brewer, 1998). See also Mary Swan and Elaine Treharne (eds.), *Rewriting Old English in the Twelfth Century*, Cambridge Studies in Anglo-Saxon England 30 (Cambridge: Cambridge University Press, 2000), 'Introduction', pp. 1–10.

[7] See e.g. Benedict Anderson, *Imagined Communities: Reflections on the Origin and Spread of Nationalism* (London: Verso Books, 1991), p. 201; and Krishan Kumar, *The Making of English National Identity* (Cambridge: Cambridge University Press, 2003), pp. 39–59, although it is difficult to agree with all the assertions made. Thanks to Andrew Prescott for discussing this with me.

[8] In J. T. Hatfield, W. Leopold and A. J. F. Ziegelschmidt (eds.), *Curme volume of linguistic studies*, Language Monographs 7 (Baltimore: Waverley Press, 1930), pp. 110–17. Chambers, *Continuity of English Prose*, p. lxxxvi, knows exactly when it began: 'if a line must be drawn between Old English and Middle English, it would, I think, have to come between the man who wrote the Peterborough annal for 1131, and the man who wrote (perhaps about 1155) the Peterborough annal for 1132.' Simon Horobin and Jeremy Smith, *An Introduction to Middle English* (Edinburgh: Edinburgh University Press, 2002), p. 1, regard Middle English as 'the form of the English language which was spoken and written in England between c.1100 and c.1500'.

Periodization and the Concept "Middle" ', tackles precisely this issue,[9] challenging scholars in the field to re-think the taxonomy that marks out the boundaries of what he calls the 'Triadomany' of 'Old', 'Middle', and 'Modern' English.[10] Such a threesome does not include the complicating and commonly-used additional labels of 'early Old', 'late Old', 'classical Old', 'Standard Old', 'transitional', 'early Middle', and 'late Middle'. Lass effectively demonstrates the arbitrary nature of the labels assigned to the evolution of English during the nineteenth century by influential scholars such as Henry Sweet and Thomas Wright. Despite subsequent attempts by linguists and anthologists to particularize moments in the development of the language, successive generations of scholars have chosen to concretize the demarcations postulated by Sweet. Yet, as Lass says, 'A little reflection shows that, crucially, if a language history is long enough, it has no middle; or, to put it another way, if it *continues* long enough, the "Middle" perpetually shifts to the right.'[11]

Textual Separation: Hierarchies

It is not only the English texts produced from *c.*1060 to 1220 that fall into the shadows, however; many English texts produced from about 1020 to 1060 also slip out of sight because of the emphasis in scholarship on 'original' literature, and particularly literature that is poetic or 'creative'. Scholars work on sources that are 'literary' (poetic or highly rhetorical and sophisticated prose) or original. But creativity is not confined to originators, and one of the real achievements of the Early English period is the very many manuscript compilers, authors or co-writers who recreated texts in new contexts. They demonstrate an ability to produce vernacular texts that are relevant to their own historical moments, evincing a belief in the prestige of English; and they clearly understand the utility of English texts for many different purposes. These are aspects of cultural and intellectual expression that have been underestimated because of a persistent scholarly focus on named authors, identifiable movements,

---

[9] In Irma Taavitsainen, Terttu Nevalainen, Päiva Pahta, and Matti Rissanen (eds.), *Placing Middle English in Context*, Topics in English Linguistics 35 (Berlin: Mouton de Gruyter, 2000), pp. 7–41.

[10] Lass, 'Language Periodization', esp. pp. 10–14.

[11] Lass, 'Language Periodization', p. 10.

intellectual distinctiveness, and, to coin Allen Frantzen's phrase, 'a desire for origins'.[12]

In our hierarchies and insistence on known origins and expressible characteristics, the many quotidian English texts manufactured in the years following the first conquest in 1016, with very few exceptions, become penumbral, uncategorizable, and easily ignored. 1016 follows the death of the greatest of Old English writers, Ælfric of Eynsham; it is the period after Wulfstan's greatest moment with his *Sermo Lupi ad Anglos* written in 1014; and it is the end of the generation that anthologized the major works of the magnificent Anglo-Saxon poetic tradition. The neglect of most texts that come after the zenith of Old English literary achievement can only be attributed to the conceptual invisibility of 'copies' or 'later versions' of the original. Such texts literally remain unseen. The derogation of the 'copy', as if such a thing could ever in fact exist in manuscript culture, initially blinkers modern readers to the interpretative possibilities of multiple functions offered by these native vernacular works. The moment of *original* composition is privileged as the only moment of significance when, really, each manifestation of a text has a great deal to reveal about its creator's intentions, purpose, and rhetorical situation. Given that from about 1020 or so there is barely any 'original' writing in English at all until about 1170, it is time to reappraise what exists, how it is classified and what its function might be, to gain, perhaps, a more nuanced and realistic picture of English literary history.

Textual Fragmentation

The manuscripts compiled from 1020 or so until the beginning of the thirteenth century have been the focus of a number of different kinds of examination. The most obvious is the edition of the text (the earliest version usually being selected as the base text) and the common appearance

---

[12] Allen Frantzen (ed.), *Desire for Origins: New Language, Old English, and Teaching the Tradition* (New Brunswick, NJ: Rutgers University Press, 1991).

of later versions as variants in the apparatus beneath the 'original' text.[13] These variants include spelling and lexical differences and differences in word order between the base text and the other versions, such that only bits and pieces of later versions of English texts appear on the edited page at all. With one or two exceptions,[14] all of these scholarly publications, important and fundamental as they are, have resulted in a fragmentation of the late eleventh- and twelfth-century English material remains. Moreover, in the work of editors, while some variant spellings or lexemes are provided in the apparatus at the foot of the page, not all are.[15] This creates the effect of a giant jigsaw puzzle, many parts of which are missing. The late witnesses to the Old English homiletic tradition are, thus, employed for what they can demonstrate from a stemmatic perspective, but have not been studied in their own right, until very recently.[16] Whereas in contemporary editorial policy, the latest version of an author's work would be used for publication (the final corrected edition of a Henry James novel, say), for Anglo-Saxon editors, the last versions of Ælfric or Wulfstan or the Vercelli Homilies are regarded as

[13] A. S. Napier (ed.), *Wulfstan: Sammlung der ihm Zugeschriebenen Homilien nebst Untersuchungen über ihre Echtheit*, Sammlung englischer Denkmäler in kritischen Ausgaben, 4 (Berlin: Weidmann,1883); Dorothy Bethurum (ed.), *The Homilies of Wulfstan* (Oxford: Clarendon Press, 1957); John C. Pope (ed.), *Homilies of Ælfric: A Supplementary Collection*, EETS o.s. 269, 260 (London: Oxford University Press, 1967–8); M. Godden (ed.), *Ælfric's Catholic Homilies: The Second Series Text*, EETS s.s. 5 (London: Oxford University Press, 1979); D. G. Scragg (ed.), *The Vercelli Homilies and Related Texts*, EETS o.s. 300 (London: Oxford University Press, 1992); S. Irvine (ed.), *Old English Homilies from MS Bodley 343*, EETS o.s. 302 (Oxford: Oxford University Press, 2003); P. Clemoes (ed.), *Ælfric's Catholic Homilies: The First Series: Text*, EETS s.s. 17 (London: Oxford University Press, 1997).

[14] Richard Morris (ed. and trans.), *Old English Homilies of the Twelfth Century*, EETS o.s. 53 (London, 1873); R.-N. Warner (ed.), *Early English Homilies from the Twelfth-Century MS. Vesp. D. XIV*, Early English Text Society o.s. 152 (London, 1917 for 1915. Only the first of two proposed volumes ever appeared.); A. O. Belfour (ed.), *Twelfth-Century Homilies in MS. Bodley 343*, EETS o.s. 118 (London: Oxford University Press 1909); and Irvine, *Old English Homilies*.

[15] Pope, *Homilies of Ælfric*, I. 178, states, for instance: 'Deviations in certain manuscripts of the twelfth century are of course much more numerous, as the apparatus shows in spite of the selectiveness with which variants from the latest ones are treated.'

[16] Mary Swan addresses this issue and demonstrates ways in which later uses of earlier homilies can be studied in 'Holiness Remodelled: Theme and Technique in Old English Composite Homilies', in Beverly Mayne Kienzle et al. (eds.), *Models of Holiness in Medieval Sermons: Proceedings of the International Symposium* (Kalamazoo, May 1995), Textes et Études du Moyen Âge 5 (Louvain-la-Neuve, 1996), pp. 35–46.

'corrupt', 'deviant' or 'too late to be of use'.[17] In many respects, this is entirely legitimate given the function of the scholarly edition to provide an *ur*-text that most closely represents the (often hypothetical) author's intended text, but it also relegates the 'eventful' text[18] of later decades to a category of textual dissolution, unreconstitutable.[19] Any reconstruction of the late text becomes impossible without impracticable recourse to each manuscript version,[20] and while ideally, all extant works would be fully edited, possibly codex by codex, no conventional publisher would contemplate such an undertaking.

Textual Reclamation

This book seeks to raise the profile of not only the significant number and variety of English texts written in the years between 1020 and 1220, but also to provide an overview of their contexts of production. It will be of key importance in my analysis to address the curious obfuscation of these English texts within contemporary scholarship; to look again at the texts as providing evidence for the motivation of their creators; and, on occasion, to speculate upon the ways in which the texts might have been received. I am interested in determining to what extent this

[17] Indeed, it is often implied that late material is uninteresting from the Anglo-Saxonists' perspective. For a stimulating discussion of the agenda in editing texts, see Clare Lees, 'Whose Text is it Anyway? Contexts for Editing Old English Prose', in D. G. Scragg and P. E. Szarmach (eds.), *The Editing of Old English: Papers from the 1990 Manchester Conference* (Woodbridge: Boydell & Brewer, 1994), pp. 97–114.

[18] One of the most sustained and pertinent discussions of the 'eventful text' is to be found in Frantzen, *Desire for Origins*. For the changing nature of the text, see also Joyce Hill's 'Ælfric, Authorial Identity and the Changing Text', in Scragg and Szarmach, *The Editing of Old English*, pp. 177–89.

[19] In the case of the numerous later versions of Ælfric's *Catholic Homilies*, Godden, *CHII*, p. xcv, states that his editorial policy determines that 'Variations in spelling...and punctuation are not recorded, and neither are variations in inflexion where these seem to reflect only the late Old English levellings of endings (though such variations in late manuscripts occasionally need to be cited where they are relevant to more significant variations in early manuscripts).' Implicit in the last clause here is that late variations are simply not significant.

[20] Made somewhat easier, though, by the publication of the ongoing *Anglo-Saxon Manuscripts in Microfiche Facsimile* series (ed. A. N. Doane and M. Hussey, Tempe, AZ: MRTS), and by the increasingly impressive and wide-ranging digitization of manuscripts.

vernacular literary compilation can be regarded as a manifestation of an English national consciousness and collective identity, and that thread underpins all the chapters here, though from many different perspectives.

Chapters 1 and 2 look at the *Letters of Cnut* written in 1020 and 1027 to ascertain how the voice of the conqueror king sought self-validation for his reign. That reign, founded on violence, had major consequences for the Anglo-Saxon political state, and Chapters 3 and 4 try to discover what English texts from the period can reveal about cultural trauma, and its articulation through history and homily. Chapter 5 takes this idea about trauma and identity into the post-Conquest period (post-*Norman* Conquest), focusing on responses to 1066 that range from the historian's to the bishop's, and highlighting the contrasting views that are elicited by the textual remnants. The final three chapters deal specifically with the large corpus of material that survives from the twelfth century, surveying the evidence for the emergence of a specifically English voice, articulating a different story to that promulgated by historians then and now. The politics of English that emerges is one of a language (and by implication, a nation) that cannot be silenced; the writers of English from 1020 to 1220 had a confidence in the authority and status of their language that is consistently shown in and by the surviving manuscripts, even if this authority and status has not been accorded the same endorsement in the modern era, until now.

| 1 |

'And change may be good or evil'[1]

The Process of Conquest

A nglo-Saxon England ceased to exist as a political entity on 14 October 1066, but of course this was not the first time in the eleventh century that the kingdom had been conquered. In 1013, the Danish king, Swein Forkbeard, took the throne from Æthelred II and sent the Anglo-Saxon king into exile; by 1016, Swein's son, Cnut, had gained control of all England in a reign that was to last for nineteen years.[2] This first conquest has received less sustained scholarly attention in comparison with that of the Normans, presumably because the consequences of Cnut's acquisition and maintenance of power seem neither as catastrophic nor as long-lasting, and, equally importantly, are not as well documented.

---

[1] Rudyard Kipling, 'The King's Task' (in C. J. Fletcher and Rudyard Kipling, *A History of England* (Oxford: Clarendon Press, 1911, pp. 51–3). In the final lines of the poem, the Saxons, addressing King Edward, state: 'And change may be good or evil—but we know not what it will bring; | Therefore our king must teach us. That is thy task, O King!'

[2] For a brief account of Cnut's reign, see Simon Keynes, 'Cnut', in Michael Lapidge, John Blair, Simon Keynes, and Donald Scragg (eds.), *The Blackwell Encyclopaedia of Anglo-Saxon England* (Oxford: Blackwell, 1999), pp. 108–9. The standard work on Cnut is M. K. Lawson, *Cnut: England's Viking King* (Stroud: Tempus, 1993). See also Timothy Bolton, *The Empire of Cnut the Great: Conquest and the Consolidation of Power in Northern Europe in the Early Eleventh Century* (Leiden: Brill, 2009).

Following the work of Dorothy Whitelock in particular, the sources
that do exist have been the focus of detailed scrutiny in the last ten years
by some of our most perceptive historians—Simon Keynes, Pauline Stafford and Patrick Wormald among them.[3] Of particular interest has been
the legislative legacy of Cnut; the administrative and political compe-
tency evinced by him and his *witan* during his reign; and the role of
Emma (Ælfgifu), his wife. Unlike the reputation of his English predecessor, Æthelred, Cnut does not seem to have suffered any sustained criticism; indeed, in his biography of Cnut Lawson commented:

> It is sufficiently clear, for example, that Cnut was, by the standards of
> his day, the most successful of all pre-Conquest rulers in Britain.[4]

This high praise, contextualized within an ostensibly objective setting of
'the standards of his day', can be paralleled by the reception often afforded
to William the Conqueror, whose administrative, political and govern-
mental abilities have generated widespread approbation, and for some,
unambiguous praise.[5] And while, from a constitutional, administrative,
and military perspective, panegyric—where it occurs—might be entirely
appropriate, it is valuable to retreat from these dominant emphases of
historical evaluation, and deliberate instead the literary and cultural
responses to the double conquest endured by England in the eleventh
century. The cultural and, particularly, textual consequences of both historical processes can fruitfully be examined for their illumination of
traumatized responses to the process of Conquest.[6] Such analysis has

---

[3] Dorothy Whitelock, 'Wulfstan and the Laws of Cnut', *English Historical Review* 63
(1948), pp. 433–52; Simon Keynes, 'Cnut's Earls', in A. R. Rumble (ed.), *The Reign of Cnut,
King of England, Denmark and Norway* (London: Leicester University Press, 1994),
pp. 43–88; Pauline Stafford, *Unification and Conquest: A Political and Social History of
England in the Tenth and Eleventh Centuries* (London: Hodder Arnold, 1989); P. Wormald,
The Making of English Law: King Alfred to the Twelfth Century. Vol. 1, *Legislation and its
Limits* (Oxford: Blackwell, 1999).

[4] M. K. Lawson, *Cnut: The Danes in England in the Early Eleventh Century*, The Medieval World (London: Longman, 1993), p. 214.

[5] There is a vast literature on the Norman Conquest and William I, and a great deal of
scholarly debate. See, for example, David Carpenter, *The Struggle for Mastery of Britain,
1066–1284* (London: Penguin, 2003); David Crouch, *The Normans: The History of a
Dynasty* (London: Hambledon, 2002); and, for a particularly engaging and sensitive
account, George Garnett, *Conquered England: Kingship, Succession, and Tenure, 1066–1166*
(Oxford: Oxford University Press, 2007).

[6] Conquest is deliberated by Stafford in *Unification and Conquest*.

important implications for issues of power and authority, for language and linguistic contexts, for social and political identities, and for aspects of perceived ethnic allegiance.

The first eleventh-century conquest has garnered far less critical analysis than the second. This may be because of the apparent scarcity of administrative and historical material emanating from the reign of Cnut. The evidence needed to piece the reign together is fragmented, disparate, and crucially limited. The king's modern biographer, M. K. Lawson, comments in relation to Cnut's reign, that:

> Only thirty-six [charters] have survived. Even adding the eight writs, his reign is the least well-represented of any between those of Æthelstan and Edward the Confessor, and seven of the documents we have are fairly definitely later forgeries, while nearly half the rest are suspect...these documents offer little on the important and possibly substantial grants of lands to Scandinavians immediately after Cnut's accession, probably because the majority were never recorded in this form.[7]

It is not just the charters that decline in numbers during Cnut's reign: the *Anglo-Saxon Chronicle*'s entries are also noticeably sparser than preceding reigns; English religious prose seems, from what one can deduce from datable manuscripts, to decline in production, too. One might wonder if this scarcity of textual output exemplifies the shock and concomitant loss occasioned by conquest—a silence that indicates a disbelieving refusal to engage in narrating unfathomable events; or whether it depicts, antithetically, a trauma-*less* period, an interpretation that appears to have gathered scholarly advocates in recent years. The conclusion that the conquest and reign of Cnut occasioned little or no trauma would seem logical, if Stafford is right that an 'increased historical consciousness' results from trauma. Thus, after the year 975:

> with renewal of Viking attacks on England...the old stimulus to the writing of contemporary history had returned. The general result of this is a mass of documentation.[8]

In other words, the trauma of conflict in the later tenth century led to a proliferation of documentation while the relative decline in textual

---

[7] Lawson, *Cnut: The Danes in England*, p. 66.
[8] Stafford, *Unification and Conquest*, p. 11.

production in Cnut's reign would suggest, conversely no, or little, trauma. Indeed, this is Stafford's view within the broader historical context: that '1016 appears less traumatic than 1066, the continuity greater, the dispossession less'; and that '1016 was too soon undone to stimulate long-term comment'.[9]

Acclaimed King

From these statements, and from the contentious conclusion reached by the great Frank Stenton that 'Cnut's reign … was so successful that contemporaries found little to say about it',[10] one would be forgiven for thinking that this first major conquest of Anglo-Saxon England and the crowning of a foreign king passed with little more than a slightly raised English eyebrow. Cnut's successes were many: his military victory over the English, and his claiming of all England after Edmund Ironside's death in 1016; his political acuity in marrying his predecessor's wife— Emma, Æthelred's queen; his intelligent acquisition of the support of Wulfstan, archbishop of York (the greatest statesman of his day, and the mouthpiece of the church in Anglo-Saxon England); his imperial aspirations, and eventual rule over Norway, Denmark, parts of Sweden, and England; and his acceptance by some of his peers in Europe as a Christian king of considerable power.

The single most significant statement of Cnut's power is not documentary, but visual. London, British Library, Stowe 944, the Winchester *Liber Vitae*, made in *c.* 1031 at Winchester, contains a variety of texts, including King Alfred's will and lists of benefactors and confreres of the New Minster.[11] Its frontispiece, at folio 6r, is one of the most discussed and widely known images of any king and queen from the medieval period. In this image (Figure 1), Cnut and his wife Emma (Ælfgifu), are depicted donating a golden cross to the New Minster in a triple horizontal register,

---

[9] Stafford, *Unification and Conquest*, p. 69.

[10] F. M. Stenton, *Anglo-Saxon England*, 3rd edn. (Oxford: Oxford University Press, 1971), p. 399.

[11] Simon Keynes (ed.), *The Liber Vitae of the New Minster and Hyde Abbey Winchester: British Library Stow 944, together with leaves from British Library Cotton Vespasian A. viii and British Library Titus D. xxvii*, Early English Manuscripts in Facsimile 26 (Copenhagen: Rosenkilde and Bagger, 1996).

standing on the earth, with the celestial sphere represented by Christ, Mary and Peter. Mary and Peter are linked by angels to Emma and Cnut in a vertical register. Among the plethora of comments on this image are those that point out how Cnut's piety, so explicit in this image, is somewhat compromised by his sword, which threateningly pierces the frame, symbolizing rule by aggression.[12] However, I propose the sword also symbolizes the power of the Emperor as the authorized temporal equivalent of the Petrine sword, itself invested in the spiritual power of the Pope.[13] This possible allusion to the symbiotic relationship of papacy and crown is the more resonant because the image postdates Cnut's visit to Rome on pilgrimage and to attend the coronation of Conrad II in 1027, when he met the Pope. The whole image is thus the expression of monarchical supremacy, spiritual validation, and imperial ambition. Cnut is at the apex of his career, the archetypal exponent of a glorious self-promotion, and in this, his depiction here is similar to that of his contemporary, Basil II, the Byzantine Emperor also known as Basil 'the Bulgar Slayer', whose famous Psalter image shows him being crowned by archangels, standing on a mound, under which are prostrate subjects.[14] In the Stowe 944 depiction of Cnut's royal generosity and devotion, he is the direct linear descendent of St Peter, with shared ownership of the keys to celestial joy; Cnut's feet are planted squarely on the symbolically global *terra firma*, the imperial heir to the manifestly stylized northern hemisphere upon which he treads. This potential allusion to the *orbis terrarum* ('circle of countries') is illustrative of Cnut's power, holding the world under his feet in a deliberate construction of imperial domination—the *Globus cruciger*

---

[12] Gale Owen-Crocker, 'Pomp, Piety, and Keeping the Woman in her Place: The Dress of Cnut and Ælfgifu-Emma', *Medieval Clothing and Textiles* 1 (2005), pp. 41–52. See, also, Catherine E. Karkov, *The Ruler Portraits of Anglo-Saxon England*, Anglo-Saxon Studies 3 (Woodbridge: Boydell and Brewer, 2004), pp. 121–45, where, at p. 131, she sees Cnut's sword as indicating his guardianship of his kingdom (as Peter's key symbolizes his guardianship of heaven); and Jan Gerchow, 'Prayers for King Cnut: The Liturgical Commemoration of a Conqueror', in Carola Hicks (ed.), *England in the Eleventh Century* (Stamford: Paul Watkins, 1992), pp. 219–38.

[13] Louis Dumont, 'A modified view of our origins: the Christian beginnings of modern individualism', in M. Carrithers, S. Collins and S. Lukes (eds.), *The Category of the Person: Anthropology, Philosophy, History* (Cambridge: Cambridge University Press, 1985), pp. 93–122, at 110–11.

[14] Depicted on the cover and as Plate I of Paul Stephenson, *The Legend of Basil the Bulgar-Slayer* (Cambridge: Cambridge University Press, 2003), from Venice, Library, Cod. Marc. Gr. 17, fol. 3r.

('cross-bearing globe' or 'orb'). This monarchical regalia is reminiscent of the Christ as *salvator mundi* ('saviour of the world') and is a symbol of the authority of other Holy Roman Emperors past—of Charlemagne, of Otto I, and Holy Roman Emperors present—Conrad II, contemporary of Cnut.[15] Interestingly, Christ is depicted as a *maiestas domini* in a mandorla, with the *orbis terrarum* beneath, as we would expect to see if this were a typically Byzantine image; only here, Cnut is interposed between Christ and the globe, a powerful projection of monarchical-imperial iconography.

This famous image in Stowe 944, then, as with much of the other textual evidence that survives to tell the story, seems to provide an impressively positive depiction of Cnut and his queen.[16] Cnut's success as king has resulted in general approbation, though some notes of caution are sounded by historians from Hemming of Worcester and William of Malmesbury to Patrick Wormald. It is thus worth assessing Cnut from the perspective of words and deeds: the actions that he took in relation to the way in which he presented himself, or had himself presented by his advisers. It may be that Cnut's construction both in Stowe 944 and a variety of other texts shows him to be the master of public relations, but this particular image is not consistently borne out by actions undertaken by the king or, indeed, by some of the descriptions of him in vernacular poetry composed in his reign. Moreover, Gale Owen-Crocker demonstrates how some of the features of Cnut's dress in this image are specifically Scandinavian, rather compromising, perhaps, his overt protestations of non-partisanship in his rule over Danish and English.[17] This complexity suggests that Cnut should be regarded as an astute and politically aware monarch, very much in control of the way in which he had himself portrayed to his subjects, and particularly concerned to advocate ethnic unity between the English and the Danes.

---

[15] Leslie Brubaker, *Dictionary of the Middle Ages* (New York, 1982–9), V, p. 564. The Byzantine emperor, Constantine IX (1042–55), is depicted holding a *Globus cruciger* and a sceptre at p. 25 of W. G. Sayles, *Ancient Coin Collecting V: The Romaion-Byzantine Culture* (Iola, WI: Krause Publications, 1998).

[16] Owen-Crocker, 'Pomp, Piety', pp. 48–52, convincingly demonstrates how Emma's role is downplayed in this depiction.

[17] Ibid., pp. 43–7.

FIG 1   London, British Library, Stowe 944, folio 6r

© The British Library Board. Reproduced with permission.

In a recent essay, Matthew Innes employs textual evidence to interpret 'shifting allegiances of local elites' in this period.[18] He perceptively discusses the manipulation of identities and of ethnicity, in part through his discussion of Wulfstan of York's role in presenting Cnut to his subjects. Innes comments on Wulfstan's iteration of 'Cnut's regime as a partnership between Danes and English' where 'the model of legal duality was a powerful one for such cooperation'.[19] Wulfstan died in *c*.1023, and can only have been responsible for advising Cnut for the first seven years of his reign. It is this earlier part of the reign that usually forms the focus for the most detailed critical analyses: those years that saw his Conquest consolidated; law codes issued in the name of Edgar; and acts of penitence and restitution, such as the building of a church at *Assandun* in 1020, the site of the battle between Cnut and Edmund Ironside in 1016.[20]

Focusing on the first decade of Cnut's reign, though, tends to overemphasize Wulfstan's role in creating the king in the image of his 'Golden Age' English predecessors at the expense of Cnut's later activities after Wulfstan's death.[21] In the latter decade of his reign from 1025 to 1035, he was no impotent monarch in need of an ecclesiastical public relations adviser, though Lyfing has been credited with this role; Cnut is not 'the intellectually challenged' king postulated by Patrick Wormald in a typically robust evaluation.[22] The later years of his reign show much more clearly how much less notably his immediate English predecessors might have influenced his actions and his all-important self-positioning.

With regard to his positioning to ensure his acceptance by his old (Danish) and new (English) subjects, the issues of ethnicity and identity are at the forefront of the investigation. Key to this is Innes's declaration that 'Political calculation, not ethnic identification, underpinned the activities...of Cnut'.[23] His ethnic identifications are national, if insular:

[18] Matthew Innes, 'Danelaw Identities: Ethnicity, Regionalism, and Political Allegiance', in Dawn Hadley, and J. D. Richards (eds.), *Cultures in Contact: Scandinavian Settlement in England in the Ninth and Tenth Centuries* (Turnhout: Brepols, 2000), pp. 65–88, at p. 76.

[19] Innes, 'Danelaw Identities', p. 77.

[20] Lawson, *Cnut*, pp. 131–3.

[21] Innes, 'Danelaw Identities', p. 73. See also Wormald, *Making of English Law*, pp. 345–66.

[22] See Wormald, *Making of English Law*, p. 348, for the discussion that Cnut's Second Letter of 1027 was written by Lyfing, as parts of the first Letter were written by Wulfstan.

[23] Innes, 'Danelaw Identities', p. 74. Innes refers specifically to the king's activities 'in the North', but it seems likely that all of England and his English affairs were influenced by 'political calculation' rather than 'ethnic identification'.

Cnut seems to think holistically, even while sub-dividing his new realm among his leading ealdormen and jarls. These identities can be decoded through the depiction of subjectivity in texts purportedly written by Cnut and those written for him. These are extant in a range of material recorded in all three languages: English, Latin, and Old Norse. Each of these linguistic media naturally operates distinctively to underscore specific ideological messages within dramatically different functional contexts.[24] The analysis of Cnut's positioning, his posturing, reveals a king whose practice is the epitome of what I shall label pragmatic ethnicity.

In the exposition of this pragmatic ethnicity, the key texts are Cnut's *Letters to the English* written in 1020 and 1027, and contemporary *Knutsdrapur*, the Old Norse Skaldic verse performed for Cnut at his court.[25] In every respect, these sets of texts could not be more different: the first, an outward-looking expression of imperial power, military might, Anglo-Danish national interests, and Christian piety, are author-ized, authenticated by the king's voice, and ecclesiastically sanctified; the second, a set of texts looking inward, is exclusive, emphatically military, elite, panegyric. The first is essentially public: originally in English, for the English, by a predominantly, though here, *mimetically*, English king. The second is fundamentally private: in Old Norse, for the Danish king and his Danish aristocracy at court, bellowing victory, subordination of foes, and domination of dynasties.

---

[24] On Old Norse, see Matthew Townend, *Language and History in Viking Age England: Linguistic Relations between Speakers of Old Norse and Old English*, Studies in the Early Middle Ages 6 (Turnhout: Brepols, 2002); on Latin court culture, see Elizabeth Tyler, 'Talking about History in Eleventh-Century England: The *Encomium Emmae Reginae* and the Court of Harthacnut', *Early Medieval Europe* 13 (2005), pp. 359–83.

[25] From the Arnamagnaean Collection, 20 d, datable to *c.*1700, and containing parts of the *Knutsdrapur* within the larger *Knytlinga saga*. These are edited by Matthew Townend as part of the *Skaldic Poetry of the Scandinavian Middle Ages*, gen. ed. Diana Whaley: http://skaldic.arts.usyd.edu.au/db.php. I am very grateful to Dr Townend for permission to use his excellent editions prior to publication. The edition and translation of Cnut's *Letter to the English* (1020) here is my own from Elaine Treharne (ed.), *Old and Middle English, An Anthology, c. 890–1450* (Oxford: Blackwell, 2009). See also D. Whitelock, M. Brett, and C. N. L. Brooke (eds.), *Councils and Synods with other Documents Relating to the English Church, I, AD 871–1204: Part I, 871–1066* (Oxford: Clarendon Press, 1981), pp. 435–41. They print the letter with accompanying translation, using chapter numbers. This is also the manner in which A. J. Robertson edits and translates the text in *The Laws of the Kings of England from Edmund to Henry I* (Cambridge: Cambridge University Press, 1925), pp. 140–5.

Cnut's Letter to the English (1020)

Cnut cyning gret his arcebiscopas and his leodbiscopas, and Þurcyl eorl and ealle his eorlas, and ealne his þeodscype, twelfhynde and twyhynde, gehadode and læwede, on Englalande, freondlice.

And Ic cyðe eow þæt Ic wylle beon hold hlaford[26] and unswicende to Godes gerihtum and to rihtre woroldlage.

Ic nam me to gemynde þa gewritu and þa word þe se arcebiscop Lyfing me fram þam papan brohte of Rome þæt Ic scolde æghwær Godes lof upp aræran, and unriht alecgan and full frið wyrcean be ðære mihte þe me God syllan wolde.

Nu ne wandode Ic na minum sceattum þa hwile þe eow unfrið on handa stod. Nu Ic, mid Godes fultume, þæt totwæmde mid minum scattum.

Ða cydde man me þæt us mara hearm to fundode þonne us wel licode. And þa for Ic me sylf mid þam mannum þe me mid foron into Denmearcon þe eow mæst hearm of com; and þæt hæbbe mid Godes fultume forene forfangen, þæt eow næfre heofonforð þanon nan unfrið to ne cymð þa hwile þe ge me rihtlice healdað and min lif byð.

Nu ðancige Ic Gode ælmihtigum his fultumes and his mildheortnesse þæt Ic þa myclan hearmas þe us to fundedon swa gelogod hæbbe, þæt we ne þurfon þanon nenes hearmes us asittan; ac us to fullan fultume and to ahreddingge, gyf us neod byð.

Nu wylle Ic þæt we ealle eadmodlice Gode ælmihtigum þancian þære mildheortnesse þe he us to fultume gedon hæfð.

Nu bidde Ic mine arcebiscopas and ealle mine leodbiscopas þæt hy ealle neodfulle beon ymbe Godes gerihta, ælc on his ende þe heom betæht is. And eac minum ealdormannum Ic beode þæt hy fylstan þam biscopum to Godes gerihtum and to minum kynescype and to ealles folces þearfe.

Gif hwa swa dyrstig sy, gehadod oððe læwede, Denisc oððe Englisc, þæt ongean Godes lage ga and ongean mine cynescype oððe ongean woroldriht, and nelle betan and geswican æfter minra biscopa tæcinge, þonne bidde Ic Þurcyl eorl and eac beode þæt he ðæne unrihtwisan to rihte gebige gyf he mæge. Gyf he ne mæge, þonne wille Ic mid uncer begra cræfte þæt he hine on earde adwæsce oððe ut of earde adræfe, sy he betera sy he wyrsa.

---

[26] See Alice Sheppard, *Families of the King: Writing Identity in the Anglo-Saxon Chronicle* (Toronto: Toronto University Press, 2004) for a broad-ranging discussion of the ideology behind 'hold hlaford'.

And eac Ic beode eallum minum gerefum, be minum freondscype and be eallum þam þe hi agon and be heora agenum life, þæt hy æghwær min folc rihtlice healdan and rihte domas deman be ðæra scira biscopa gewitnesse, and swylce mildheortnesse þæron don swylce þære scire biscope riht þince, and se man acuman mæge.

And gyf hwa þeof friðige oððe forena forlicge sy he emscyldig wið me þam ðe þeof scolde, buton he hine mid fulre lade wið me geclænsian mæge.

And Ic wylle þæt eal þeodscype, gehadode and læwede, fæstlice Eadgares lage healde, þe ealle men habbað gecoren and to gesworen on Oxenaforda, forðamþe ealle biscopas secgað þæt hit swyþe deop wið God to betanne þæt manaðas oððe wedd tobrece.

And eac hy us furðor lærað þæt we sceolon, eallan mægene and eallon myhton, þone ecan mildan God inlice secan, lufian, and weorðian and ælc unriht ascunian. Ðæt synd mægslagan, and morðslagan, and manswoworan, and wiccean, and wælcyrian, and æwbrecan, and syblegeru.

And eac we beodað, on Godes ælmihtiges naman and on ealra his haligra, þæt nan man swa dyrstig ne sy þæt on gehadodre nunnan oððe on mynecenan gewifige. And gyf hit hwa gedon hæbbe, beo he utlah wið God and amansumod fram eallum Cristendome, and wið þone cyning scyldig ealles þæs þe he age, buton he ðe raðor geswice and þe deopplicor gebete wið God.

And gyt we furðor maniað þæt man Sunnandæges freols mid eallum mægene healde and weorðige fram Sæternesdæges none oð Monandæges lyhtinge; and nan man swa dyrstig ne sy þæt he aðor oððe cypinge wyrce oððe ænig mot gesece þam halgan dæge.

And ealle men, earme and eadige, heora cyrcan secean and for heora synnum þingian, and ælc beboden fæsten geornlice healdan, and þa halgan georne weorðian, þe us mæssepreostas beodan sceolan, þæt we magan and moton ealle samod þurh þæs ecean Godes mildheortnesse, and his halgena þingrædene, to heofena rices myrhðe becuman, and mid him wunian þe leofað and rihxað, a butan ende. Amen.

Cnut's Letter to the English (1020)

King Cnut cordially greets his archbishops and his people's bishops and Eorl Thurkel and all his eorls, and all his nation, whether men of a twelve-hundred wergild or of a two-hundred, ecclesiastical and lay, in England.

And I reveal to you that I wish to be a loyal lord and loyal to God's rights and to just worldly laws.

I have kept in mind the letters and messages which Archbishop Lyfing brought me from the Pope in Rome, that I should raise God's praise up everywhere, and curb injustice and establish complete peace by the might which God wishes to give me.

Now I did not spare my treasures while you had hostilities in hand. Now, with God's help, I removed that threat with my treasures.

When it was revealed to me that a greater danger was intended to us than was at all pleasing, then I, myself, travelled with the men who journeyed with me into Denmark, from where the most harm came to you; and then with God's help have taken a stand, so that from now on, no hostility shall ever come to you from there, as long as you are justly ruled by me, and as long as my life lasts.

Now I thank almighty God for his help and his mercy, in that I have disposed of the great dangers, which were intended against us in this way so that we do not need to fear any danger to us from there, but there will be abundant help and deliverance,[27] if it is needed by us.

Now it is my desire that we all humbly thank God almighty for the mercy that he has given to help us.

Now I pray that my archbishops and all my people's bishops will be ardent about God's causes, each in the part that is entrusted to them; and also I instruct my ealdormen that they assist the bishops in God's cause, and in my royal honour, and for the need of all people.

If anyone, ecclesiastic or lay, Danish or English, is so foolish that he goes against God's law and my royal authority or against secular law, and will not amend it and cease from it after my bishops' instruction, then I shall urge and also command Eorl Thorkel to force the unjust man to do right, if he is able. If he is not able, then I insist that, with the power of us both, he shall destroy him within this land or drive him out of this land, whether he is of the higher or the lower rank.

And I also command all my reeves, by my friendship and by all that which they own and by their own lives, that they justly protect my people everywhere and give just judgements by the witness of the diocesan bishops, and practice such mercy therein as seems right to the bishop of the diocese, and as that person is able to sustain.

---

[27] 'ahreddan' seems to have biblical connotations (i.e. the deliverance of the chosen people).

And if anyone harbours a thief or stands in the way of the pursuit, he is to be held accountable to me in the same way as the thief, unless he is able to clear himself to me with the full process.

And I desire that the entire nation, those in orders and laymen, shall steadfastly hold to Edgar's law, which all people have chosen and sworn to at Oxford,[28] because all the bishops say that perjury and the breaking of oaths have to be very deeply atoned with God.

And also they further teach us that we should, with all our strength and our might, thoroughly seek, love and honour the eternal, merciful God, and shun all evil ones; those are, slayers of kin, and murderers, and perjurers, and wizards, and witches, and adulterers and the incestuous.

And also we command in the name of God almighty and of all of his saints that no man is to be so foolish as to take as a wife a woman dedicated to God or a nun. And if anyone has done so, he is to be an outlaw against God and excommunicated from all Christendom, and to forfeit to the king all that he owns, unless he ceases quickly and makes remedy all the more deeply with God.

And in addition, we further warn that the Sunday festival is to be held with all might and honourably so from noon on Saturday until dawn on Monday, and that no one is to be so foolish that he either practise trading or attend any meeting on that holy day.

And all men, poor and rich, are to go to their church and seek forgiveness for their sins and to earnestly observe each required fast, and eagerly honour those saints as the mass-priests shall command to us, so that we may and might all together through the mercy of that eternal God and his saints' intercession come to the joy of the heavenly kingdom and live with him who lives and reigns, ever without end. Amen.

This *Letter of Cnut to the English*, written in 1020, was sent from Denmark when Cnut was occupied with gaining control of his inheritance, and, with the exception of the work of one or two scholars, has enjoyed virtually no sustained scholarship. Yet it might be regarded as one of the most important indicators of English's status in early medieval England.[29]

---

[28] At a great meeting in 1018, all the nobles of England—Danish and English—had sworn to uphold the Laws of Edgar, issued under that king in the 960s.

[29] I have written more fully on this Letter, and its role in the ideological history of early written English in 'The Politics of Early English', The Toller Memorial Lecture, *Bulletin of the John Rylands University Library of Manchester* (2010 for 2006), pp. 101–22. Parts of the discussion here are reworkings of some of that discussion.

The Sacred Word

Cnut's Letter or Writ or Proclamation to the English is contained in the manuscript, York Gospels, York Minster, Additional 1 (See Figure 2).[30] This *de luxe* manuscript, datable to the first decades of the eleventh century, was made at Christ Church, Canterbury, before becoming the personal property of Wulfstan of York. Cnut and Emma might have given the book to Wulfstan in 1020 as a thank-you for Wulfstan's consecration of Æthelnoth to the archbishopric of Canterbury. Wulfstan could have kept the book in his minster at York as is commonly believed, or, as more recently argued, Wulfstan might have retained it at his estate at Sherburn-in-Elmet in Yorkshire.[31]

The Latin gospels, with illustrated evangelist pages, form the core of the book. Two folded sheets of membrane were added to the Gospel book in the years following its acquisition by Wulfstan, which expand the function of the book from a *de luxe* liturgical volume to a repository of archiepiscopal documents—inventories, prayers, and homiletic-legal works, among which are four items closely associated with Wulfstan at folios 158r to 160. The complete set of additional texts is:

> folio 156v Survey of Sherburn-in-Elmet
> folio 157r Surveys of Otley and Ripon
> folio 158r–v *Sermo Lupi*
> folio 159r *Be Hæðendome*
> folio 159v *Be Cristendome*
> folio 160r–v Cnut's *Letter to the English 1020*
> folio 161r Church treasures at Sherburn
> folio 161v Bidding Prayers
> folio 161v List of Archbishop Ælfric Puttoc's *festermen*, or liegemen.

---

[30] Nicholas Barker (ed.), *The York Gospels: A facsimile with introductory essays by Jonathan Alexander, Patrick McGurk, Simon Keynes, and Bernard Barr* (London: Roxburghe Club, 1986); Wormald, *The Making of English Law*; Patrick Wormald, *Legal Culture in the Early Medieval West: Law as Text, Image and Experience* (London: Hambledon, 1999); M. Townend (ed.), *Wulfstan, Archbishop of York: The Proceedings of the Second Alcuin Conference*, Studies in the Early Middle Ages 10 (Turnhout: Brepols, 2004).

[31] Christopher Norton, 'York Minster in the Time of Wulfstan', in Townend, *Wulfstan, Archbishop of York*, pp. 207–34, at pp. 207–18. T. A. Heslop in 'Art and the Man: Archbishop Wulfstan and the York Gospelbook', in the same volume (pp. 279–308), believes the York Gospels to have been made specifically for Wulfstan.

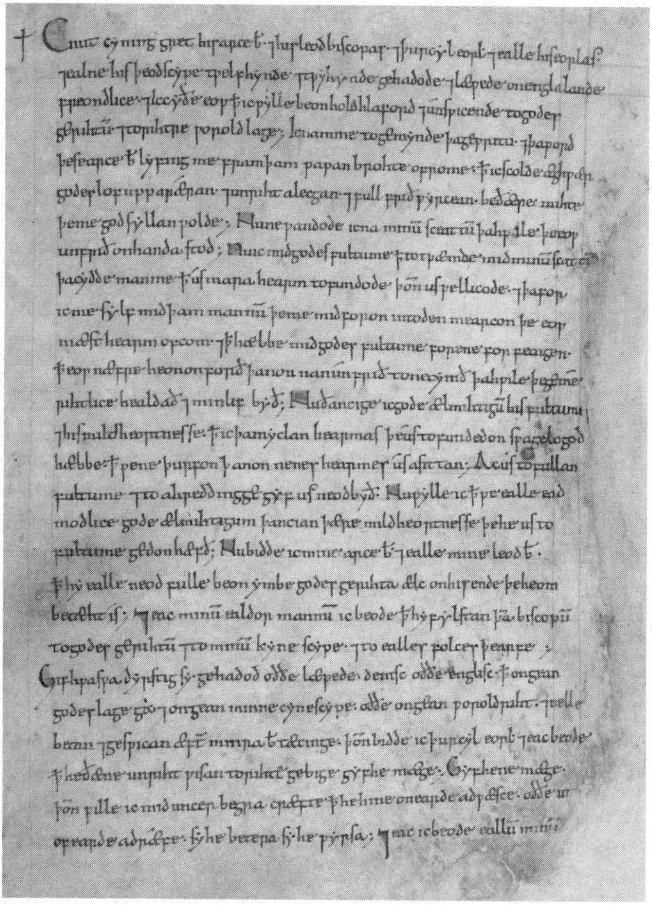

FIG 2   York Minster 1, folio 160r
© By kind permission of the Dean and Chapter of York.

The Old English texts are of great significance for a variety of reasons,[32] not least of which is that the sermons, derived from excerpts of Wulfstan's previous writings, are amongst the last that he wrote—between 1020 and his death in 1023—and they contain annotations in his own

[32] For the surveys of estates, see Stephen Baxter, 'Archbishop Wulfstan and the Administration of God's Property', in Townend, *Wulfstan: Archbishop of York*, pp. 161–206.

hand.[33] These sermons will form the centre of discussion in Chapter 3 as articulations of Wulfstan's anxiety about the state of England, seven years after Cnut's ascent to the throne. The palpably anxious words in the sermons are nowhere evident in the juxtaposed *Letter of Cnut*, written, ostensibly, by the king himself as a declaration of his intentions for his English kingdom.

This letter is clearly intended for every subject in England, the country 'Englaland' emphatically closing the salutation. Cnut's greeting hierarchically addresses the archbishops, bishops, Earl Thorkell, noblemen, religious subjects, and laymen throughout the land. He reveals that he has carefully considered letters and messages from the Pope that request him to encourage the veneration of God and enforce justice in temporal and spiritual affairs, as the divinely appointed monarch. One might argue that his promise to uphold law and follow the Pope's urgings suggests he has not done so thus far in his reign. Words therefore become the permanent record of an intention of remedy, a remedy that will reinstate the inheritance of Anglo-Saxon kings through the promulgation of the 'law of Edgar...given under oath at Oxford' in 1018. As beneficiary of his predecessor's law code, he takes upon himself the role of law-giver; and as both subject and cipher of the Pope's injunctions, he is simultaneously representative of the Holy Father and mediator between Rome and England.

Just as the Letter shows Cnut's mediation with Rome, it also mediates between Cnut and his subjects, and it is significant that the chosen language of delivery is English. Cnut is certainly, then, cognizant of the function and prestige of English as an authorized language of regal declaration, even from the mouth of a foreign king. Moreover, English is here sacralized by its quire's contiguity with the Holy Gospels, the word of God. There is no better place to put critically valuable texts than adjacent to, and so under the protection afforded by, the Gospels;[34]

---

[33] Among the many concerns these evince are issues of church scot and Peter's Pence in *Be Cristendome*, for example. Notably, these also form a focus of Cnut's *Letter to the English* in 1027.

[34] See David Dumville, *Liturgy and the Ecclesiastical History of Late Anglo-Saxon England: Four Studies*, Studies in Anglo-Saxon History 5 (Woodbridge: Boydell, 1992), pp. 119–23. Dumville states at p. 119 'the addition of documentary texts to gospel-books... is...a widely observed phenomenon, and has been taken to be a means both of sanctifying the transaction (and its attendant written record) and of enhancing the record's chances of survival and its integrity as a point of reference.'

Wulfstan's desire for the permanence of the record in having it copied in the Gospels seems of paramount concern, as it was for others who similarly used Gospelbooks for the safe-keeping of legal and documentary materials.

As with most of the texts copied into Gospelbooks, it is apparent that the original context of textual dissemination is lost in the recopying. In the case of manumissions of slaves copied into the Bodmin Gospels,[35] for example, these ceremonies would have been performed liturgically, and the words recording the procedure were thence inscribed into the margins of the Gospels and canon tables. The sacred setting of the manumission ceremony is transferred into the physical context of the book, though, as if the book symbolically represented the church itself. In the case of Cnut's Letter and the York Gospels, one wonders if the same kind of analogy could be made: that the writ or letter would be read to the people in an ecclesiastical setting, notionally replicated by its copying into the back of the Gospels. Presumably issued by the king and carried to England, its intended materiality would have been a single leaf document, existing independently, to be read out loud in some public forum, which could equally well have been the shire court.[36]

As I have argued elsewhere,[37] these English additions to the York Gospels insist on the sanctity of the vernacular, and claim a direct association of this elevation with the very highest levels of the church in the figure of Wulfstan. They bespeak a confidence in the official status of English and its usefulness for disseminating any message, whether evangelical or regal, didactic or legal. Moreover, like the Latin Gospel texts that host the English writings in the York manuscript, Cnut's Letter anticipates public performance. This performative element is enhanced by its placement adjacent to three sermons that were clearly written for public reading. In Cnut's Letter, then, the permeability of genre so typical of Wulfstan himself is evident: it is part letter, part sermon, part royal

[35] London, British Library, Additional 9381, a ninth-century Latin Gospelbook from St Petroc, Cornwall, containing a considerable number of Latin and English manumission documents, apparently freeing slaves.

[36] Florence Harmer (ed.), *Anglo-Saxon Writs*, 2nd edn. (Stamford: Paul Watkins, 1989), p. 56, states: 'Cnut's two Proclamations of 1020 and 1027 ... which are in epistolary form, and employ the writ protocol, are addressed generally ... [and] may have been sent round to the shire courts.' There is no doubt that eleventh-century English additions to the Hereford Gospels (Hereford Cathedral P. i. 2) were recordings of court proceedings.

[37] Treharne, 'The Politics of Early English'.

writ.[38] The work has the outward shape of a homily with a typical closure including the letters of 'Amen' spread out across the final line of the manuscript; but the actual form of the piece, introduced with the sign of a cross is legal, a writ.

Wulfstan wrote Cnut's Law Codes, and thus his immense influence in creating the image of Cnut as lawmaker is unquestionable. Simon Keynes has proposed the Archbishop may also have been the writer of the last third of the *Letter of 1020*,[39] beginning at the point following the reference to 'Edgar's law, which all people have chosen and sworn to at Oxford'. After this, the form of first-person address moves from singular 'Ic' ('I') to plural 'We', and the admonitions move from the general to the naming of specific Christian and unchristian actions, typically illustrated in Wulfstan's many other sermons. Wulfstan thus effectively altered the tenor of the Letter: Cnut declares a personal promise of future good government through the synergistic efforts of secular and ecclesiastical arms of the law; Wulfstan enumerates present wrongdoings within the nation, and names the remedy as a return to church-going, absolution from sins, and prayer. Both parts of the Letter promote the respective speakers, Wulfstan, though, ventriloquizing the king's voice to reinforce his own requests for pious action by the people in the closing stages of the text.

Whether read as one long document, or stripped of its closing Wulfstanian section, Cnut's Letter explicitly represents a politics of 'acceptance' through its vernacularity, of ostensible assimilation of colonizer to colonized. There is a wonderful irony in Cnut's claim that he has travelled into Denmark to eliminate any danger from that country towards

---

[38] Wormald, *The Making of English Law*, pp. 195–7, discusses the English additions to the York Gospels. It is worth citing his view at pp. 196–7 in full: 'Immediately after the three tracts comes the sole surviving copy of Cnut's letter to the English (1019/20). For the reasons just given, this essentially legislative statement closely resembles the preceding homilies…But it should be said that their resemblances extend to their presentation on the page. The Letter is in the same hand as the tracts and may have been copied at the same time. It lacks the heading they have but instead has a pictorial invocation of a cross that they do not. Otherwise, it is laid out in just the same way. In both, continuous prose is broken up by the punctus versus, its impact reinforced by initials shaded in red ink. If these were designed to guide readers to beginnings of new clauses, then the tracts were also meant to be read as sets of clauses. Unanimity of message outweighed the distinction between "law" and "homily", "official" and "unofficial".'

[39] Simon Keynes, 'The Additions in Old English', in Barker (ed.), *The York Gospels*, pp. 95–6.

England, when he himself brought conflict from the former to the latter. But building on this allegiance of Cnut with the inhabitants of his new kingdom, there is a very clear sense of an emergent nation of Danish and English forming an 'us' against other common enemies. Indeed, this Letter's main function is likely to be the creation of a sense of unity through the joint efforts of all to ensure the rule of law. Confirming this, Cnut issues his Letter in English, the language of the land he has conquered, and English is assumed to be the dominant voice of kingship and the language of those who sign up to Cnut's mandate for peace. There is recognition that the real power of being integrated comes from using the powerful tool of the English language, not Latin and not, at the level of the written word, Scandinavian. This rejection of his own language demonstrates the political acuity of Cnut; his is the utterance of one who co-opts the language of the major native indigenous presence while simultaneously casting himself in the role of just Christian king, of saviour of the beleaguered English nation, a nation that was, however, beleaguered by the very creator of this text.

| 2 |

'Some would drink and deny it, and some would pray and atone'[1]

The Propaganda of Conquest

Cnut's *Letter to the English* of 1020 very much projects the image of an Anglocentric *miles Christi*,[2] advised by the Pope, supported by loyal subjects throughout the state. This public construct seems to have been partially created and maintained by Wulfstan in the first few years of Cnut's reign. However, despite the Letter's obvious significance for establishing Cnut's agenda and his authority, it appears to have sunk without trace beyond its unique survival in the York Gospels, for it seems not to have been known at all beyond its immediate physical context. In his *Gesta Regum Anglorum*, for example, the thorough source-hunter William of Malmesbury shows no knowledge at all of the *Letter of 1020*, yet he knows and translates a second Letter, written by Cnut to his people in

[1] Rudyard Kipling, 'The King's Task', in *A History of England*, pp. 51–3.
[2] As he is depicted in the famous portrait in the Winchester *Liber Vitae*, London, British Library, Stowe 944, discussed earlier. This portrait is widely reproduced and discussed; see, for example, Owen-Crocker, 'Pomp, Piety, and Keeping the Woman in her Place'; Karkov, *Ruler Portraits of Anglo-Saxon England*, p. 124; and Gerchow, 'Prayers for King Cnut', pp. 219–38.

1027.[3] Again, in relation to the first Letter, it is known that William of Malmesbury visited York,[4] but he obviously did not come across the 1020 text, providing further evidence that the manuscript was kept elsewhere (such as Sherburn-in-Elmet) in the twelfth century. Similarly, in his much fuller twelfth-century *Chronicle* account, the laudatory John of Worcester also translated Cnut's *Letter of 1027*, but seems to have been unaware of any earlier, similar document; he also did not know the *Letter of 1020*.[5] Given that Wulfstan's links with Worcester were supposedly maintained after he relinquished his incumbency, it is strange that the extensive Worcester archive does not seem to have had a copy of the crucial 1020 Letter; if it had, it seems improbable that both John of Worcester and William of Malmesbury could have missed it.

The 1027 Letter, apparently written in English by Cnut after he had visited Rome to attend the coronation of the Emperor Conrad II, is an extraordinary statement of imperial ambition, which illustrates effectively how far this king had come in only seven years. The Letter survives now only in twelfth-century Latin versions in John of Worcester's *Chronicle* and William of Malmesbury's *Gesta Regum Anglorum*, where it erroneously occurs in the annal for 1031.[6] Wormald suggests that as well as bringing the Letter to the nation, Lyfing, Bishop of Crediton and then Worcester, actually wrote it too.[7] This is an imponderable, given its survival in a converted language and form, embedded in post-Conquest historiography.

[3] R. A. B. Mynors, R. M. Thomson, and M. Winterbottom (eds. and trans.), *William of Malmesbury, Gesta Regum Anglorum: The History of the English Kings*, Oxford Medieval Texts, 2 vols. (Oxford: Oxford University Press, 1998), i. 327.

[4] R. M. Thomson, 'Malmesbury, William of (*b. c.*1090, *d.* in or after 1142)', *Oxford Dictionary of National Biography* (Oxford: Oxford University Press, 2004) [http://www.oxforddnb.com/view/article/29461]

[5] R. R. Darlington and P. McGurk (eds.), Jennifer Bray and P. McGurk (trans.), *The Chronicle of John of Worcester*, vol. ii: *The Annals from 450 to 1066*, Oxford Medieval Texts (Oxford, 1995), ii. 513–19, s.a. 1031. At p. 513, Annal 1031: '[Cnut] also swore to God before the sepulchre of the apostles to amend his life and ways, and from there he sent to England an epistle [*epistolam memorie dignam*] worth remembering delivered by the hand of that most prudent man Lyfing, then abbot of Tavistock but soon after, in the same year, successor to the episcopacy at Crediton of Eadnoth...and by the hands of other ambassadors...We considered the text of his letter worthy of being subjoined.'

[6] *The Chronicle of John of Worcester*, ii. 512–19; *Gesta Regum Anglorum*, i. 324–31.

[7] Wormald, *Making of English Law*, p. 348.

Cnut's Letter to the English, 1027

Canutus, rex totius Anglie et Denemarcie et Norreganorum et partis Suanorum, Athelnotho metropolitano et Alfrico Eboracensi archiepiscopo omnibusque episcopis et primatibus, et toti genti Anglorum, tam nobilibus quam plebeiis, salutem.[8]

Cnut, king of all England and Denmark and the Norwegians and part of the Swedes, to Æthelnoth the metropolitan and Ælfric, archbishop of York, and to all his bishops and chief men, and to all the English people, both nobles and ceorls, greetings.

I make it known to you that I have recently gone to Rome and have prayed[9] for the redemption of my sins, and for the salvation [*et pro salute*] of the kingdoms whose people are subject to my rule. I had vowed to God to make this journey a long time ago, but I could not perform it earlier because of the affairs of the kingdom and other impediments. Now, however, I most humbly thank my omnipotent God, who has allowed me, in my lifetime, to visit His blessed apostles, Peter and Paul, and every sanctuary which I could find within the city of Rome or outside it, and according to my desire, to worship and adore in my own person. The most particular reason why I did this was that I learnt from wise men that St Peter the Apostle received from God the great power of binding and loosing, and carries the keys of the kingdom of heaven, and so more particularly I considered it very profitable to seek his special advocacy with God diligently.

And I make it known to you that a great congregation of nobles was there at that same Easter celebration with the lord Pope John and the Emperor Conrad, namely all the princes of the peoples from Mount Gargano to the nearest sea, who all both received me with honour and honoured me with precious gifts. I was honoured most, though, by the emperor with sundry gifts and priceless presents, both gold and silver vessels and cloaks and extremely precious garments. Therefore, I spoke with the emperor himself and the lord pope and the princes who were there about the needs of all the people of my entire

---

[8] *The Chronicle of John of Worcester*, ii. 512. The translation here is based on that in *The Chronicle of John of Worcester*, pp. 512–19, but with a number of modifications.

[9] The MS versions printed both use 'oratum' here, the first supine of 'oro' 'have prayed', but two MS variants of John of Worcester's Chronicle have 'orare' 'to pray' (*Chronicle*, ii. 512, note a). Both of these extant versions provide a strong penitential and intercessory motivation for Cnut's journey to Rome.

realm, both English and Danes, that they concede fairer law and securer peace to them on the road to Rome, and that they should not be hindered by so many barriers along the road and vexed by unjust tolls; and the emperor consented, and likewise Rudolf, the king who controls most of these said barriers; and all the princes confirmed with edicts that my people, both merchants and others who journey to make their prayers, might go to and return from Rome without any hindrance of barriers and toll-collectors, in firm peace and secure in a just law.[10]

Another time, I complained in my lord pope's presence and stated my great displeasure that my archbishops were so much constrained by the immense amount of money which was demanded of them when they journeyed to the apostolic seat, according to custom, to receive the pallium; and it was decreed that this should not occur in future. For all that I requested from the lord pope and the emperor and King [Rudolf], and the other princes through whose lands our road to Rome passes, for the benefit of my people, they most liberally granted, and confirmed these concessions with an oath, testified by four archbishops and twenty bishops and an innumerable multitude of dukes and nobles who were present there. Consequently, I give great thanks to Almighty God, because all that I wished—just as I had determined in my mind—I have carried out successfully, and I have completely fulfilled my vows.

Let it be known to you then that I humbly vowed to Almighty God to lead my life justly in all things from now on, and to rule justly and piously the kingdoms and peoples subject to me, and to observe just judgement in all things (*et regna mihi subdita populosque iuste et pie regere, equumque iudicium per omnes obseruare*).[11] If anything has been done previously through the intemperance of my youth or through my negligence, other than what was just, I intend with God's help to make amends for it completely.

For that reason, I enjoin upon and command my counsellors to whom I have entrusted the counsels of my kingdom that in no way either from fear of me or to obtain the favour of any powerful person shall they consent to any injustice or allow it to emerge in all of my kingdom from now on. I also instruct all the sheriffs and reeves within my entire realm, just as they want to have my friendship or their own

---

[10] William of Malmesbury has *cum firma pace*, *Gesta Regum Anglorum*, i. 326.
[11] *The Chronicle of John of Worcester*, ii. 516.

safety, to employ no unjust violence against any man whether he is rich or poor; but all people, whether noble or ordinary, rich or poor, shall be able to receive just law. From this they shall not deviate either to gain the favour of the king, or because of any powerful person, or for the reason of gathering money for me, because I have no need for money gathered by unjust exaction.

Therefore I wish it to be made known to you that, returning by the same route by which I came out, I am going to Denmark, to establish peace and a firm pact, on the counsel of all the Danes, with those nations and peoples who, if they might have, wanted to deprive us of kingdom and life; but they were not able to, God destroying their power. May He preserve our rule and honour through His benign compassion, and thereafter dissipate and destroy all of our enemies' power and strength. Finally, when peace has been established with those nations who live around us and my whole kingdom here in the east is in proper order and peaceful so that we have no war to fear from any part, nor any hostility from anyone, I intend to come to England as early this summer as I can have a fleet equipped. I have now sent this letter on ahead so that all the people in my kingdom might be happy at my prosperity, because, as you yourselves know, I have never abstained, nor will I ever abstain, from giving of myself and all my effort for the necessary service of my entire people.

Now therefore I instruct and appeal to all my bishops and the reeves of the kingdom, by the loyalty that you owe to me and to God, to make sure that before my arrival in England, as far as you can, all the dues of that we owe to God under ancient law are paid; namely plough-alms and tithes on animals born in the same year, and the pence which we owe to St Peter in Rome, whether from towns or from villages; and in the middle of August a tithe of produce, and on the feast of St Martin the first fruits of the seed to the parish church where a person lives, which is called 'church-scot' in English. If these and other similar payments have not been paid by the time I come, the royal payment shall be exacted strictly in accordance with the law that fits the crime without any hope of pardon from the defaulter. Farewell.

In the first Letter issued in 1019–20 while Cnut was away in Denmark, as *cyning* he greets archbishops, bishops, Earl Thorkell, all the earls and all the people *freondlice*, 'in friendship'. In this second Letter, composed while he was travelling from Rome to Denmark in 1027, Cnut styles himself *rex totius Anglie et Denemarcie et Norreganorum et partis Suorum*;[12] he greets his archbishops, but no nobles, by name; and he salutes *toti genti Anglorum, tam nobilibus quam plebeiis*. He tells the English people that he has visited Rome for two reasons: principally, in order to redeem his sins; and then to secure the safety of all of his kingdoms. He reveals that he has visited all the shrines he could because Peter has the power to loose and bind on this earth; that he met with the Pope and the Emperor in Rome, who showered him with gifts, and promised to redeem all taxes and tolls faced by English pilgrims; and to dispense with the English archbishops' expensive and arduous requirement to obtain the *pallium* from the Pope by journeying to Rome.

Notably, despite greeting the bishops and leading men and all the English people, or *genti Anglorum*, 'people of England', the disparate ethnic groups are singled out later in the Letter, when Cnut reveals that he spoke to the Pope and Emperor about the needs of all the people of my entire realm (*totius populi universi regni mei*)—*tam Anglorum quam Danorum*, 'whether English or Danish'. That these separated ethnic groups are explicitly provided in the Letter is probable recognition of their reality in the shires throughout England: it is thus not simply a hierarchical delineation—from archbishop down—that is adumbrated here. It is also the case, though, that Cnut refers to his two main kingdoms of Denmark and England, showing clearly that *et Norreganorum* in the opening of the Letter is an addition.

The ethnic division of English and Danish is also seen in other English documents issued during Cnut's reign, including his earliest Law Codes of 1018, when peace was ostensibly established between conquerors and conquered, brokered through the joint work of King and Witan.[13]

---

[12] The editors of *The Chronicle of John of Worcester*, ii.. 513, fn. 4, rightly point out that 'et Norreganorum' must be an addition if this letter is datable to 1027, since, at that time, Cnut was not king of Norway, despite his assistance in the exile of the sainted King Olaf in 1028; Olaf's death at the Battle of Stiklestad in 1030 ensured that he became king himself for a few years, before Olaf's son, Magnus, reclaimed the throne. The Norwegian throne would have been added to the English Letter, because both John of Worcester and William of Malmesbury believed the Letter to be datable to 1031. On Olaf, see Sverre Bagge, 'Warrior, King and Saint: The Medieval Histories about St Óláfr Haroldsson', *Journal of English and Germanic Philology* 109 (2010), pp. 281–321.

[13] The Prologue of the slightly later Law Code, I Cnut (datable to about 1020 and based in part on the 1018 Law Code) reads: 'þis is seo gerædnys, þe Cnut ciningc, ealles Englalandes ciningc 7 Dena cining mid his witena geþeahte gerædde' ('This is the ordinance which King Cnut, king of all England and king of the Danes, ordained with the advice of

In English, then—understood, of course, by his subjected people—Cnut is at pains to be an advocate of equal opportunities: English and Danish are given their own textual space. This formula in insular documents like law codes is extended to the more international scale of the *Letter of 1027*, supporting the careful construction of the penitent conqueror, keen to project equity, eager to ensure fairness on the continent for his fellow English pilgrims, a friend and confidant of popes and emperors, senior among the princes of Europe.

This proclamation by Cnut of his own legitimization and trans-formation—from Viking usurper to authorized Christian emperor—is the major success of the king's public relations activities. The performative utterance itself, from the outset, effectively re-enthrones Cnut on the international stage, just as much as the Letter recounts the actual coronation of the Emperor Conrad II. Moreover, an analysis of Cnut's second Letter to the English demonstrates unequivocally how his visit to Rome has come to dominate the modern understanding of the second half of his reign, and, ultimately, all subsequent readings of this most politically astute of all kings.[14] This is, in part, a result of the scarcity of other, datable sources, and the Letter's inclusion, in full, in both William of Malmesbury and John of Worcester's historiographical works, two of the most widely used primary sources for the period 1000–1140.[15] In its entirety, the Letter is so successful a strategy of identity construction that the image of the devout, but powerful, penitent forms the deepest imprint of Cnut's reign.

The Letter is extant only in the two very similar, twelfth-century Latin versions. Since the days of Liebermann's *Gesetze der Angelsachsen*,[16] scholars have assumed this Letter to have been composed originally in

his councillors'). See Dorothy Whitelock, 'Wulfstan and the Laws of Cnut', *English Historical Review* 63 (1948), pp. 433–52, and A. G. Kennedy, 'Cnut's Law Code of 1018', *Anglo-Saxon England* 11 (1983), pp. 57–81. Elsewhere, Cnut styles himself 'Cnut, enthroned king of the English' in a grant to Burhwold, bishop of Cornwall, emphasizing his legal right to rule; and 'Cnut, ruler and *basileus* of the noble and fair race of the English', in his grant to New Minster in 1019. See Whitelock, *EHD* i. 551 and 553.

[14] See further, Elaine Treharne, 'The Performance of Piety: Cnut, Rome and England', in Francesca Tinti (ed.), *England and Rome in the Early Middle Ages: Piety, Politics and Culture* (Brepols: Turnhout, 2013)

[15] These two historians were employed very widely by later historians, as they still are to this day.

[16] F. Liebermann (ed.), *Die Gesetze der Angelsachsen*, 3 vols. (Halle, 1903–06)

Old English, a vernacular version subsequently lost to posterity, but fortunately translated by both John of Worcester and William of Malmesbury, probably from the same source.[17] Dorothy Whitelock, Patrick
Wormald, and most commentators who have worked on the piece reit-
erate its vernacular origin.[18] Given the Letter's survival only in a translated form, decontextualized in its post-Conquest historiographical
framework, one wonders how vernacularity can be determined for the
piece. Perhaps the use of the English taxation term, 'church-scot', marked
out as 'Anglice' in both texts, is a trace of the Letter's linguistic origins,[19]
though it seems odd, if the Letter *were* English to note that 'church-scot'
is the term *in* English. Perhaps this phrase is another addition by the
Latin translator to the original text. This issue of language matters, too: if
it was conceived and delivered in Old English, its imperial declarations
become somewhat undermined by its linguistic exclusivity for the English (and only the English) subjects of the king; if Latin was the Letter's
language of composition, its potential audience could be expanded to
encompass all of those to whom one imagines Cnut's self-promotion
really mattered—insular and continental princes and churchmen, the
Pope among them.

In the Letter, Cnut, through the declared fulfilment of his vow to visit
Rome to worship Peter and the saints, absolves himself of the sins committed to this point in his reign, making that absolution a point of continuity for the remainder of his life. Through the covenant that he makes
with the recipients of the Letter, he promises to compensate his people if
he has been inequitable or intemperate: 'If anything has been done previously through the intemperance of my youth or through my negligence, other than what was just, I intend with God's help to make amends

---

[17] *The Chronicle of John of Worcester*, i. 512–19; *Gesta Regum Anglorum*, i. 325–9. See
Councils and Synods, i. 506–13 for text and commentary.

[18] *Councils and Synods*, i. 506; Lawson, *Cnut*, p. 66; Wormald, *Making of English Law*,
p. 348, reconstructs the address of the ' "vicecomitibus et prepositis", who were presumably "scirgerefan 7 gerefan" in the Old English original'. Wormald suggests that as well as
bringing the letter to the nation, Lyfing, Bishop of Crediton and then Worcester, wrote
it too.

[19] [Many taxes are owed, one of them being] 'in festiuitate sancti Martini primitie sem-
inum ad ecclesiam sub cuius parrochia quisque deget, que Anglice ciricsceatt nominan-
tur' ('at the festival of St Martin, the first-fruits of seed owed by each man to his parish
church, which is called in English "church-scot" ') from *The Chronicle of John of Worcester*,
ii. 518–19; *Gesta Regum Anglorum*, i. 328, has 'cyrcscet'.

for it completely.' Here, he establishes himself as *iustus rex*, 'a just king' seeking absolution not only from God and his apostles, but from his subjects throughout his kingdoms.

The concessive clause here ('if anything...'), one might argue, makes his past deeds seem only possibly damnable, and suggests little self-awareness or acknowledgement of the claims of bribery, murder, aggression, adultery, and usurpation that might be made against him. The clause is easily missed among the overwhelmingly legal and penitential rhetoric of the first half of the Letter. If the Old English original survived, it might tell us much more about the formula being employed here: whether 'be it known to you all now' (*Nunc itaque notum sit omnibus uobis*) translated the notification clause of the authoritative Old English writ—a legally binding promise or covenant—which was, according to Bishop and Chaplais, invariably worded '⁊ ic cyðe eow þæt' ('And I make known to you that');[20] and whether the final clause in the quotation above where 'I intend, henceforth, with God's help, to amend it entirely' (*totum, Deo auxiliante, deinceps dispono emendare*) must translate something like 'ealle, mid [or 'þurh'] Godes fultum, Ic wylle betan', directly emulating the liturgically binding penitential conventions. Moreover, numerous lexical and phrasal echoes of Old English homiletic and legal formulae pepper the *Letter of 1027*; thus, for example, in his emphasis on justice, Cnut confirms that travellers and merchants will now be able to journey through the continent to Rome 'in firm peace and secure in a just law' (*firmaque pace et iusta lege secure*), which in a small part echoes Wulfstanian lexis, including 'rihtlaga' ('just law'),[21] and perhaps some collocation of 'fæste' and 'frið' or, less likely, 'grið' ('firm peace', 'fixed peace').

Having made the sequence of statements concerning his desire to amend any previous wrongdoing, Cnut presents a temporal shift from the narration of the events in Rome to the commands (and threats) to English counsellors, sheriffs, and reeves to function justly and gather all taxes in Cnut's absence. As a written document, this Letter was presumably a writ, like its 1020 predecessor seems to have been. As such, its formal function would be a binding covenant, with all those participants

---

[20] T. A. M. Bishop and P. Chaplais (eds.), *Facsimiles of English Royal Writs to A.D. 1100 presented to Vivian Hunter Galbraith* (Oxford: Clarendon Press, 1957), p. xii.

[21] See Bosworth-Toller, s.v. *rihtlaga, rihtlagu*.

equally bound.[22] The Letter is, of course, also a statement of Cnut's personal salvation, his epiphanic moment when he apprehends that *perhaps* the acts of his first twelve years as king require a public acknowledgement, bound closely with the promise that from now he will rule in the appropriate manner for a Christian king, or the Christian emperor in the northernmost parts of Europe. The trajectory of Cnut's career thus rather curiously parallels Olaf's in Norway, as described by Bagge in his sensitive analysis of the primary sources: warrior Viking king, to *iustus rex*, to saint.[23]

Despite the fact that this Letter has been read as a straightforward statement of event and intent, there is much more to be discovered in it. In every sense, it magnificently manifests the inherent contradictions of the king himself both as murderous usurper, tyrant and adulterer, and as pious, devout, divinely inspired king. These apparent irreconcilables are not untypical of the early medieval period, of course, for one could apply similar descriptions to Cnut's continental counterpart, Conrad II; in fact, the contradiction of warrior and martyr is well illustrated by King Olaf Haroldsson of Norway, exiled and usurped by Cnut.[24] Even so, besides the apparently accurate account it provides of Cnut's visit to Rome in 1027, and his subsequent commands to England's caretakers, the Letter of 1027 evinces a discursive ambivalence that reflects its owner's voice: it is simultaneously genuine conversion narrative and Germanic boast. The vow or boast is, in fact, made explicit in the Letter, when Cnut reveals his thanks to God for success in his desires: 'because all that I wished—just as I had determined in my mind—I have carried out successfully, and I have completely fulfilled my vows'.[25] This thought-word-deed triad is reminiscent of the Germanic heroic warrior before battle,[26] though Cnut's apparent battle here is a spiritual one (even while its pious events are surrounded by years of hostilities intended to expand his empire into Norway and Sweden). His are the words of the penitent

[22] On the performative nature of such public, testimonial material, see Benjamin Withers, 'Unfulfilled promise: the rubrics of the Old English Prose Genesis', *Anglo-Saxon England* 28 (1999), pp. 111–39.

[23] Bagge, 'Warrior, King and Saint', esp. pp. 316–21.

[24] Bagge, 'Warrior, King and Saint', discusses this very aspect of Olaf's life and legend.

[25] *The Chronicle of John of Worcester*, i. 516: *prout mente decreueram, prospere perfeci, uotisque meis ad uellis satisfeci.*

[26] See, among others, Andy Orchard, *A Critical Companion to Beowulf* (Cambridge: D. S. Brewer, 2003), p. 146 fn. 75 and references therein.

pilgrim, conscious of sins past and the need for future salvation, and concurrently a brag-sheet of well-made friends and new networks, political battles won and crowning ceremonies attended.

The text provides us with an excellent example of the ambivalence of Cnut himself. It is easy to be absorbed into the comfortable world of good kingship that he depicts with its repeated emphases on Christian piety, equity and right rule. The major theme of the Letter is justice—the necessity of ruling justly, dealing with peers and subjects justly, and the giving and receiving of justice for all orders of society. Repetition of 'law' 'justice', 'rule', injustice', 'equity', 'just law' (*iusta lege*) reinforce the image of the king as law-maker and peace-maker first seen in the Lawcodes issued in 1018, then again in the *Letter to the English* of 1020. It is particularly interesting, then, that William of Malmesbury highlights the issue of justice in his summation of Cnut:

> *iniuste quidem regnum ingressus sed magna ciuilitate et fortitudine uitam componens*;
>
> There was no justice in his succession to the throne, but he arranged his life with great statesmanship and courage.[27]

Malmesbury's account goes on to depict a king whose piousness, equity, and magnanimity is to be much admired, and following the publication of Cnut's *Letter of 1027*, Malmesbury comments that the king 'was as good as his word', establishing the observance of England's ancient laws.[28] The king's Christian devotion is evinced at Winchester, for example, where Cnut gave a golden cross to the New Minster (the same cross depicted as the frontispiece of the minster's *Liber Vitae*, discussed earlier); and his generous gifts to Chartres are recounted.[29] William notes that Cnut's donations resulted in a scene that might be interpreted as one of startling excess: Cnut 'exhibited the munificence of his generosity, where his offerings were such that strangers are alarmed by the masses of precious metal and their eyes dazzled as they look at the flashing gems.'[30]

---

[27] *Gesta Regum Anglorum*, i. 320–1.

[28] Ibid. i. 328–9.

[29] Ibid. i. 330–2.

[30] Ibid. i. 323: *Wintoniae maxime munificentiae suae magnificentiam ostendit, ubi tanta intulit ut moles metallorum terreat aduenarum animos, splendor gemmarum reuerberet intuentium oculos.* The present tense here reminds William's contemporary readers that Cnut's beneficence was still very much in evidence at Winchester.

Despite the praise of Cnut, though, Malmesbury, perhaps surprisingly, spends little time on his death, simply stating: 'Cnut...reaching the end of his life, died at Shaftesbury, and was buried at Winchester'.[31] And the Cnut in the *Gesta Regum Anglorum* is a rather more glorious monarch than the one portrayed in William of Malmesbury's other great contemporary work, *Gesta Pontificum Anglorum* finished, like the *Gesta Regum*, in 1125.[32] Here, Cnut is shown as a 'barbarian', clearly in need of miraculous intervention to hasten his rehabilitation:

> [Æthelred's] successor Cnut was a Dane, a man of action but one who had no affection for English saints because of the enmity between the two races. The cast of mind made him wilful, and when at Wilton one Whitsun he poured out his customary jeers at Eadgyth herself: he would never credit the sanctity of the daughter of King Edgar, a vicious man, an especial slave to lust, and more tyrant than king. He belched out taunts like this with the uncouthness characteristic of a barbarian, just to indulge his ill temper; but Archbishop Æthelnoth, who was present, spoke up against him. Cnut became even more excited, and ordered the opening of the grave to see what the dead girl could provide in the way of holiness. When the tomb was broken into, Eadgyth was seen to emerge as far as the waist, though her face was veiled, and to launch herself at the contumacious king. In his fright, he drew his head right back; his knees gave way, and he collapsed to the ground. The fall so shattered him that for some time his breathing was impeded, and he was judged dead. But gradually strength returned and he felt both shame and joy that despite his stern punishment he had lived to repent.[33]

There is no historical record of Cnut's visit to Wilton at Pentecost but his subsequent veneration of the saint is documented through his

[31] Ibid. i. 335.

[32] M. Winterbottom (ed. and trans.), *William of Malmesbury, Gesta Pontificum Anglorum*, vol. i: *Text and Translation*, Oxford Medieval Texts (Oxford: Oxford University Press, 2007), pp. 299–301; see also David Preest (trans.), *William of Malmesbury: The Deeds of the Bishops of England [Gesta Pontificum Anglorum]* (Woodbridge: Boydell and Brewer, 2002).

[33] *Gesta Pontificum Anglorum*, trans. Preest, p. 127. Quite what one is supposed to make of William of Malmesbury's account of Eadgyth in his *Gesta Regum Anglorum* (i. 402–5) in the light of this story is difficult to say. In the *Gesta Regum Anglorum*, William tells us that the virgin's body 'was found all fallen into dust except the finger and the belly and the parts beneath it'.

commission of a shrine to house her relics.[34] Having the year of this miraculous event might permit us to determine the real moment of Cnut's moral conversion, prior to his visit to Rome, but it has to be post-1020, when Æthelnoth was consecrated as archbishop of Canterbury by Wulfstan, archbishop of York. In this episode in the *Gesta Pontificum*, Cnut's 'barbarism', his 'contumacy', and his disregard for a saint strongly suggest his lack of Christian impulse, even after the date of the first *Letter to the English* in 1020. Indeed, there is more than a hint of prurience in Cnut's desire to penetrate the tomb and see Eadgyth (even though this might seem quite formulaic within this genre), a voyeurism that suggests a lack of control reflected in Cnut's insistence throughout his reign on maintaining Emma as his queen and Ælfgifu of Northampton as his mistress. This is despite his overly Christian statements, from his Law-codes to his *Letter* of 1020. Though it is generally believed that Cnut was already a Christian when he took the English throne in 1016, the date of his baptism has long been debated. A recent suggestion is that he was baptized as a child, and took the name Lambert by which he was remembered in his obit in the Leofric Missal—Oxford, Bodleian Library, Bodley 579—a manuscript of Exeter provenance.[35] Still, whether Cnut was Christian in deed, in name only or not at all, William of Malmesbury, at this early point in the king's reign, depicts a miraculous (and presumably fantastical) conversion narrative that goes some way to explaining, perhaps, the emergence of Cnut as a king who had learned, and subsequently practised, a genuine piety. The king's virtual death and metaphorical resurrection here at the hands of the virgin saint Eadgyth (Edith) transforms him into a new, repentant Christian—a king who subsequently endowed Wilton with a shrine to Eadgyth, the fame of which helped consolidate his penitence and devotion, and very much intimated and reinforced the image that Cnut wished to portray of himself in the second decade of his reign.

[34] Andre Wilmart, 'La legende de Ste Edith en prose et vers par le moine Goscelin', *Analecta Bollandiana* 56 (1938), pp. 5–101 and 265–307; see also Stephanie Hollis with Bill Barnes, Rebecca Hayward, Kathleen Loncar, and Michael Wright (eds.), *Writing the Wilton Women: Goscelin's Legend of Edith and Liber Confortatorius*, Medieval Women Texts and Contexts, 9 (Turnhout: Brepols, 2004).

[35] Michael Hare, 'Cnut and Lotharingia: Two Notes', *Anglo-Saxon England* 33 (2002), pp. 261–78, in a careful study of the available evidence, suggests that Cnut was baptized as a child, taking the Lotharingian name Lambert as his baptismal name.

Baptism into Christianity is one thing; actually living a Christian life is another as the Wilton narrative suggests. There is no doubt that Cnut did not always behave in the pious, benevolent manner that he explicitly constructs for himself in his Letters of 1020 and 1027. Although the sequence of events around 1026 to 1030 is not clear in the various sources, it seems certain that Cnut instigated the deposition of the Norwegian king, Olaf. John of Worcester comments that Olaf was 'greatly despised' by Cnut because of 'his simplicity and mildness, justice and piety'.[36] Given that Cnut focused on justice in his *Letter of 1027*, the irony is obvious. In 1027 or thereabouts, Cnut bribed disaffected Norwegians to assist him at the Battle of Holy River in Skåne, Sweden, when he fought against Olaf, and Önund of Sweden, resulting in the casting out of Olaf, and the acquisition of the throne of Norway for Cnut himself.[37] Following the battle, Cnut appears to have arranged the murder of his traitorous brother-in-law, Ulf, who had foolishly taken one of the king's pieces while playing chess with him, according to one version of the story.[38] Whether the penitence announced as a reason for the pilgrimage to Rome was meaningful or otherwise, its declaration at the head of the Letter is obviously a sound religious and political manoeuvre. Of more pressing import than the need for forgiveness, though, was the urgent requirement for alliances with major European rulers in the light of Cnut's attacks against Norwegian and Swedish forces in the months immediately prior to his departure for Rome. The *Letter of 1027* thus becomes an explicit statement of penance, politics and public relations quite unlike anything else that survives from the pre-Conquest period in England.

The authenticity of Cnut's declarations from the more personal perspective is difficult to judge, but the efficacy of the Letter's covenanted claims is dubious, since within a decade favours acquired by Cnut seem to have disappeared. In the case of the archbishops of Canterbury, for example, Cnut's promise in the 1027 Letter appears to be that they need not travel to Rome for the pallium, because of the exorbitant cost of the journey: 'constrained by the immense amount of money which was

---

[36] *Chronicle of John of Worcester*, ii. 511.

[37] On the difficulty of dating these events, see Lawson, *Cnut*, pp. 56–7.

[38] See L. M. Larson, *Canute the Great, 995–1035* (New York: Putnam, 1912), 220–2; Whitelock, *EHD*, i. 309; and for Olaf, see Bagge, 'Warrior, King and Saint', p. 305.

demanded of them when they journeyed to the apostolic seat, according to custom, to receive the pallium... it was decreed that this should not occur in future'. Yet in 1040, after Eadsige was ordained archbishop following Æthelnoth's death in 1038, the A-version of the *Anglo-Saxon Chronicle* reads 'Her Eadsige arcebiscop for to Rome. 7 Harold cing forðferde' ('In this year, archbishop Eadsige went to Rome, and king Harold died').[39] This indicates that any deal made by Cnut on this issue of the pallium and the English archbishops failed to have any lasting impact. His self-congratulatory description of the reception he received at Rome does seem to have some basis in fact, however, as other contemporary writers confirm that he was given a significant role in the order of election ceremony. According to 'The Deeds of Conrad II', written by Wipo in 1046:

> And on the holy day of Easter [1027], [Conrad] was elected emperor by the Romans, and he received the imperial benediction from the Pope,
>   Called Caesar and Augustus by the Roman name.
> And more, Queen Gisela received at the same time the consecration and the name of empress. After these things were done thus in the presence of two kings—of Rudolf, king of Burgundy, and of Canute, king of the Angles—and after the divine office was ended, the Emperor was led to his chamber in the place of honor between the two kings.[40]

But even as Cnut's ceremonial role is acknowledged, his imperial pretensions are dismissed with Wipo's carefully orchestrated demotion of Cnut to 'King of the Angles'. Still, it would hardly do to advertise Cnut's full range of titles and clear success in gathering kingdoms to himself at the moment when the principal emperor on the European stage was being crowned. That as a king Cnut was considered significant cannot be doubted, and his alliance with Conrad, visually demonstrated through ceremonial procession, was further cemented by the betrothal of Cnut's daughter to Conrad's son, and by the secession of land in Northern Germany to bolster Cnut's Danish holdings. From the political perspective,

---

[39] Janet Bately (ed.), *The Anglo-Saxon Chronicle, A Collaborative Edition, MS A* (Cambridge: D. S. Brewer, 1986), s.a. 1040.

[40] Theodor E. Mommsen and Karl F. Morrison (trans.), *Imperial Lives and Letters of the Eleventh Century* (New York: Columbia University Press, 2000), p. 79.

Cnut must have thought himself invincible: darling of the Church, friend of kings and emperor, ally of sundry monastic and ecclesiastical institutions from the North Sea to the Mediterranean.

Masterful Rhetoric

In contrast to the international drama played out in the Letter of 1027 is another elite set of texts and their courtly audience: the Old Norse *Knutsdrapur* performed for Cnut and his Danish housecarls. Matt Townend's research on the Skaldic verse of Cnut's reign has established beyond doubt the importance of this under-used corpus of literature.[41] Indeed, as Townend puts it, this Old Norse material is 'remarkable in terms of its sheer quantity'.[42] The corpus throws into sharp relief the near-silence of the reign's traditional documentary material and demands the concurrent reappraisal of the nature of the English materials that survive. For while the Norse praise-poetry is panegyric of the most ostentatious kind, there is little similar praising of the king in the other recorded vernacular of English, other than through the king's own self-promotional Letters. The success of this king's reign, *pace* Stenton's interpretation of 'silence being golden',[43] thus cannot be measured by the response of the stunned and ostensibly gagged English. More significant are the works of his inventive Danish followers and their elaborate word games. The considerable corpus of Skaldic poetry dating from Cnut's reign seems to refute Innes's view that:

> It was only in… [the] most exceptional circumstances that 'Danish-ness' intruded into the domain of high politics; typically, it remained politically inert, rooted in local right.[44]

This Danishness, expressed through the exclusive medium of Old Norse, symbolizes high politics indeed, for its rhetorical situation was most likely the court. The *Knutsdrapur* are far from 'politically inert', and they range in date throughout Cnut's reign, flourishing most at the period of

---

[41] Matthew Townend, 'Contextualizing the *Knútsdrápur*: Skaldic praise-poetry at the court of Cnut', *Anglo-Saxon England* 30 (2001), pp. 145–79.
[42] Townend, 'Contextualizing the *Knútsdrápur*'.
[43] See above, p. 12.
[44] Innes, 'Danelaw Identities', in Hadley (ed.), *Cultures in Contact*, p. 85.

heightened political consciousness and activity—1027–31—when Norway stood to be gained and imperial status was being sought and manufactured so explicitly in the *Letter of 1027*.

In this poetry of the court, based in the Wessex capital of Winchester, the old centre of the English kings, Cnut was regaled by his skalds, highlighting his military prowess and his proud Danish lineage. Immediately after, and for some dozen and more years after Cnut's conquest, when scholars envisage a peaceful assimilation of English and Dane, we find the elite aristocracy of the court still profoundly alert to the significance of their king's unmatched victory. Sighvatr Þórðarson's *Knutsdrapa* performs the role of renewer of victories at just the time when Cnut's Letter evincing international diplomacy *par excellence* is disseminated. But Sighvatr's poem glorifies no mere conquest of a kingdom: it is the conquest of an entire dynasty, a race; it is the affirmation of the prospect of Danish longevity, a blow to the English aristocracy who might have listened, half-understanding:[45]

Ok senn sonu	And Knútr soon defeated
sló, hvern ok þó,	or drove out the sons of Æthelred,
Aðalráðs eða	and, indeed, each one.
út flæmði Knútr.[46]	

While such panegyric, with its syntactic emphasis on Cnut, has a specialized and obvious eulogistic function, the consistency of the corpus and its specific performative context suggests that the ethnic pragmatism of the king—simultaneously English, Danish, and international—is remarkably complex. At precisely the time when the king was propounding his own status as pious politician, his poets can be found lauding his unparalleled prowess as a warrior in seeing off an Anglo-Saxon predecessor (which included the exile of Edward and Alfred, the sons of his wife, Emma, and her former husband, Æthelred). Óttarr svarti's contemporary *Knútsdrápa*, similarly, transmits not simply an elevation of Cnut's kingship and martial skills, but a wholesale dynastic takeover:

---

[45] It is unlikely, given the highly complex and condensed nature of Skaldic verse that a contemporary Anglo-Saxon would apprehend the poetry easily. On the debate of mutual intelligibility, see Townend, *Language and History in Viking Age England*.

[46] Edited and translated by Matthew Townend, in the forthcoming major project, *Skaldic Poetry of the Scandinavian Middle Ages* (http://skaldic.arts.usyd.edu.au), ed. Diana Whaley. Very many thanks to Dr Townend for sending me these editions and translations prior to publication, and for permission to use them here.

Herskjöld bart ok helduð
Hilmir, ríkr af slíku;
Hykkat, þengill, þekkðust
þik kyrrsetu mikla.
Ætt drap, Jóta dróttinn,

Játgeirs í för þeiri;
þveit rakt—þrár est heitinn—
þeim, stillis konr, illan.
Brunnu byggðir manna,

Buðlungr, fyr þér ungum;
opt lézt húss of heiptar

herkall búendr gerva.

You carried the warshield
prince, and prevailed;
I do not think, lord, you
cared much for sitting in peace.
The lord of the Jótar [Cnut],
struck the kindred
of Edgar on that expedition;
ruler's son [Cnut], you dealt them
a harsh blow; you are called defiant.
King, settlements of people
burned
before you in your youth;
often you caused the residents to
make a war-cry
on account of the destroyer of the
house [fire].

… Skjöldungr, vant und skildi
skœru verk, inn sterki;
fekk blóðtrani bráðir
brúnar Assatúnum.
Vátt, en valfall þótti

verðung, jöfurr, sverði
nær fyr norðan stóru
nafn gnógt Danaskóga.

Strong Scylding, you performed
a feat of battle under the shield;
the blood-crane [raven] received
dark morsels at Ashingdon.
Prince, you won by fighting a great
enough name
with a mighty sword nearby
to the north of the Forest of Dean,
and it seemed a slaughter to the
retinue. [47]

This poem makes concrete the achievement of Cnut. Where it might have seemed transient, it now becomes potentially eternal with the epithet 'Skjöldungr' placing the king firmly in the long line of the legendary founders of Denmark, the Scyldings.[48] The piling up of lordly nomenclature—'hilmir' ('leader', 'king'), 'þengill' ('leader', 'prince'), 'Jóta dróttinn' ('lord of the Jutes'), and so on—reinforces the magnificent achievements of Cnut, placing him among the greatest of his race. The specificity of his battle-deeds at Assundun in 1016, and defeat not just of Æthelred but of the 'family of Edgar' encapsulates both the precise detail

[47] Stanzas 3, 4, and 10 of the eleven of B6 Óttarr svarti III: Knútsdrápa. Edited and translated by Matthew Townend (as n. 45).
[48] See Alexander M. Bruce, Scyld and Scef: Expanding the Analogues (London, 2002).

of Cnut's conquest, and the sweeping consequences of his displacement of the Anglo-Saxon line. That this takes place in the later 1020s is notable. Just as Cnut publicly, in his English writings, declares himself penitent, devoted to justice and to his subjects as a whole, in the private, oral sphere of Old Norse Skaldic verse, his Viking glories and defeat of the English monarchy are applauded in terms common to the Germanic heroic ethos. As Townend perceptively points out, 'the precincts of the royal palace [at Winchester] are a remarkable location' for these Skalds 'to be celebrating Cnut's triumph over named West Saxon kings.'[49]

Townend sees this courtly pursuit of Skaldic poetry as signifying 'that any...English audience must have aligned their interests with the Danish perspective of the conquerors.'[50] On the contrary, though, I would see this as firm evidence for the reality and reinforcement of the distinction drawn between Danish and English. While Cnut's *Letter of 1027* seems to employ those obvious ethnic divisions for the sake of political expediency and rhetorical equality, it is clear that such easily overlooked indicators of identity represent simply the king's pragmatic ethnicity, masking his (unsurprising) allegiance to his own traditions and people, elucidated so magnificently through his Skalds' endeavours.

This contrast is worth focusing upon for a moment, as its implications may be significant. While the English might have had very little to say about Cnut, the Scandinavian court poets were effusively noisy about his victories. Russell Poole rightly comments that in the *Knutsdrapa* (within the *Knytling saga*) it is interesting that Cnut is praised for causing sorrow to 'the English people'. Moreover, casting his eyes back on the poetry of the reign as a whole, Poole notes that the *Eiriksdrapa* may have been read out to an elite force in 1018 created by Cnut: the *þingamenn*.[51] This is perhaps similar to the elite courtly context of the later *Knutsdrapur*. Thus, we may search for the positive outcome optimistically put forward by Stafford and others—that '1016 appears less traumatic than 1066',[52] but if the poetry resonates with the tenor of the reign, the evidence of these two vernaculars, Old Norse and English, and the anticipated reception of their intended audiences, suggests otherwise. Throughout Cnut's

[49] Townend, 'Contextualizing the *Knútsdrápur*', p. 174.

[50] Ibid., p. 175.

[51] Russell Poole, 'Skaldic Verse and Anglo-Saxon History: Some Aspects of the Period 1009–1016', *Speculum* 62 (1987), pp. 265–98, at pp. 271–3.

[52] Stafford, *Unification and Conquest*, p. 69.

reign and beyond, traceable disparate and potentially irreconcilable elite textual communities existed uneasily. How much this reflected the situation at large—the unrecorded communities—is difficult to say, though the next chapter will address precisely that. Cnut may have appeared to sail a steady course between the conquered English and his victorious Danes, but this was a carefully stage-managed exercise, successfully demonstrated by his *Letter of 1027*, and not so obviously supported by other kinds of evidence usually overlooked in accounts of Cnut's reign.

| 3 |

'The end of that game is oppression and shame'[1]

The Silence of Conquest

Imaginatively reconstructing the years immediately prior to Cnut's reign, Rudyard Kipling wrote *Danegeld* (1911) as a wise warning against the dangers of a nation paying tribute to an invading army. His poem, written at the height of British imperialism of which he was both a product and supporter, highlights the danger of paying ransom to any potential blackmailer in order to stave off a threat of molestation and invasion. Given the expansionist nature of British foreign policy in the previous half century, this warning to the threatened nation is nicely ironic, though here, despite the obvious context of German aggression against Britain, the implication is that the opponents in the poem are more evenly matched than any colonial encounter that had faced British forces: 'an armed and agile nation' in the Danes versus a 'rich and lazy one' in the Anglo-Saxons—energy and opportunism versus material resource and complacency (this view of the slothful English might, in fact, derive from William of Malmesbury, among others[2]). The dates

---

[1] Rudyard Kipling, 'Dane-Geld', in *A History of England*, pp. 39–40.
[2] See Elaine Treharne, *Gluttons for Punishment: The Drunk and Disorderly in Old English Sermons*, The Annual Brixworth Lecture, 2nd series, 6 (University of Leicester, 2007).

encompassed by the sweep of this poem are precisely 980 to 1016—beginning with the renewed attacks on Anglo-Saxon England by the Vikings, who raided Chester and Southampton, and ending with the accession of Cnut to the English throne. Danegeld did not, of course, cease at Cnut's accession; on the contrary, he continued to raise punitive taxes for many years.[3] However, with his foundation of the Anglo-Scandinavian Empire, in Kipling's imaginative evaluation, Cnut's crowning effectively marked the loss of the nation, and the 'oppression and shame' of the English. Given that we can undoubtedly read the entire process of Cnut's conquest as a complex form of colonization, what evidence can be found to evoke the actual responses of the Anglo-Saxons to the sequence of events that culminated in the crowing of a foreign king? Is it possible to imagine 'oppression and shame' as real consequences? This is certainly what Wulfstan's rhetorically charged *Sermo Lupi ad Anglos* had revealed about the situation in Anglo-Saxon England during the Viking raids in 1014, which had led to 'a sharpening of perceptions of difference between "English" and "Dane"', as Matthew Innes notes.[4]

Multiple Narratives: Colonizer, Colonized

Thinking about the postcolonial in relation to early England is, in itself, quite tricky. Many modern scholars would deny there was any connection, since the colonial and postcolonial are thought to be properties of modern society replete with national borders and a clear sense of political distinction. This implies, however, that there was no sense of England as a nation or as a discrete social and political unit in the pre-modern period, when recent scholarship has shown unambiguously that there was a keenly developed and explicitly expressed English identity in this late Anglo-Saxon period.[5] In addition, it denies the people of England,

---

[3] Stafford, *Unification and Conquest*, p. 70. See also *Anglo-Saxon Chronicle*, Annal 1040, p. 234: 'C(D) In this year King Harold died. Then they sent to Bruges for Hardacnut, thinking that they were acting wisely, and he then came here with 60 ships, before midsummer, and then imposed a very severe tax, which was endured with difficulty, namely eight marks to the rowlock. And all who had wanted him before were then ill-disposed towards him.'

[4] Matthew Innes, 'Danelaw Identities', p. 77.

[5] See Sarah Foot, 'The Making of *Angelcynn*: English Identity before the Norman Conquest', *Transactions of the Royal Historical Society* 6th ser., 6 (1996), pp. 25–49.

or elsewhere, a consciousness of political relationships, an apprehension of dominations both within England and without. At the same time, the concept of England itself is problematic, partly because of the long and poorly recorded decades of Danish settlement, and because structures of power and ethnic interaction in Danelaw are unclear. Partly, too, we are unable to determine easily the reaction of the majority of the English's response to Conquest, though it has to be the case that silence does not equal compliance, and an untroubled surface can still conceal agitated undercurrents.

Interpretation is made the more complicated by the overwhelming nature of the Norman Conquest. Both processes of conquest—1016 and 1066—tend to be melded in scholarly writing, the earlier subsumed under the latter's apparently greater significance. But this is a perspective that can only be ascertained retrospectively. One quite typical historical reading of the consequences of the English conquests is Henry Loyn's:

> We can all see that the notion of the king's peace, rooted in Carolingian precedent, blossomed and burgeoned in the eleventh century, dramatically so under new direction, first by Cnut and then under William the Conqueror.[6]

One might be forgiven for reading these two cataclysmic 'new directions' as an obvious, and very desirable, pairing. I've argued elsewhere that this is anachronistic and teleological, and it denies the first conquest any of the significance it had in its own historical moment. In the very early years of Cnut's reign, the majority of English ealdormen and thanes were killed, the country divided into four, Anglo-Scandinavian jarls given positions of power, and many changes brought about in governance at national and local level, the impact of which was still felt into the Norman period.[7] Yet, there seems to have been almost no concerted domestic response, little by way of obvious protest.

---

[6] Henry Loyn, 'De Iure Domini Regis: A Comment on Royal Authority in Eleventh-Century England', in Carola Hicks (ed.), England in the Eleventh Century (Stamford: Paul Watkins, 1992), pp. 17–24, at 21.

[7] Katherin Mack, 'Changing Thegns: Cnut's Conquest and the English Aristocracy', North American Conference on British Studies 16, 4 (1984), 375–87. See also the Anglo-Saxon Chronicle, s.a. 1016: p. 227, 'When the king learnt that the [Danish] army had gone inland, for the fifth time he collected all the English nation; and pursued them and overtook them in Essex at the hill which is called Ashingdon…and all the nobility of England was there destroyed.'

And at the same time as we have to hunt for English responses to Cnut, and Cnut's response to the English, the fact that there is more than one narrative is important, as the discussion of Skaldic verse in Chapter 2 has already shown. It therefore becomes imperative to try and untangle the voices of colonizer, colonized, vocal, silenced, recorded, and ghostly. This is complex, though, in part because of the difficulties in reconciling the external and internal faces of Cnut and in disentangling the views of commentators on Cnut, who themselves seem variously to practise a politics of praise or of sensationalism.

Major difficulties arise, unsurprisingly, in reading through the texts of postconquest historians. Aware that a great deal of writing, and particularly public writing, is ideological, it is easy to assume that what was written in this period emanated from an agenda of either resistance or imperialized propaganda. This binary is simplistic. One can detect multiple narratives in play, some themselves hybridized by the problematic bifurcation of individual writers, like William of Malmesbury, whose views vacillate, at times radically, across his extensive and important corpus. The various depictions of Cnut in Malmesbury (such as those discussed in Chapter 2) can be read at face value, such that one can interpret from the episode with the virgin Eadgyth a petulant king, chastened and made pious by a local saint. Or, one might highlight the consistently derogatory comparisons to Cnut's English predecessors in Malmesbury's writings: the slothful Æthelred; the tyrannical, lustful and vicious Edgar; and the evilness of the treacherous Anglo-Saxon Eadric Streona, defeated and executed by Cnut, as if he were a metonym for a sinful nation.[8]

Other historians, none as revered and over-employed as William, paint a different picture of Cnut's reign. Hugh Candidus, chronicler of Peterborough, comments that:

---

[8] *Gesta Regum Anglorum*, i. 321. Should we also, then, believe that Cnut chooses 'shameless' prelates to guide him and be his 'influential confidant'? *Gesta Pontificum Anglorum*, i. 314–15, reveals about Lyfing, bishop of Crediton that: 'Lyfing, who was a monk of Winchester and abbot of Tavistock before becoming bishop of Crediton, was an influential confidant of King Cnut, (2) spending much time with him in Denmark and accompanying him on his journey to Rome. Accordingly, after the king had finished his business in Rome and set off by land for Denmark, Lyfing sailed to England with the king's letters, charged to carry out his instructions. He showed remarkable wisdom in performing before Cnut's arrival all that had been required of him, and won such favour with the king that on the death of his uncle Brihtwold bishop of Cornwall he combined the two sees under his rule. (3) Ambitious and shameless [*ambitiosus et proteruus*], he is said to have lorded it like some irresistible tyrant over the laws of the Church, with no scruple in doing all he wished.'

Grievous and excessive was the tribute which the English were paying to the army of the Danes, who in the time of Æthelred the king and Edmund, for the space of nearly forty years, plundered, and sorely afflicted all England, with fire and sword, as the histories do testify, until Sweyn, or Canute his son, of the Danish race was exalted to the throne. For the English had always to pay this tribute, and it was yearly increased until it became seventy two thousand pounds and more, not to mention the eleven thousand which London alone paid. And yet it availed them little or nothing, for the Danes never ceased to do all manner of mischief. Those who had money enough to pay such mighty tribute paid it, but those who had it not lost beyond recovery their lands and possessions, and all things they had. Thus this church [Peterborough] like divers others, did suffer great loss.'[9]

Here, the differences in power are seen to be those of national identity—ethnic distinction, a distinction whose chronology is not clear: Danes and decades are melded, such that it becomes difficult to determine how much the Danish oppression continued under Cnut, if any. Even so, the 'great loss' looked, to some at least, permanent.[10]

'Great loss' and 'The Politics of the Witness'

[*Anglo-Saxon Chronicle* D, 1014:] Þa sende se cyning his sunu Eadweard hider mid his ærenddracan 7 het gretan ealne his leodscype, 7 cwæð þæt he him hold hlaford beon wolde, 7 ælc þæra þinga betan þe hi ealle

---

[9] W.T. Mellows (ed.), *The Peterborough Chronicle of Hugh Candidus*, Peterborough Museum Society (Glossop: Paul Bush, 1941; rep. 1997), p. 29.

[10] M. R. James (trans.), E. S. Hartland (ed.), *Walter Map's 'De Nugis Curialium'*, Cymmrodorion Record Series 9 (London: Society of Cymmrodorion, 1923). Such oppression is explicit in Walter Map's *De Nugis Curialium*, a later twelfth-century, often romanticized account of various episodes in history that he thought entertaining. Calling Cnut 'the richest and bravest of all the kings at that time', he reveals that Cnut 'continued a free monarch for a long time, and the Danes spread over all the provinces everywhere, and prevailed over the English and forced them into the worst of slaveries, ill-using their wives, daughters and nieces.' *De Nugis Curialium*, Distinction V, Chapter IV, p. 237. For oppression, see also the account of Cnut in Frank Barlow (ed.), *Vita Ædwardi Regis*, Oxford Medieval Texts (Oxford: Oxford University Press, 1992), at Bk I. i, pp. 12–13: 'so God's loving kindness, sparing the English after the heavy weight of rebuke [the Danish reigns of Cnut etc.], showed them a flower preserved from the root of their ancient kings' [*sic dei pietas Anglis post grauem sue correptionis pressuram parcens, de antiquorum regum stripe seruatum florem ostendit*].

ascunodon, 7 ælc þara þinga forgyfon beon sceolde þe him gedon oððe
cwæden wære, wið þam þe hi ealle anrædlice butan swicdome to him
gecyrdon. 7 man þa fulne freondscipe gefæstnode mid worde 7 mid
wedde on ægþre healfe, 7 æfre ælcne Dæniscne cyning utlah of ængla-
lande gecwædon. Þa com Æþelred cyning innan þam Lænctentid ham
to his agenre þeode, 7 he glædlice fram him eallum onfangen wæs. Þa
syþþan Swegen dead wæs, sæt Cnut mid his here on Gæignesburuh oð
ða Eastron, 7 gewearð him 7 þæt folc on Lindesige anes þæt he hine
horsian sceoldon, 7 wið þan ealle ætgædere faran 7 hergian. Ða com se
cyning Æþelred mid fulre fyrde þyder ær hi gearwe wæron to Lindesige,
7 man þa hergode 7 bærnde 7 sloh eall þæt mancynn þæt man geræcan
mihte. 7 se Cnut gewende him ut mid his flotan, 7 wearð þæt earme folc
þus beswicen þurh hine, 7 wende þa suðweard oð he com to Sandwic, 7
læt man þær up þa gislas þe his fæder gesealde wæron, 7 cearf of heora
handa 7 earan 7 nosa. 7 buton eallum þissum yfelum se cyng het gyldan
þam here þe on Grenewic læg .xxi. þusend punda. 7 on þissum geare on
Sancte Michaeles mæsseæfen com þæt mycle sæflod geond wide þisne
eard, 7 earn swa feor up swa næfre ær ne dyde, 7 adrencte fela tuna, 7
manncynnes unarimedlic getel.

Then the king [Æthelred] sent his son Edward here with his messengers and commanded all his people to be greeted, and said that he
would be a faithful lord to them, and would make each of the things
that they all detested better; and each of the things that had been
done or said against him should be forgiven, assuming that they all
unanimously and without treachery turned to him. And then full
friendship was established on either side in word and pledge. And
they said that every Danish king was to be outlawed from England.
Then King Æthelred came home to his own people at Lenten-time,
and he was gladly received by them all. Then, after Swein was dead,
Cnut settled with his raiding army in Gainsborough until Easter, and
the people in Lindsey came to an agreement with him that they
should provide him with horses and afterwards all go together and
raid. Then, before they were ready, King Æthelred came there with
the whole army into Lindsey, and then all human kind that could be
got at were raided and burned and killed. Cnut himself went out with
his fleet—and thus the wretched people were betrayed through him—
and then turned southwards until he came to Sandwich, and there
put ashore the hostages who were granted to his father, and cut off
their hands and ears and noses. And besides all these evils, the
king ordered the raiding party that lay at Greenwich to be paid
21 thousand pounds. And in this year on St Michael's Eve, that great

> sea-flood came widely throughout this country, and ran further inland than it ever did before, and drowned many settlements and a countless number of human beings.[11]

This lengthy and detailed description of the tumultuous events of 1014, included in the C, D, and E versions of the *Anglo-Saxon Chronicle*,[12] provides the contextual backdrop to Cnut's eventual succession to the throne of England in 1016, after the deaths of King Æthelred and his son, Edmund Ironside. Together with the annals for 1015 and 1016, it forms a relatively full account of the political tension and high-level negotiation in England after Swein's death.[13] The fraught nature of the situation is evident not only in the rapidity of the relation of events, with the piling up of clauses introduced by 'and', but also in the swift alternation between the death of the pagan Swein, consecration of a Christian bishop, selection of Cnut, rejection of Cnut and reconfirmation of commitment to Æthelred. The movement takes us from outside the realm to inside, outside to inside in a rhetorical reflection of the vacillation of a nation. At every turn, until the silent ending of the annal, the noise of imagined word and deed is traceable—the acclamation of Cnut's fleet, the debate of the *witan*, the reporting of the sets of messengers, the clatter of raiding horses, the shrieking of the wretched people. An account that begins with one natural death, ends with the natural disaster of countless victims' drowning; sandwiched in between are the killings of 'all human kind that could be reached' and the mutilations of the hostages caught up in the conflict.

Representing the Unrepresentable

The *Chronicle*'s dramatic and intense account of the suffering of the English is evident from this annal and it sets the scene for the arrival

[11] Edited from London, BL Cotton Tiberius B. iv, folio 65r. See also G. P. Cubbin (ed.), *The Anglo-Saxon Chronicle, A Collaborative Edition, 6: MS D* (Cambridge, 1996), p. 59, and Michael Swanton (ed. and trans.), *The Anglo-Saxon Chronicle* (London: Dent, 1998), p. 145.

[12] London, BL Cotton Tiberius C.i is manuscript C (the *Abingdon Chronicle*); Tiberius B. iv is manuscript D; and Oxford, Bodleian Library, Laud 636 is E (the *Peterborough Chronicle*). See Cubbin, *MS D*; Susan Irvine (ed.), *The Anglo-Saxon Chronicle, 7: MS E* (Cambridge: D. S. Brewer, 2004); Katherine O'Brien O'Keeffe (ed.), *The Anglo-Saxon Chronicle, 5: MS C* (Cambridge: D. S. Brewer, 2000).

[13] So dramatically complemented by Wulfstan's *Sermo Lupi ad Anglos*, of course. See Jonathan Wilcox, 'Wulfstan's *Sermo Lupi ad Anglos* as Political Performance', in Townend (ed.), *Wulfstan, Archbishop of York*, pp. 375–96.

of Cnut into national history. Amidst the noise of the competing voices embedded in this monastic narration is the assured statement of the historian, self-authorized to recount the formative events of the nation. Yet from here to the D-*Chronicle's* lament for the *earm folc* in 1066—a lament for those for whom what was already catastrophic grew 'always afterwards very much worse'[14]—one might wonder about the absence and silence of the sufferers themselves, particularly of the faceless (noseless, earless) dispossessed and 'wretched people'. I wonder, given the large gaps in our evidence, what these literal lacunae hide, what these absences of articulation force us to miss? And yet, I wonder more about the clamour of the evidence we *do* have, about the detectable ghosts that we *can* trace in the texts that survive, and I wonder why scholars do so much to erase those who were already half-erased—the silent, voiceless human hubbub behind the land-grabbers, psalm-singers and sword-wielders.

These concerns insist on a consideration of the perspective of the normally silenced survivor, a 'politics of the witness', or 'a representation of the unrepresentable', terms I borrow from Marc Nichanian in his moving and significant work on the late nineteenth- and early twentieth-century Armenian Catastrophe.[15] This is tricky work, partly because to find the articulations of horror and resistance, it is essential to use textual reflections that are themselves, at times, inarticulate or indirect, often incapable of putting into words that which is ineffable, inexpressible. Moreover, in relation to the conquests of the eleventh century, there are multiple sets of witnesses. There are those authorized and politicized, often hierarchized, contemporary responses to the events that saw foreign kings displace their English predecessors, with the full acquiescence of God and with right on their side. There are also those accounts that shout loudly, but briefly,

---

[14] '7 Oda biscop 7 Wyllelm eorl belifen her æfter 7 worhton castelas wide geond þas þeode, 7 earm folc swencte, 7 a syððan hit yflade swiðe. Wurðe god se ende þonne God wylle' ('And [in England] Bishop Odo and Earl William were left here and they built castles widely throughout the nation, and wretched people were afflicted, and it always afterwards became very much worse. May the outcome be good, when God wills it'). See Cubbin, *MS D*, p. 81.

[15] Marc Nichanian, 'Catastrophic Mourning', and David Kazanjian and Marc Nichanian, 'Beween Genocide and Catastrophe', in David L. Eng and David Kazanjian (eds.), *Loss* (Berkeley: University of California Press, 2003), pp. 99–124 and pp. 125–47, respectively. A 'politics of the witness' appears at pp. 140–1.

about the change in the political landscape and the replacement of the top and middling echelons of Anglo-Saxon society. And there are the accounts accessible to the silenced, mediated by a church whose role is as the inscriber of cultural memory. Finally, and perhaps most significantly, there are the responses of modern scholars, whose apparent objectivity and distance mutes the voices of those beneath the highest echelons of society, and denies any potential articulation of catastrophe and mourning.

The turbulent events of Cnut's accession and William's fifty years later are well rehearsed. Both conquests followed periods of disruption and bloodshed, though that of 1066, in contrast to the decades prior to 1016, was swift and came from the north with revolt by Tostig, Harold Godwineson's brother, and invasion by the Norwegian king, Harold Hardrada; both conquests were followed by further acts of violence and suppression, particularly in the case of the Norman, where active resistance to William lasted for some years after 1066.[16] In the very early years of Cnut's reign, many changes were brought about in governance and personnel at national and local level, the impact of which was still felt into the Norman period.[17] On the one hand, one might easily assume that with Cnut's accession to England's throne, its people continued much as they had done, with a king who depicted himself as pious, generous, and politically astute; on the other hand, a number of his deeds were actions of a brutal, tax-raising, regicidal, fratricidal, adulterous usurper.[18] Should one assume that none of the violence or demands for increased taxes throughout the almost two-decade reign of Cnut was of concern to his Anglo-Saxon subjects? Indeed, how can we ever know? Mark Lawson may perhaps speak on behalf of an imagined Anglo-Saxon response, for as he reminds us:

> The Danish conquest is relatively forgotten today not only because it was short-lived and without significant consequences, but because a

[16] On 1066 and events leading up to the Battle of Hastings, see, among many others, David Bates, *William the Conqueror* (London: Tempus, 1989); F. Barlow, *The Godwins: The Rise and Fall of a Noble Dynasty* (Harlow: Longman, 2002).

[17] Katherin Mack, 'Changing Thegns', pp. 375–87.

[18] Cnut harshly punished London for its support of Æthelred and Edmund Ironside, and the east of England was subdued for years. See esp. Bolton, *Cnut the Great*, pp. 86–94. Cnut also maintained an adulterous relationship with Ælfgifu of Northampton.

scarcity of sources makes elucidation of its nature, and not least that of its main figure, arduous and frequently inconclusive.[19]

For Lawson, it is the 'short-lived' and inconsequential nature of Cnut's conquest—a conclusion based principally on the lack of documented narrative—that makes this major historical event so easily elided; the more so, of course, because events fifty years afterwards have seemed to later historians more shattering. In addition, the declared adherence to Edgar's law in Cnut's reign manufactured by a familiar statesman like Wulfstan I facilitates the appearance of 1016 as seamless continuity. Ultimately, the reinstatement of Æthelred's line on the return of Edward the Confessor in 1042, allows us, with our anachronistic perspective, to sublate that first conquest of 1016.

Lawson suggests that if there were more evidence, more incontrovertible proof of consequences, the 1016 conquest would become significant.[20] But the claims of silence[21] are focused upon the relative absence of traditional forms of monarchical administration—royal charters, writs and diplomas, and the detailed record of the *Anglo-Saxon Chronicle* as witnessed from the years around Cnut's reign. As will become apparent, there is no dearth of testimony to Cnut's reign; the abundance of commentary is subsumed beneath the superficially atemporal homilies and saints' lives copied in English throughout the years 1016–35, and beyond. These English materials mediate the tension in the political landscape, tensions that are manifested explicitly through the Skaldic verse, eulogizing the king's brutal regime and his *own* epistolary declarations of law-making, diplomatic negotiation, and revivification through

[19] Lawson, *Cnut*, p. 214. At http://www.the-orb.net/textbooks/muhlberger/canute .html, the author writes: 'Cnut made a more important commitment the next year, when he was on expedition to Denmark. He told them that he would rule as a good Christian monarch and an upholder of law and order; but further, he told the English that if they supported him, he would make sure that England would no longer be troubled by Vikings. This was a deal that everyone could approve of, and Cnut had little trouble in England for the twenty years that he reigned.'

[20] This issue of consequences, or continuities, in 1016 and 1066 is also discussed by Patrick Wormald, 'Archbishop Wulfstan: Eleventh-Century State-Builder', in Townend (ed.), *Wulfstan, Archbishop of York*, pp. 9–27, at p. 15.

[21] Which seem ubiquitous; thus, Anne Williams, 'England in the Eleventh Century', in Christopher Harper-Bill and Elisabeth Van Houts (eds.), *A Companion to the Anglo-Norman World* (Woodbridge: Boydell, 2003), pp. 1–18, at p. 8 states: 'Lack of material for Cnut's reign (especially the latter half) prevents us from seeing how Leofric and Godwine attained their eminence.'

penitence. In this middle space, resolving the paradox of ambivalent kingship, are the many English texts that utilize familiar tropes of societal fragmentation and spiritual damnation, but with specific historical positioning and determinable cultural referencing, which raises their value as the vicarious articulation of the voiceless, the ventriloquized testimony of those who could themselves never bear witness.

In the York Gospels, York Minster Library 1, Wulfstan effectively appropriated and reconfigured that volume by providing his own additions in an added quire. Among the additions is the famous *Letter to the English* of Cnut from 1020, discussed in Chapter 1, preceded by new pastiche homilies by Wulfstan, datable to *c*.1020–3, and plausibly his last public words.[22] At folio 161v there is a set of four complete, and one unfinished, Bidding Prayers, the earliest of their kind.[23] Since Wulfstan's own hand appears within the sermons, and since the sermons were copied by the same scribe that wrote out the prayers, it seems reasonable to assume that Wulfstan himself was responsible for the prayers in his personal Gospelbook.[24] More to the point, particular elements of the lexis and rhetoric suggest very strongly that these are all, or partly, Wulfstan's compositions. Marked out by a marginal cross similar to that which opens Cnut's *Letter of 1020*, these prayers range from the universal to the particular, taking in all of Christian time from Adam's day onwards, and praying for the nation as well as the named individual:

> Wutan we gebiddan God ealmihtine, heofena heah cyning, 7 Sancta Marian, 7 ealle Godes halgan þæt we moton Godes ælmihtiges willan gewyrcan þa hwil þe we on þyssan lænan life wunian þæt hy us

[22] Keynes, 'The Additions in Old English', pp. 81–99.

[23] Edited by W. H. Stevenson, 'Yorkshire Surveys and other eleventh-century documents in the York Gospels', *English Historical Review* 27 (1912), pp. 1–25, and Keynes, 'The Additions in Old English', p. 97.

[24] Joyce Tally Lionarons, *The Homiletic Writings of Archbishop Wulfstan* (Woodbridge: Boydell and Brewer, 2010), p. 18, suggests these prayers are mid to late eleventh century, but that does not make sense if the scribe of the prayers is the same as the one who writes the homilies. Christopher A. Jones, 'Wulfstan's Liturgical Interests', in Townend (ed.), *Wulfstan, Archbishop of York*, pp. 325–52, at p. 334, fn 40, comments: 'It is far from certain that the so-called bidding prayers in Old English ... were intended for public use. Their relation to Wulfstan is in any case unknowable.' It is difficult to see these prayers with their first person plural address and imperative 'Wutan' as intentionally private. On the language of and influences on these prayers, see Thomas Bredehoft, *Authors, Audiences and Old English Verse* (Toronto: University of Toronto Press, 2009), Appendix, esp. p. 215.

gehealdan 7 gescyldan wið ealra feonda costnunga, gesenelicra and ungesenelicra, *Pater noster.*

Wutan we gebiddan for urne papan on Rome, 7 for urne cyning, 7 for urne arcebiscop and for urne ealdorman, 7 for ealle þa þe us gehealdað frið and freondscype on feower healfe into þysse halgan stowe, 7 for ealle þa ðe us fore gebiddað binnan Angelcynne 7 butan Angelcynne, *Pater noster.*

Wutan we gebiddan for ure godsybbas 7 for ure cumpæðran, 7 for ure gildan and gildsweostra, 7 ealles þæs folces gebed þe þas halgan stowe mid ælmesan seceð, mid lihte 7 mid tigeðinge, 7 for ealle ða þe we æfre heora ælmessan befonde wæron, ær life 7 æfter life, *Pater.*

Bidde we […]

For Þorferþes saule bidde we *Pater noster*, 7 for Mælmære saule, 7 for ealle þa saula þe fulluht underfengan 7 on Crist gelyfdan fram Adames dæge to þisum dæge, *Pater noster.*

Let us pray God almighty, high king of heaven, and Saint Mary, and all God's saints that we might do almighty God's will as long as we live in this transitory life that they might protect us and shield us against all the fiend's temptations, seen and unseen. Our Father.

Let us pray for our pope in Rome, and for our king, and for our archbishop, and for our ealdorman, and for all those who defend peace and friendship for us in the four parts of this holy place, and for all those who pray for us among the English nation and outside the English nation. Our Father.

Let us pray for our sponsors and for our godfathers and for our gildsmen and gildswomen, and for the prayers of all those people who seek this holy place with alms, with light and with tithes, and for all those from whom we ever received alms, during life or after life. Our Father.

Let us pray…

We pray Our Father for the soul of Thurferth and for the soul of Mælmære, and for all the souls who have received baptism and believed in Christ from Adam's day to this day. Our Father.

These prayers, or the first three at least, share lexical similarities with texts known to have been written by Wulfstan; namely the law codes for King Æthelred, V and X Æthelred,[25] where the second prayer's collocation

---

[25] See, most conveniently, Patrick Wormald, 'Wulfstan (*d.* 1023)', *Oxford Dictionary of National Biography*, Oxford University Press, 2004 [http://www.oxforddnb.com.proxy.lib. fsu.edu/view/article/30098, accessed 18 July 2010].

'frið 7 freondscype' only occurs otherwise.[26] Echoing Wulfstanian language, the pairing of near synonyms, 'gehealdan and gescyldan', emphasizes the need for celestial protection, while the legal language (also reminiscent of certain charms) of the second prayer seeks temporal protection in 'feower healfe' of 'this holy place', probably the church itself, but also, metonymically, England with its 'the four parts' or, perhaps, 'all four corners'.[27] Like its use in the homilies and charms in which it occurs, 'feower healfe' emphasizes the blanket covering of an expanse; in this specific context, the four parts of England may also be a direct political reference to the quarters of the land created by Cnut on his accession, and given to his senior ealdormen to administer.[28] The first three prayers, which probably form a unit, move from the outside in—from beseeching protection from God and his saints, to the protection of secular Christian leaders, to the individual's godparents, and the locality's collective gilds and parishioners. This atemporal and pyramidal structure beseeching the safeguarding of peace, friendship, and salvation is reinforced by the final typological plea for the souls of all baptized from Adam's day onwards, but dramatically disrupted by the presentness of the prayer for the souls of specific individuals, presumably benefactors, whose names were added to the list of more general prayers.

The function of these prayers seems explicitly to encourage unity, a unity that focuses on the English recipients of much-needed protection who belong to the congregation of the particular church, but who, in effect, represent all Christians. The performative nature of these brief texts underscores the public nature of the Gospels that host them. It seems likely, given the marks in the Gospel texts themselves, that this manuscript was used liturgically. Preachers' marks occur, for example, at folios 53v–54r and 120 onwards, including small crosses above particular words meant to be emphasized, *c*-shaped marks indicating stress, and *s*-shaped indicators. That this Gospelbook appears to have been in use within an ecclesiastical setting at York and possibly

---

[26] *Dictionary of Old English*, s.v. 'frið 7 freondscype'.

[27] The phrase occurs in *Pax*, a one-line law code appended to Æthelred's Wantage Code in *Quadripartitus*, formulated, Wormald thinks, before Wulfstan's influence. See Wormald, *Making of English Law*, p. 372. On Wulfstan's rhetoric, see Raachel Jurovics, '*Sermo Lupi* and the Moral Purpose of Rhetoric', in Paul E. Szarmach and Bernard Huppe (eds.), *The Old English Homily and its Backgrounds* (Albany, NY: SUNY, 1978), pp. 203–20.

[28] Keynes, 'Cnut's Earls', p. 81.

Worcester, too, and in direct contact with Wulfstan between 1020 and 1023, means it should be considered an anchor-codex for Cnut's reign and for our understanding of cultural responses to the reign within the very formulaic context of the liturgy and Wulfstan's own writings. Homiletic English thus becomes a mediator between the formal, authorized and self-authenticating utterances of Cnut in his charters (including his writ-like Letters), the ecclesiastically official *Anglo-Saxon Chronicle*, and the king's subjects by conquest. That this church-going audience is the imagined construct of the pastor does not mean they are thought to have no agency; on the contrary, the audience is urged to activity, to right and proper Christian behaviour in order the more effectively to negotiate the decades of hardship and turbulence. The audience is thus taught to respond in a way that is entirely appropriate given contemporary received wisdom on the turmoil of conquest, which viewed these events as the visitation of God's anger on a people encumbered by sinfulness and looks to individuals within this wider Christian community to bring about a collective redemption.

'Leofan men, doð swa ic lære':[29] the lessons of conquest

In *The Homilies of Wulfstan*, Bethurum comments on the three texts in the York Gospels, *Sermo Lupi*, *Be Hæðendome*, and *Be Cristendome* (Napier 59, 60, and 61) that she had decided to exclude them from her edition of Wulfstan's homiletic works because they are not homilies, but are, rather, made up of combinations of Wulfstan's other works.[30] Since then, few scholars have commented on these texts, exceptions being Simon Keynes, Patrick Wormald, and Audrey L. Meaney.[31] Keynes judges these pieces to be significant:

[29] Wulfstan, *Sermo Lupi*, York Gospels, folio 158r: 'Beloved people, do what I instruct'. The text is also edited by A. Napier, *Sammlung der ihm zugeschriebenen homilien nebst untersuchungen über ihre echtheit* (Berlin: Weidmann, 1883).

[30] Dorothy Bethurum (ed.), *The Homilies of Wulfstan* (Oxford: Oxford University Press, 1957), 38–9.

[31] Keynes, 'The Additions in Old English', p. 92; Wormald, *Making of English Law*, p. 196; Audrey L. Meaney, '"And we forbeodað eornostlice ælcne hæðenscipe": Wulfstan and Late Anglo-Saxon and Norse "Heathenism"', in Townend, *Wulfstan, Archbishop of York*, pp. 460–500. Meaney edits and translates *Be Hæðendome* at pp. 481–3, and offers a very substantial reading of this and analogous texts.

> The three homiletic tracts at the end of the York Gospels were prob-
> ably compiled especially for inclusion in the manuscript...they rep-
> resented a considered summary of Wulfstan's views on the proper
> ordering of a Christian society, and by placing them in the gospel
> book Wulfstan evidently intended not only to enhance the authority
> behind them but also to ensure that his message would not be
> forgotten.

These texts represent, in language that echoes the *Sermo Lupi*, Wulfstan's
final view of the society he strove so hard to shape and sustain, and it is a
picture that suggests continued turmoil and continued need for reform
years into Cnut's reign. In what follows, the two of the three short homi-
letico-legal works that seem directed to a general audience are presented,
but all three statements can be considered the final distillation of Wulfstan's words and thoughts both as statesman and as archbishop. They
offer a catena of his own writings, sourced by him from his law code of
I Cnut and from his own major synthesis of political and theological
theory, the *Institutes of Polity*.

In a rare move, the first tract is named as Wulfstan's and authorized
by that name; this *Sermo Lupi* demands that the listeners—specifically, those in orders who teach—adhere to the core duties of God's
servants in ensuring the right Christian behaviour of the laity, and of
others in orders. This hierarchy suggests that this text was prepared
for bishops, who oversee the work of priests, and who are ultimately
responsible for ensuring the proper baptismal preparation of parishioners. The short, emphatic and highly organized text encapsulates
the major principles of how a bishop and priest might best go about
their business, and it is abundant with the typical rhetorical devices
favoured by Wulfstan in his admonitions and exhortations to the
righteous Christian.

The same forceful oratorically adept style pervades *Be Hæðendome*
too. Keynes comments on this piece that

> The heading '*Be Hæðendome*' is thus misleading, for in effect the
> tract is concerned with a far wider range of social ills. If we may
> assume that Wulfstan himself compiled the tract from his own writ-
> ings, specifically for inclusion in the York Gospels, it is interesting
> to find that he should still be adopting the tone of his *Sermo ad
> Anglos* in the reign of Cnut. It could be that he was particularly wor-
> ried by the state of affairs in the diocese of York, but one suspects

that he would propound such views regardless of the conditions prevailing.[32]

It is more than 'interesting' to see Wulfstan commenting on England at this point and in this critical way, it is compelling, and particularly so when one considers the juxtaposition of this piece with Cnut's *Letter of 1020*. This homily, like the Letter, has a particular rhetorical situation, which is certainly post-1020, and which thus suggests that the attendant horrors of the process of conquest were still very apparent five or more years into Cnut's ascendancy.[33] Wulfstan, adopting a stern hortatory tone, instructs those responsible for upholding ecclesiastical law to implement it properly and to identify and deal with those who do not adhere to it.

Be Hæðendome

Nemo cristianorum 'vel nullus cristianus' paganas superstitiones intendat, sed gentilium inquinamenta omnia omnino contemnat.

Eala, mycel is nydþearf manna gehwylcum þæt he wið deofles larswice warnige symle, and þæt he hæðenscype georne æfre forbuge, þæs þe he gedon mæge. And gyf hit geweorðe þæt cristen man æfre heonanforð ahwar heðendom begange oððon ahwar on lande idola weorðige, gebete þæt deope for Gode and for worolde. And se ðe to gelome þæt unriht begange, gylde mid Englum swa wer swa wite and on Dena lage lahslite, be ðam þe seo dæd sy. And, gyf wiccean oððe wigelearas, horingas oððe horcwenan, morðwyrhtan oððe mansworan innan þysan eared weorðan agytene, fyse hy man georne ut of þysan earde and clænsige þas þeode oððon on earde forfare hy mid ealle, butan hi geswicon and þe deoppor gebetan. And do man swa hit þearf is, manfulra dæda on æghwylcan ende styre man swyðe.

---

[32] Keynes, 'The Additions in Old English', p. 94. This homily has been discussed recently by Jonathan Davis-Secord, 'Rhetoric and Politics in Archbishop Wulfstan's Old English Homilies', *Anglia* 126 (2008), pp. 65–96, at pp. 69–71.

[33] In relation to Wulfsige, bishop of Sherborne, Simon Keynes ('Wulfsige, bishop of Sherborne', in Katherine Barker, David A. Hinton and Alan Hunt (eds.), *St Wulfsige and Sherborne: Essays to Celebrate the Millennium of the Benedictine Abbey 998–1998* (Oxford: Oxbow, 2005), pp. 53–94, at pp. 62–3) points out the contemporary applicability of a letter of an archbishop to a bishop, actually written by Alcuin originally, but copied into the Pontifical of Dunstan in the later tenth century and thereafter in Wulfsige's possession.

Her syndan on earde godcundnesse wiðersacan and Godes lage ofer-hogan, manslagan and mægslagan, cyrichatan and sacerdbanan, had-brecan and æwbrecan, myltestran and bearnmyrðran, þeofas and þeodscaðan, ryperas and reaferas, leogeras and licceteras and leodha-tan hetele ealles to manege, þe ðurh mansylene bariað þas þeode, and wedlogan and wærlogan and lytle getrywða to wide mid mannum. And ne byrhð se gesibba hwilan gesibban þe ma, þe ðam fremdan, ne broðor his breðere oþre hwile; ne bearn for oft his fæder ne meder, ne nafela manna ne healt his getrywða swa wel swa he scolde for gode and for worolde, ac do man, swa hit þearf is, gebete hit georne and clænsige þas þeode, gyf man Godes miltse geearnian wylle.

None of the Christians 'or no Christian' should pay attention to pagan superstitions, but should entirely condemn all the iniquities of the Gentiles.

Listen, there is a great need for each person that they should always protect themselves against the devil's seduction, and should always eagerly shun heathenism, as far as they are able. And if it happens that a Christian person ever afterwards practises heathenism anywhere, or worships idols anywhere in this land, let them make up for that sin-cerely before God and the world. And those who too frequently prac-tise that sin, let those among the English pay the wergild for breaking the law, and those in the Danelaw the fine payable for violating the law, appropriate to whatever the deed might be. And, if witches or wizards, whores or prostitutes, murderers or perjurers are found within this land, they should be eagerly driven out of this country and these peo-ple should be cleansed, or they should be entirely destroyed within the country, unless they stop and make amends the more sincerely. And let someone deal with evil deeds in every area, just as the need arises.

Here in the land there are enemies of the divine and those who despise God's law, murderers and killers of kinsmen, those who hate the church and priest-killers, violators of holy orders and adulterers, pros-titutes and murderers of children, robbers and those who despoil the community, hypocrites and criminals and those who hate the people all too much, who, by selling into slavery decrease the people, and those who break pledges and the faithless, and there is too little truth among men. And it is no longer the case that the kinsman protects his kinsman any more than a stranger, nor does a brother his brother sometimes; neither too often, a child his father or his mother. Nor do many people keep their faith as well as they should, before God and the world. But people should do as is needed: make amends for it eagerly, and cleanse this people, if they want to earn God's mercy.

Be Cristendome

A Cristo enim cristiani sunt nominati, Cristus autem capud nostrum est et nos membra eius. Crist is ealra Cristenra manna heafod and ealle Cristene men syndon to Cristes limum getealde, gyf hy heora drihtne gecwemað mid rihte.[34] And hy scylan swyþe georne Cristendom æfre healdan mid rihte and Cristes cyrcan secan gelome heom sylfum to þearfe and Cristes gerihta rihtlice gelæstan. And þæt is an ærest þæt man geteoðige æghwylce geare þæt þæt God sende þonne on geare folce to þearfe on corne and on flexe and on gewelhwylcon wæstme. And arise seo æcerteoðung a be ðam þe seo sulh þone teoðan ær geeode, be Godes miltse and be ðæs cynges and be ealles Cristenes folces and be ðære steore þe Eadgar cyng gelagode.

And sy ælcere geogoðe teoðung gelæst be Pentecosten be wite and eorðwæstma be ealra halgena mæssan. And Romfeoh gelæste man æghwylce geare be Petres mæssan; and se ðe hit ne gelæste, sylle þærtoeacan xxx peninga and bringe 'vel sende' to Rome and gylde þam cynge on Engla lage cxx scillinga; and cyricsceat gelæsten on Engla Lage and to Martines mæssan; and se ðe þæt ne gelæste, forgylde hine mid twelffealdan and þam cynge cxx scillinga and sulhælmessan gebyrað, þæt man gelæste be wite æghwylce geare þonne huru xv niht beoð agan ofer Eastertid. And leohtgescot gelæste man be wite to Cristesmæssan and to Candelmæssan and to Eastron, do oftor se ðe wylle. And saulscat is rihtast þæt man gelæste aa æt openum græfe. And freolsa and fæstena bewite healde man rihtlice. And ealle Godes gerihta fyrðrige man georne, ealswa hit þearf is,[35] and gyf hwa swa nelle, gewylde man hine to rihte mid woroldlicre steore.

Indeed, from Christ are Christians named, for Christ is our head, and we his body. Christ is the head of all Christian people and all Christian people are reckoned as Christ's limbs if they support their lord with justness. And they should very eagerly maintain Christianity with right, and should seek Christ's church frequently as is needful for them, and Christ's dues rightly perform. And that is firstly that a person gives a tenth each year of what God sends to people annually for their needs in grain and flax and each kind of produce. And the field tithe is always produced from the tenth acre that the plough has previously gone over,

---

[34] See Andy Orchard, 'Re-editing Wulfstan: Where's the Point?' in Townend, *Wulfstan: Archbishop of York*, pp. 63–91, at p. 72, for a similar passage in other homilies. This opening, with its organological view of the body of Christian believers, also opens Bethurum, *Homilies of Wulfstan*, Xc, p. 200.

[35] On 'soulscot' derives from V Aethelred 12.

according to God's mercy and the king's and all Christian people's and according to the regulation laid down by King Edgar.

And each tithe on all young animals should be paid by Pentecost in fine or produce and that (tithe) on the earth's produce by the feast of All Saints. And St Peter's Pence should be gathered each year by St Peter's feastday; and should it not be paid, thirty pennies[36] besides that will be given and brought 'or sent' to Rome and 120 shillings paid to the king, by English law; and churchscot should be paid, as is English law, by Martinmas and should that not be paid, he is to pay a twelvefold penalty and 120 shillings to the king, and bear ploughalms, so that it is paid by fine every year then by at least fifteen nights after the Easter. And the tax for light should be paid at Christmas and Candlemas and Easter, or more often if one desires. And it is most proper that the tax for the soul always be paid at the open grave. And let festivals and fast-days be properly observed and held. And all of God's dues should be diligently furthered, just as is needed, and if anyone will not do this, have him be made subject to secular regulation.

These tracts weave doctrine, moral, political statement, and practical advice into a comprehensive, if brief, exposition of regulation and observation. Since they are so closely allied with Wulfstan himself,[37] utilize his own work in a cogent reworking of law and homily, and exhibit many of the stylistic features associated with the archbishop's English writings, there seems little doubt that Wulfstan composed them. It is possible that the *Sermo Lupi, Be Haðendome*, and *Be Cristendome* with the Bidding Prayers and Cnut's *Letter to the English of 1020* form a set of five short texts exemplifying Wulfstan's own final thoughts in the early 1020s on the state of the nation, perhaps deliberately providing his successor, Ælfric Puttoc (d. 1051) with a set of work that is itself a snapshot of major archiepiscopal duties and concerns. The sequence of prose texts moves from the statement of what issues the archbishop and his delegated pastors should focus

---

[36] Tally Lionarons, *Homiletic Writings*, transcribes this as 'three hundred' at p. 170.

[37] This is a point also made by Stephen Baxter in 'Archbishop Wulfstan and the Administration of God's Property', in Townend (ed.), *Wulfstan, Archbishop of York*, pp. 161–205, at pp. 188–9. Baxter argues that among the additional texts brought together by Wulfstan are the surveys of archiepiscopal estates at folios 156v–157v of the York Gospels. This may be the case, though the scribe is different to the one copying the texts discussed here. I argue that the Bidding Prayers, three homilies, and Letter of Cnut form a discrete unit of material specifically composed by Wulfstan for public and pastoral use.

upon, to the traumatic inheritance of a country in dire need of assistance, to the ideal, orderly society which functions as a single body working to assure the healthy future of the church. It is interesting in *Be Cristendome* that the lawcodes referred to specifically are those of Edgar, and not Cnut.

The suggestion that these texts form a sequence is speculative, but the appearance of the texts in the manuscript suggests a deliberate overall cogency. Each begins on a new folio with plenty of space on the page, indicating a compiler's overview of the room available for copying and the generous use of membrane. The titles of the homiletic works are written in Rustic Capitals which are ink-filled and take up a full line that ends with a *positura* matching the *positura* at the text's close. The initial capitals of the texts are offset slightly to the left, features that are paralleled by the cross that begins Cnut's Letter at folio 160r, though the Letter has no title (see Figure 2). Cnut's Letter is tied thematically to the homilies that precede it, though: *Be Cristendome* ends with the instruction to hand over a repeat offender to 'woroldlicre steore' if they do not pay their tithes or give the just dues, and immediately following this, is Cnut's Letter, with its promises to uphold and encourage law and foster the close relationship of Church and State. That the Letter forms the final element to this sequence of prelate's responsibility, ordinary Christian's responsibility and then king's responsibility creates a group of texts that offers insight into current conditions and future hopes in England in the earlier 1020s. The assessment would not be wholly laudatory: the evidence cumulatively amassed testifies to continuing cultural trauma[38] in the 1020s. It seems clear that trends can be discerned, trends that focus on establishing behaviours, encouraging cohesion, and trying to offset the apparent causes of conquest (in this case, the ongoing sins of the nation). Social solidarity becomes critical, with particular ceremonies and traditions central to this, and with the emergence of a narrative both reflecting and contributing to formulation of collective memory.[39] At the same time, though, the unvoiced find some articulacy through their being part of Wulfstan's imagined audience here, together with the provision of a core of model demands for supervisory consistency of Christian

---

[38] Ron Eyerman, 'The Past in the Present: Culture and the Transmission of Memory', *Acta Sociologica* 47. 2 (2004), pp. 159–69, at p. 160, talks about 'cultural trauma'.

[39] Ibid., p. 161.

conduct. While these texts, datable to 1020–3, are clearly pertinent to and reflective of the national situation at hand, they are yet barely distinguishable from the decades of homilies that preceded the reign of Cnut and that spoke so urgently and articulately about the imminent perils of the state and its people. This indicates that little had improved in the years since Cnut's accession, despite the assumption that the silence of the traditional documents of government might suggest a golden age.

| 4 |

'Shame and Wrath had the Saxons'[1]

The Trauma of Conquest

'Frecenfulle tida': Dangerous times

Wulfstan of York wrote in both English and Latin, although his Latin writings are only now being published and studied.[2] The York Gospels represent, as far as can be deduced, Wulfstan's final set of homiletic work, distilled from his years as a legislator, administrator and leading churchman. The picture he presents to his successor is a grim one of a country still struggling with sin and conflict, and a church still seeking to rebuild itself. Wulfstan's parting shots are composed in the vernacular, a language he recognized for its official authority, its national significance, and its public efficacy. The writing of prayers, sermons, and the promise of a king into a Gospelbook has the effect not only of preserving the works, but of changing the nature of the book into a personal repository

---

[1] Kipling, 'The King's Task', in *Traffics and Discoveries* (London: Doubleday, Page & Company, 1904), p. 146.

[2] Thomas N. Hall, 'Wulfstan's Latin Sermons', in Townend (ed.), *Wulfstan, Archbishop of York*, pp. 93–139, discusses Wulfstan's writings in Latin, and publishes editions of a number of interesting sermons, which can usefully be compared with the three in the York Gospels.

of wisdom and instruction, of extending the function of the Gospels, of sacralizing the English materials juxtaposed with the word of God.[3] From the York Gospels one can glean that English was a politically mature language by the eleventh century, the use of which by the foreign king Cnut underpins its significance, and assists in eliding the conquest of 1016, since this conquest involved the overt embrace of English and all of its rich literary and legal traditions.

As far as English materials other than those associated with Wulfstan and Cnut himself are concerned, there is little that can easily be dated with certainty to the years of Cnut's reign, which might seem surprising given the validation of English by archbishop and king. Part of the problem is our inability to date manuscripts surviving from c.1010 to c.1050. Careful palaeographical scrutiny of all the available evidence by Peter Stokes has resulted in the identification of a style of writing at the Winchester Minsters that is probably datable to the 1020s and 1030s. The scribes sharing characteristics of script—one of whom is Ælfsige—copied not only Ælfwine's Prayerbook (London, BL Cotton Titus D. xxvi and xxvii), but also most of London, BL Stowe 944 (with the frontispiece of Cnut mentioned in Chapter 1), Gloucester Cathedral 35 (Ælfric's *Catholic Homilies*), a forged charter (S. 443.1: London, BL Cotton Charter viii.17), and a copy of the Old English *Historia adversus paganos* in London, BL Cotton Tiberius B. i.[4] It is tempting to see the forged charter as a response to conquest, a visible and audible insistence on the rightful ownership and subsequent gifting of Winchester's monastic lands. And as for the Old English homiliaries and hagiographic collections copied in the years 1010–1040, Gloucester Cathedral 35 is now fragmentary, and contains parts of Ælfric's Lives of St Swithun and Mary of Egypt, and the Passion of SS Peter and Paul.[5] It is thus impossible to reconstruct the full extent of this manuscript, but the survival of an English saint's life, a repentant saint's, and apostolic saints' indicate the popularity of the genre with its emphasis on exemplary models

---

[3] See Treharne, 'The Politics of Early English'. See also Baxter, 'Archbishop Wulfstan and the Administration of God's Property', p. 189.

[4] Peter Stokes, 'English Vernacular Minuscule', 2 vols. (Unpub. PhD diss., Cambridge, 2005), I, 80–1.

[5] N. R. Ker, *Catalogue of Manuscripts Containing Anglo-Saxon* (Oxford: Clarendon Press, 1957; repr. with supplement, 1991), pp. 154–5. John Earle (ed.), *Gloucester Fragments I: Legends of St Swiðhun and Sancta Maria Ægyptiaca* (London: Longman, 1861), which contains plates of the fragments.

of grace and perseverance, reinforcing the very practical guides to Christian behaviour produced in the homiletic corpus, as illustrated by Wulfstan. In addition to these Winchester manuscripts, written in the city of Cnut's court, others compiled wholly in English, or containing English texts and notes among Latin works survive from the period of Cnut's reign. One, Cambridge, Corpus Christi College (henceforth CCCC) 188 stands out for its extensiveness, and perhaps the more so for its sequence of *First Series* Ælfric homilies, many of which are apostolic hagiographies, again, though consistently copied by scribes from the late tenth century until the end of the twelfth, surely particularly pertinent for a people under threat as examples of persistence in the face of persecution.

CCCC 188 represents the latest stage in the First Series of *Catholic Homilies*, and contains a number of revisions made by Ælfric sometime between 1005 and his death around 1014–20.[6] Its copying in or about 1030 represents a manuscript compiler's view of the most appropriate vernacular pastoral material available for transmission in the middle years of Cnut's reign. It is no surprise that Ælfric's works form the focus of this literary effort, given the immediate authority with which his homiletic series were invested, and their lengthy dissemination from monastic centres such as Worcester and Canterbury. CCCC 188 is the only surviving manuscript of Ælfric's *Catholic Homilies* (expanded with other texts) that can reasonably be assigned to the period of Cnut's rule, and from that perspective alone it is worth investigating here to listen for possible responses to conquest and all that that process entails.[7]

CCCC 188 might have been produced at Christ Church, Canterbury or at Sherborne, if Stokes's palaeographical analysis is correct, though in Donald Scragg's forthcoming *Conspectus of Scribes*, he posits Hereford as the place of origin.[8] It is a very significant manuscript, barely

---

[6] K. Sisam, 'Mss. Bodley 340 and 342: Ælfric's *Catholic Homilies*', in K. Sisam, *Studies in the History of Old English Literature* (Oxford: Clarendon Press, 1953), pp. 148–98, at pp. 175–8 [originally published in *RES* vii (1931)].

[7] Ker, *Catalogue*, item 43, 65–70.

[8] Stokes, 'English Vernacular Minuscule', pp. 141, 156, where he describes the scribe of CCCC 188 as practising a script deliberately emulating the hand of Eadui Basan; Donald G. Scragg, *A Conspectus of Scribal Hands Writing English, 960–1100* (Woodbridge: Boydell & Brewer, 2012). Thank you to Professor Scragg for sending me his *Conspectus* prior to publication. Helmut Gneuss, *Handlist of Anglo-Saxon Manuscripts: A List of Manuscripts and Manuscript Fragments Written or Owned in England up to 1100* (Tempe, AZ: MRTS, 2001), p. 32, also suggests Hereford, but as the possible provenance.

scrutinized from a holistic perspective, and never, I believe, interpreted as an important witness to its specific historical moment of production in or around the 1030s. Since it testifies to Ælfric's latest revisions of his First Series of *Catholic Homilies* sometime after 1006,[9] it might be regarded as of great value in determining that author's most polished sets of statements for his constructed audiences. It contains neither of the prefaces usually associated with the First Series of *Catholic Homilies*, nor does it contain *De initio creaturae*, with which the Series usually begins.[10] Currently, the opening text is Ælfric's *Hexameron*, and Clemoes supposes that *CH* I.i would have been present prior to the now acephalous opening item. Homilies added here in relation to the earlier manuscripts containing the First Series include Pope iv—the Third Sunday in Lent (which includes a discussion of the eight capital sins); Pope xi—*In Octavis Pentecosten* (on death and judgement); Assmann iii on the Nativity of St Mary; and Assmann iv, a homily for the Nativity of a Confessor, which focuses predominantly on an exposition of Matthew 13: 35, 'Uigilate ergo'.[11] Other homilies have been expanded, including *Catholic Homilies I* viii, xvi, xvii and xxxix (Third Sunday after Epiphany, First Sunday after Easter, Second Sunday after Easter, and the First Sunday in Advent, respectively). The last of these, for the First Sunday in Advent, incorporates a passage from Ælfric's *Preface* to the First Series of *Catholic Homilies*, arguably making up for the loss of the original prefatory matter in this, and other manuscripts,[12] though the extrapolated *Preface* takes on a very different function in CCCC 188—integral here to a discussion of living a good life in thought and deed.[13] CCCC 188's version of *Catholic Homilies I* xvii, *Dominica II post Pascha*, contains a long addition printed by Clemoes,[14] which is shared with Cambridge University Library Ii. 4. 6, London, BL Cotton Faustina A. ix, Cambridge, Corpus Christi College 302, and Cambridge, Trinity College B. 15. 34. This

---

[9] Pope, *Homilies of Ælfric*, i. 62: one of the homilies in CCCC 188 is prefaced with a Latin note naming Æthelwold II of Winchester as the recipient. See also Clemoes, *CHI*, pp. 36–7 and 83–5.

[10] See Clemoes, *CHI*, pp. 36–7 and Pope, *Homilies of Ælfric*, i. 59–62 for descriptions of the volume upon which this analysis is based. Their siglum for this manuscript is Q.

[11] Bruno Assmann (ed.), *Angelsächsischen Homilien und Heiligenleben*, Bibliotek der angelsächsischen Prosa, 13 (Kassel: Wigand, 1889; repr. 1964).

[12] Clemoes, *CHI*, p. 520.

[13] Ibid., p. 523/106–11, and thence *CHI*, pp. 174/57–176/119.

[14] Ibid., Appendix B. 3, pp. 535–42.

addition, attributed to Ælfric,[15] is of considerable interest in its somewhat pessimistic reaction to the state of affairs at the time of its composition in the years after 1006,[16] but it is of even more interest as a vernacular witness to events in the years surrounding the production of the manuscript in *c.* 1030. It might be noted, here, that each manuscript can, and should, be studied in its own right as a product of its specific historical moment. There are no mere copies or mindless replicative textual events in this period; each manuscript represents its compiler's requirements to attend to the needs of the intended audience, and it has become increasingly clear in recent years that homilies functioned as contemporary commentary, just as much as other sources regarded as more traditionally historical might do.[17] While scholars struggle to find the dates of texts that exist in manuscripts later than the texts' composition, the only certainty is that particular texts copied at specific times were chosen for their then-contemporaneity, as much as for any historical value with which the texts might have been imbued.

Since CCCC 188 represents a rare example of a revised sequence of texts, it is possible to discern within the additions made by Ælfric an enhanced political engagement in relation to the earlier versions of his First Series homilies. In the major additions to homilies xvi and, particularly, xvii, for the First and Second Sunday after Easter respectively, Ælfric adds considerably to a focus on pastoral care, with a number of key politically aware statements. What he felt needed saying in the turbulent years of the new millennium, during the frequent Viking raids and demands for tributes, the compiler of CCCC 188 clearly felt worth repeating some twenty or more years later, during the final, and, apparently, quiet decade of Cnut's reign. In the homily for the Second Sunday after Easter, this amounts to a measured criticism of the role of the bishop, priest, and congregation in their behaviour in this life. Ælfric condemns those who do not assist their flock ('Se yfela hyrde, þæt is se ungetrywa lareow, ofsnið ða fættan scep, for ðan ðe he amyrð þa Cristenan þonne he unrihtlice

[15] Godden, *Ælfric's Catholic Homilies, Introduction*, pp. 136–7.
[16] Ibid.
[17] See e.g. Robert Upchurch, 'A Big Dog Barks: Ælfric of Eynsham's Indictment of the English Pastorate and *Witan*', *Speculum* 85 (2010), pp. 505–33; Elaine Treharne, 'The Life and Times of Old English Homilies for the First Sunday in Lent', in H. Magennis and J. Wilcox (eds.), *The Power of Words: Anglo-Saxon Studies Presented to Donald G. Scragg on His Seventieth Birthday* (Morgantown: West Virginia University Press, 2006), pp. 205–42.

leofað and him yfele bysnað'[18]) and moves, in this homily, from a third person instruction to a first person plural plea: 'We moton eow secgan eowre sawle þearfe, licige eow ne licige eow, þæt we ne beon lease hyrdas, for ðan ðe us is uncuð ure geendung and þeos weoruld næfð fornean nane wynsumnysse nu ...'[19] These direct words to the church's pastors are common enough in Ælfric's homiletic and epistolary works,[20] but less common is the lengthy sequence of criticisms of contemporary society—a society that was ravaged by Viking depredations in the first decade of the new millennium when the expanded homily was written, but clearly felt to be appropriate in around 1030 or slightly later, when CCCC 188 was compiled. The added passage in CCCC 188, which must have resonated with its audiences during difficult times, makes clear that in the 'last days there are dangerous times':

Nu is eac se tima þe se ylca apostol Paulus foresæde gefyrn Timotheae þam bisceope þæt on ðam endenextan dagum beoð frecenfulle tida 7 menn lufiað to swiðe þas swicolan woruld and hi beoð grædige goldes and seolfres, on modignysse ahafene and huxlice tælende. Heora fæderum and moddrum hi beoð ungehyrsume; unðancwyrðe on ðeawum and forscyldgode on dædum butan ælcere trywðe and butan soðre sibbe, mid leahtrum afyllede and unliðe him betwynan, ungehealdsume and butan welwillendnysse, melderas and toðundene and heora lustas lufigende swiðor þonne hi lufion ðone lyfiendan god. Hi habbað arfæstnysse hiw and wiðsacað þære mihte.

Nu is ðeos woruld gemencged mid swylcum mannum to swiðe and hi þa bilewitan men mid heora menigfealdum leahtrum to yfelneysse tihtað and to arleasum dædum, for ðan ðe se awyrgeda gast wunað on swylcum mannum and hi synd deofles lima swa swa heora dæda swuteliað. Micele selre us wære þæt we unswicole wæron and wordfæste us betwynan and on weorcum rædfæste þonne ure ælc oðrum ungetrywðe cydde 7 swa us sylfe and ure sawle forpærndon for ðan ðe

[18] Adapted from Clemoes, *CHI*, p. 537/62–4: 'The evil shepherd, that is the unfaithful teacher, slaughters the fat sheep because he corrupts Christians when he lives wickedly and sets an evil example for them.'
[19] Clemoes, *CHI*, p. 539/123–5: 'We must tell you about your soul's need, whether you like it or not: that we should not be not false shepherds, because our ending is unknown to us, and this world has just about no pleasantness now.'
[20] For Ælfric's addresses to his audiences, see Mary Swan, 'Identity and Ideology in Ælfric's Prefaces', in Hugh Magennis and Mary Swan (eds.), *A Companion to Ælfric* (Leiden: Brill, 2010), pp. 247–69.

ælcum menn his agen dom cymð to. Gesælig bið þæt folc ðe fela witan hæfð gif hi riht wyllað and rædfæste beoð 7 se is wita geteald þe wyle rihtwisnysse 7 se is unwita ðe wohnysse lufað þeah ðe he for worulde wita beo geteald for ðan ðe his snotornyss hine sylfne beswicð.[21]

Now, moreover, is the time that the same apostle Paul long ago predicted to Timothy the bishop that in the last days there are dangerous times, and people love this deceitful world too much; and they are greedy for gold and silver, swollen in pride and shamefully speaking evil; to their fathers and mothers they are disobedient, thoughtless in their habits, and ungrateful in actions, without any loyalty and without true affection; filled with sins and cruel among themselves, out-of-control and without kindness, the traitors and the pride-swollen, and those loving lusts more than they love the living God—they have the appearance of piety and they deny its virtue.

Now such people disturb this world too much, and with their manifold sins they exhort the simple people to evilness, because the cursed spirit lives in such men and they are the devil's limbs, just as their deeds make clear. It would be much better for us if we were not treacherous and kept our word among ourselves, and were thoughtful in deeds rather than showed bad faith to each other and thus perverted ourselves and our souls, because to each man will come his own judgement. Happy is the nation that has many wise men if they desire justice and are thoughtful, and he who desires justice is considered a wise man, and he who loves wrongdoing is unwise, even though he is considered a wise man in worldly things, because his worldly-wisdom will betray him.'[22]

In this dystopic scenario, a world approaching its end, where appearances promise piety, but actions deliver evil, Ælfric seems most at pains to highlight deceit, pride, and betrayal. This is a betrayal that functions

---

[21] Clemoes, *CHI*, p.540/157-78 The first half of this same passage, and its source (2 Timothy 3:1–5), is discussed by Andy Orchard, 'Wulfstan as Reader, Writer, and Rewriter', in Aaron J. Kleist (ed.), *The Old English Homily: Precedent, Practice and Appropriation* (Turnhout: Brepols, 2007), pp. 311–41, at pp. 336–7. At 336, line 19, Orchard misquotes Clemoes, omitting a line-and-a-half of the Old English at the end; he also comments that this 'passage on Doomsday...is not found elsewhere', when it is also included in Trinity College, B. 15.34, CCCC 302, and Cotton Faustina A. ix. Orchard supposes the homiliary might once have been kept at Hereford, but gives no evidence for this (presumably using Gneuss's supposition, for which, see above, n. 8).

[22] 'snotornyss' seems specifically to mean worldly wisdom here, and Ælfric goes on to cite 1 Corinthians 3:19: 'For the wisdom of this world is foolishness with God. For it is written: I will catch the wise in their own craftiness.'

at all levels, compromising counsellors, parents, and all of the relationships that bind society. There is a particular emphasis on the 'wise', the adviser, and the contemporary worldliness hampering the well being of society. And whereas Wulfstan urged the unity of the Christian community as the 'limbs of Christ' with Christ in *Be Cristendome*, here, the sinful are 'deofles lima' ('the limbs of the devil') through their evil deeds. The repetition of 'Nu' ('Now') creates a sense of forceful immediacy, which would have had as much impact upon the homily's audiences at the time of its copying in CCCC 188, as in the opening years of the new century when it was originally composed. This is particularly the case if the homilies were used in a performative context, preached in some full or partial form to a congregation of laity, for one might be fairly certain that the earlier eleventh-century origins of the words being delivered would be unknown to the audience; the words would be new to the assembly, and, for the compiler of CCCC 188, at the very least, of particular contemporary resonance.

The detail of threats from the treacherous and from those who lead others into sin becomes evidence of social disorder as dramatic as that in the later part of Æthelred's reign, when Ælfric was writing. The appeal of Ælfric's homilies—an appeal that continues into the thirteenth century—is their usability, their continuing relevance to a society in formation through tumultuous years. Because Ælfric does not often supply precise referents, it seems easy enough to think of his corpus as of little specific temporal reference, and, from this, to forget that each instantiation of an Ælfric homily (or Wulfstan's sermons) has genuine impact at its reading, its delivery. That the 1020s and 1030s were decades of turmoil is suggested not just by Wulfstan's final words in the York Gospels, but also by the recopying of Ælfric's homilies. The intense social criticism of these texts is reinforced by others throughout the first half of the eleventh century, from the laments of the Anglo-Saxon chronicler, to the very familiar denouncements of Wulfstan in his *Sermo Lupi ad Anglos*, composed in 1014 and delivered to the king's assembled counsel, the *witan*.[23] Here, in CCCC 188, in about 1030[24]—after Cnut had visited

---

[24] Sisam, 'Mss. Bodley 340 and 342', states at p. 175 that CCCC 188 'is written in two hands that would normally be dated round about the year 1025'. It is a pity that it is impossible to be absolutely precise about the date of the origin of CCCC 188.

Rome and returned rehabilitated and spiritually revivified, just as the Winchester *Liber Vitae* was being planned with its glorious image of Cnut and Emma (see Figure 1)—the words of condemnation of evil leadership must have seemed meaningful and timely. The homily must, moreover, have increased significance as an indicator of a crisis in governance, because, as Godden points out, this expansive sequence of instruction seems particularly aimed 'against treachery among the governing class, the *witan*.'[25] It is, then, striking that Wulfstan adapted parts of this text in his work, and that this work of Wulfstan was then itself rewritten some decades later in what is now Cambridge, Corpus Christi College 201.[26] This is a composite manuscript, originating probably from Winchester, parts of which may well be attributable to the last years of Cnut's reign. CCCC 201 includes a large number of Wulfstan's law codes, legislative and prescriptive texts, such as the *Institutes of Polity* and *Canons of Edgar*; numerous sermons regarding proper Christian behaviour; poetry; and a possibly politically-charged tale of positive leadership, and its antithesis of tyrannical kingship, in the earliest English romance, *Apollonius of Tyre*.[27] If CCCC 201 were copied at New Minster, Winchester, as 'a textbook on Christian government', perhaps for those men, as Wormald suggests, who were 'trained to serve kings of both earth and heaven',[28] then its many texts focusing on reforming society, maintaining law and Christian propriety, show a genuine *need* for instruction and regulation. This governing class of ecclesiastical advisors are precisely those who counselled Cnut and his advisors, among those perhaps who heard the Skaldic verses praising Cnut's successes against the English kings, recited even while he donated crosses and crowns to English monasteries; those, then, who witnessed the man behind the public acts of piety and penitence. Perhaps it is *through* these English homilies and

---

[25] Godden, *Ælfric's Catholic Homilies, Commentary*, p. 144.

[26] Orchard, 'Wulfstan as Reader', pp. 337–40. For an excellent analysis of CCCC 201 and its very deliberate compilatory method, see Wormald, *Making of English Law*, pp. 204–10.

[27] Treharne, *Old and Middle English, c.890–1450*, pp. 234–53. On the inclusion of poetry in the volume, see Elaine Treharne, 'Manuscript Sources of Old English Poetry', in Gale Owen-Crocker (ed.), *Working with Anglo-Saxon Manuscripts* (Exeter: Exeter University Press, 2009), pp. 88–111. My thoughts on this manuscript have benefitted from conversations with Mark Atherton (who is publishing on this manuscript shortly), Elizabeth Tyler, and Matt Townend.

[28] Wormald, *Making of English Law*, p. 210.

laws that tensions in the political and public, personal and private aspects of Cnut and his reign are reconciled within the spiritual message of unity and salvation and proper Christian behaviour. These tensions are both cause and effect of the cultural trauma suffered by Anglo-Saxon England, effectively silenced except through the depiction of a broken society in the law codes and sermons, which are overlooked because of their status as 'copies' or 'pastiches' of earlier work.[29]

Other evidence for the trauma suffered before and during the reign of Cnut is not hard to come by in contemporary and later texts.[30] Thietmar of Merseburg's *Chronicle* describes Cnut, in the earliest years of his reign as an erstwhile 'invader and assiduous destroyer of' England, but now 'its sole defender, as in the desolate Lybian desert [reigns] the basilik'.[31] This rather unappealing bestial image of Cnut is paralleled by the savagery of Danes in the much later narrative of Walter Map, a highly imaginative twelfth-century writer, who, even so, relates that 'Cnut... continued a free monarch for a long time, and the Danes spread over all the provinces everywhere, and prevailed over the English and forced them into the worst of slaveries, ill-using their wives, daughters and nieces,'[32] which, in turn, echoes the negative light in which Cnut's earlier years as king are portrayed by John of Worcester, the twelfth-century monastic historian.[33] More contemporary sources suggest the longer-term effects of Cnut's violent acquisition of the throne, when, according to William of Jumièges, 'the king had encouraged the spirits of his troops [and] fell savagely upon the English, and killed so many that no one could count how many thousands of English fell that day'.[34] This shock of battle and victory by a foreign king and his sons is depicted as God's

---

[29] See Lawson, *Cnut*, p. 221, who comments that in Cnut's reign 'there seems to have been more rewriting than new writing', and that there is little writing in comparison with subsequent reigns that survives.

[30] See also Lawson, *Cnut*, pp. 218–19, on negative portrayals of Cnut. For the alternative view, albeit one with a highly politicized agenda, see Alistair Campell (ed.), *Encomium Emmae Reginae*, with supplementary introduction by Simon Keynes (Cambridge: Royal Historical Society and Cambridge University Press, 1998).

[31] Whitelock, *EHD*, i. 321.

[32] James and Hartland, *Walter Map's 'De Nugis Curialium'*, p. 237.

[33] *The Chronicle of John of Worcester*, ii. 485 (with its reference to 2 Kings 12, and reign of alien powers) and pp. 501–7.

[34] Elisabeth M. C. Van Houts (ed. and trans.), *The 'Gesta Normannorum Ducum' of William of Jumièges, Orderic Vitalis, and Robert of Torigni*, Oxford Medieval Texts, 2 vols. (Clarendon Press: Oxford, 1992, 1995; repr. 2003), i. 21.

retribution by the propagandistic author of the *Vita Ædwardi Regis*, who, unsurprisingly, given that the text is hagiographic, portrays Edward the Confessor's accession as the natural restoration of ancient order: 'so God's loving kindness, sparing the English after the heavy weight of rebuke [the reigns of Cnut and his sons], showed them a flower preserved from the root of their ancient kings'.[35]

If the violence of Cnut's accession were as severe and long-lived as then-contemporary and modern historians suggest, the social tumult for those affected by actions of the Conquerors would merit the acknowledgement of Wulfstan and the instruction offered by Ælfric's homilies. These writings, promulgated by monastic scriptoria, reflect the compilers' perceived needs of their imagined lay or clerical audiences; the vernacular becomes the voice of the conquered English, who, for most historians then and now, are mere ciphers.

The Delay of Mourning

We do, then, have some extant cultural and, particularly, textual consequences of this first conquest that might be illustrative of the response of the traumatized to the process of Conquest,[36] a 'politics of the witness', as Nichanian proposes.[37] In his work on societal trauma, Peter Seudfeld discusses the responses to a macro-level trauma—one that affects an entire people.[38] The response involves not panic or hedonism or a breakdown in social control (so evident in the pre-conquest period, in Wulfstan's *Sermo Lupi ad Anglos*),

[35] Frank Barlow (ed.), *Vita Ædwardi Regis* (Oxford: Oxford University Press, 1992), pp. 12–13.

[36] Conquest as a process is mooted first by Stafford, *Unification and Conquest*. See also Mack, 'Changing Thegns', pp. 375–87. For Mack, who intelligently reviews the positive response to Cnut's reign from contemporary and modern historians: 'Even so, an examination of the fragmentary and diverse evidence of chronicles, charters, wills and laws demonstrates that Cnut's reign witnessed major alterations in the composition of the Old English aristocracy, and further that these changes radically altered certain traditional practices of Saxon governance' (p. 377). Mack shows how all the major English ealdormen were replaced by Cnut, and that the allegiances of the newly promoted earls were to Cnut only—not to pre-existing English familial or royal ties. Moreover (p. 378), the thegnly class was similarly decimated, if the thin evidence is carefully scrutinized.

[37] Nichanian, 'Catastrophic Mourning', pp. 140–1.

[38] Peter Suedfeld, 'Reactions to Societal Trauma: Distress and/or Eustress', *Political Psychology* 18.4 (1997), pp. 849–61.

but a 'greater emphasis…on proper behavior, self-control and social conformity'.[39] In Wulfstan's attempts to lay down the ecclesiastical law in the 1014 *Sermo Lupi*, one can see this control being taken by him personally and issued to his various audiences, including the *witan*. But it is the post-conquest legislation of 1018, and the insistence on tradition seen in the decade and more after Cnut's victory in 1016, that evince the recognition of the need for adherence to law, for the protection of society, and for the control of individual behaviour. Since explicit ground-level responses to trauma are simply not written down, and are nearly always silenced within the texts created by the elite literate communities, such responses can only be discovered in between the lines. In Cnut's Law Codes, conservatively insisting on his direct inheritance from Edgar (conveniently erasing Æthelred, just as William the Conqueror erased Harold[40]), there are a number of new laws aimed principally at widows and those who have lost land. This implies, clearly, that there were increased numbers of widows, or at least, a great need for their provision, and that land tenure was threatened as a result of the process of conquest and displacement of the tenurial classes.[41] It is through this kind of revelation gleaned by analysing what particular kinds of law, or homiletic focal points might mean in their actual historical moment that silence can be rectified and the shock of a reeling society discerned.

Drawing out the occurrence and implications of trauma is difficult in any circumstances, but the more so when sources are relatively scarce, as they are for Cnut's reign. It is more straightforward to detect a society in shock after the Norman Conquest, since overt declarations of distress and fear exist to anchor other kinds of textual evidence. In the years of Cnut's reign up to the Norman Conquest itself, however, there is further textual material that might suggest widespread insecurity. This again counters the view that the events of Cnut's accession and reign had little impact on the population at large, and that the overwhelming silence from the charters, and historical sources is symbolic of a general peacefulness.[42] Indeed, Lawson reminds readers that Cnut's grants to

---

[39] Ibid., p. 855.

[40] See George Garnett, *Conquered England: Kingship, Succession, and Tenure 1066–1166* (Oxford: Oxford University Press, 2007), esp. chapter 1.

[41] This material is well analysed in Mack, 'Changing Thegns'.

[42] Such as Frank Barlow, *The English Church, 1000–1066* (Hamden, CT: Archon, 1963), p. 36, sees the silence of the reign as equating to 'a deep peace', 'devoid of great incident'. See also Lawson, *Cnut*, p. 66.

Scandinavians may never have been recorded in writing, since his culture was predominantly non-literate.[43] But, later in the eleventh century, in that most literate of centres of textual production, Worcester (possible place of origin of the D-version of the *Anglo-Saxon Chronicle*), the remembering of Danish depredations is noteworthy, as Anne Williams indicates:

> Hemming claims that Worcestershire...was ravaged by the Danes, who seized the estates of nobles and commoners, rich and poor alike, so that they held almost the entire province by force...As well as the passage of armies, the west midlands suffered frequent demands for geld, which Hemming claims were heavy enough to require the melting-down and sale of church plate and treasure.[44]

These accounts of spoliation and theft, extortion and subjection are recorded by the Worcester monk, Hemming, in his compilation of part of London, BL, Cotton Tiberius A. xiii, otherwise known as Hemming's Cartulary, created at Bishop Wulfstan II's request.[45] Wulfstan's prescience and appreciation of the permanence of the written word led to this cartulary's production, and it was made, perhaps, as a direct result of the insecurity brought about by the Norman Conquest, with the losses of lands, possessions and ecclesiastical privileges it caused.[46]

That same sense of insecurity and fear for the future might be evinced after the conquest of 1016, too. Here, it can be traced in the literal silencing of some of the records, particularly those produced through ecclesiastical authority—once again, the *Anglo-Saxon Chronicle*, on which we depend so heavily for the reconstruction of the period. The silence can be most easily illustrated by surveying the appropriate pages from some of the manuscripts that make up the *Anglo-Saxon Chronicle*, and with a particular emphasis on the *Parker Chronicle*, the earliest witness of the text, now Cambridge, Corpus Christi College 173, folios 1v–32r.[47] This manuscript, dating from the end of the ninth century to the later

[43] Lawson, *Cnut*, p. 66.

[44] Anne Williams, 'The Spoliation of Worcester', *Anglo-Norman Studies* 19 (1999), pp. 383–408, at p. 384.

[45] Francesca Tinti, 'From episcopal conception to monastic compilation: Hemming's Cartulary in context', *Early Medieval Europe*, 11 (2002), pp. 233–61.

[46] Ibid.

[47] Bately, *MS A*; and Janet Bately, 'Manuscript Layout', in Donald G. Scragg (ed.), *Textual and Material Culture in Anglo-Saxon England: Thomas Northcote Toller and the Toller Memorial Lectures* (Cambridge: Brewer; 2003), pp. 1–21.

eleventh, records events not quite year-by-year, but for notable years, with short entries for the majority of annals, such as 962 and 963; poetic entries for other years, such as 937 (*The Battle of Brunanburh*) and 975 (*The Death of Edgar*); and fuller entries for a few annals, such as 1001. Unlike the *D*-version of the *Chronicle*, discussed in Chapter 3, which documents the early decades of the eleventh century in considerable detail,[48] the *Parker Chronicle*'s recording of the eleventh century is sparse indeed. At some point in the eleventh century, it was transferred from Winchester to Christ Church, Canterbury,[49] perhaps, when Ælfheah, bishop of Winchester, became archbishop of Canterbury in 1006. At this point, entries are, essentially, abandoned, the manuscript set aside; visually, the manuscript is testimony to a rather startling absence, which is most dramatically evident when turning folio 30 from its recto to its verso and 31r (see Figures 3 and 4). At 30v, the page has all the annal numbers already present, with the expectation of one line of writing per annal (though the first and second ruled lines of the page are completely blank). The annals are numbered from i. vii to i. xxviiii (1007–29), but the only entry, alone and in the middle of the folio is i. xvii (1017): 'Her cnut wearð gecoran to kinge' ('In this year, Cnut was accepted as king') in a hand of the twelfth century. The compact, and often densely packed, *mise-en-page* of the manuscript up this point now becomes a membranous wasteland, with only the one entry on folio 30v for the succession of Cnut as king.

Indeed, in the nineteen years of Cnut's reign, only three *Chronicle* entries exist, all made later than the years in which events occur and entered onto folios 30v and 31r:

> 1017: Her Cnut wearð gecoran to kinge.
> 1031: Her com Cnut [agean to Englalande[50]]. Sona swa he becom to Englalande, he geaf into Cristes cyrican on Cantwarebyri þa hæfenan on Sandwic 7 ealla þa gerihta þe þarof arisaþ of æiðre healfe ðare hæfene, swa þæt loc whenne þæt flot byþ ealra hehst 7 ealra fullest 'beo' an scip flotigende swa neh þan lande swa hit nyxt [mæge] 7 þar beo an mann stande on þan scipe 7 habbe ane taper æx on his...[51]

[48] Cubbin, *MS D*.
[49] Ker, *Catalogue*, p. 59.
[50] Visible under rapid and rough erasure made by a round-edged implement.
[51] Five and a half lines of text have been erased very roughly.

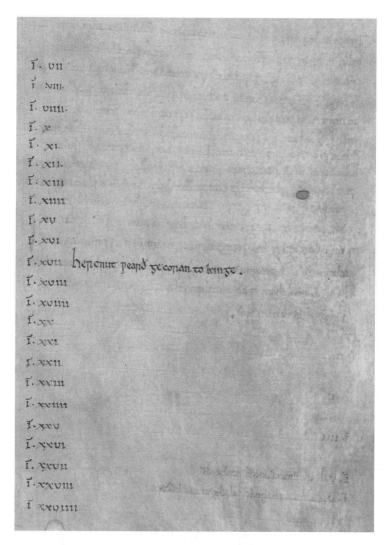

FIG 3   Cambridge, Corpus Christi College, 173, folio 30v

© Reproduced by permission of the Masters and Fellows, Corpus Christi College Cambridge.

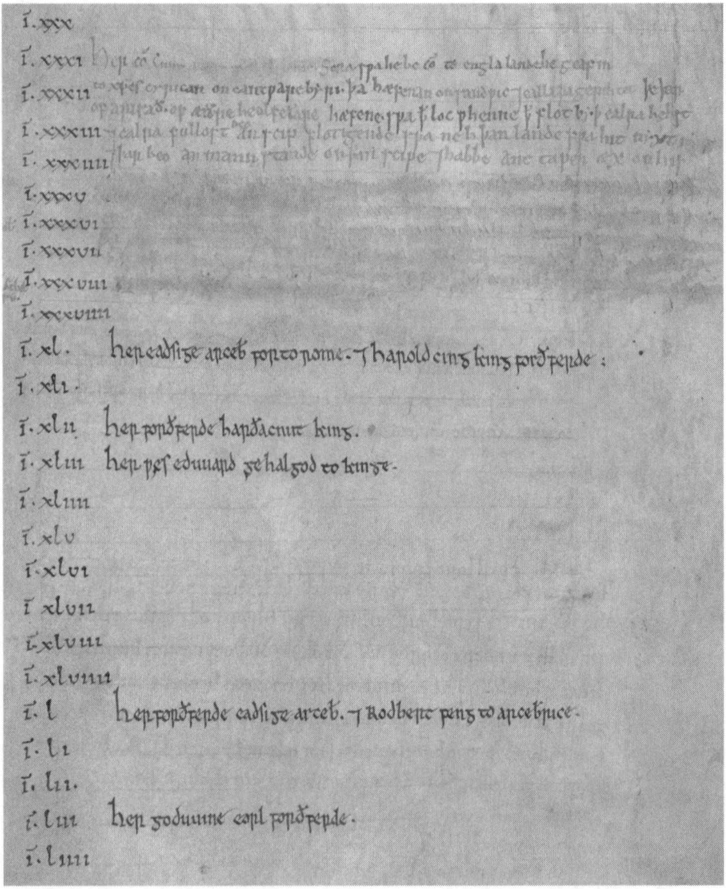

FIG 4 Cambridge, Corpus Christi College, 173, folio 31r

© Reproduced by permission of the Masters and Fellows, Corpus Christi College Cambridge.

[handa ...wyrpe up swa feorr on þæt land of swiðre healfe swa he... mæge. Swa feorr ..gað þa munekas Cristes cyrican þa gerihta þe þarof cumað. Ne nan mann nah þ... nanes... es þing... eon þa... ða... heora... ofer bates ...ber... 7 of ea... þ... cumað ...uðe.]
1036: 'Cnut obiit'

1017: In this year, Cnut was accepted as king.

1031: This year Cnut [came back to England]. As soon as he came to England, he gave to Christ Church in Canterbury the haven of Sandwich and all the rights that arise from it on either side of the haven, so that when the tide is at its highest and fullest of all, and there is a ship floating as near the land as it might, and there is a man standing on the ship who has a tapor-axe in his [hand, who has thrown it as far as he possibly can onto the land on both sides. Thus far the monks of Christ Church can enjoy the rights that come from this. Nor can any man have any …][52]

1036: 'Cnut died'

Of this sum total of recorded history in the *Parker Chronicle* about Cnut's reign, nothing was written in the manuscript contemporary with the events themselves; the three entries are retrospective, and were completed in Christ Church. In other words, there is nothing that could be said after 1001, to narrate fresh history. What, if anything can be deduced from this literal silence, a silence not replicated in the other versions of the *Chronicle*[53] that functioned through the first half of the eleventh century? First and foremost, blank space in any context always represents absence, of course—absence and the loss of that which should be present. Here, on these folios, there is poignancy about the annal numbers entered, but never filled, as if those years, in fact, have been lost to the English historians recording even the most meagre details; the skeletal structure of order presents itself, but none of the fleshy substance. Along with the absence of a narrative that someone expected to be present is the fragmentation created by the scattered annals that are entered by the later scribes. Even the longest one of these, however, is deliberately and quite violently erased from the folio: at folio 31r, at the annal for 1031, the scraping of the membrane, performed with a round-edged implement is roughly and deeply made, suggesting a very concerted effort to eviscerate the privilege of Christ Church that is the subject of the entry.[54]

---

[52] See further, Bately, *MS A.*

[53] Versions C and D: London, BL Cotton Tiberius B. i, folios 115v–64; London, BL Cotton Tiberius B. iv, folios 3–86.

[54] It is difficult to see from any reproduction of the folio, but the erasure is almost gouged out of the membrane, with the skin raised and rough as a result.

The forger of this annal entry also wrote numerous other entries in the *Parker Chronicle*. He seems to have been a member of the Christ Church community in the early twelfth century, adept at forging—particularly in the vernacular, if his work on two charters is anything to go by. As Peter Baker demonstrates, this scribe made a palimpsest of London, BL Cotton Charter x. 11 and London, BL Campbell Charter xxi. 5, which were originally parchment documents dated to the ninth and mid-eleventh centuries respectively. In the second case, Campbell Charter xxi. 5 (Sawyer 1088), the scribe palimpsests seven of the ten lines of the original writ from Edward the Confessor to Christ Church granting financial and judicial rights over their own men in all the shires where Christ Church holds lands, just as Cnut had done.[55] The writ retains its original seal, and there seems to be some attempt to emulate the palaeographical forms of the original scribe at lines 1–3. This scribe was thus intensely aware of the need to be convincing, and to retain the material form of the original, particularly. This adherence to the *real* physical object is fascinating. The same concerns seem in play in his work on the *Parker Chronicle*. Moreover, this is the scribe who wrote the bilingual F-version of the *Anglo-Saxon Chronicle*, London, BL Cotton Domitian viii, folios 30–70.[56] He derived his English and Latin texts from multiple sources for this exceptional project, working, Baker surmises, not as 'one of those scribes whose business it was to reproduce texts day in and day out', but as a monk 'whose labour was primarily intellectual or administrative'.[57] This scribe is memorably described by Baker as sometimes producing 'poor quality' work that might be explained by old age, 'cold fingers, illness, haste, and strong drink',[58] but whatever the reason behind the scribe's rather irregularly formed script with its varying aspect it is clear that he felt authorized not only to intervene in the *Parker Chronicle*, but also to rewrite history; to fill a silence with some written noise.

[55] Harmer, *Anglo-Saxon Writs*, no. 33, pp. 186–97, and Plate 1.

[56] Peter Baker (ed.), *The Anglo-Saxon Chronicle, A Collaborative Edition MS F* (Cambridge: Brewer, 2000), pp. xvii–xxiii. See, in addition, David Dumville (ed.), *The Anglo-Saxon Chronicle, A Collaborative Edition, I: MS F, Facsimile Edition* (Cambridge: Brewer, 1995). See also the Electronic Sawyer 1221 and 1088 [http://www.trin.cam.ac.uk/chartwww/charthome.html]

[57] Baker, *MS F*, p. xviii.

[58] Ibid., p. xxii.

In his entry for 1031, the scribe focuses on an elaborately designed privilege for Christ Church, Canterbury, given to the institution by Cnut on his return to England from Denmark, presumably.[59] It's impossible to know who might have been responsible for the erasure of the second half of the text, but it seems unlikely to be the scribe himself, since he had squeezed the notices of Cnut and Æthelnoth's deaths into the margin, on the other side of the annal numbers. If he had performed the erasure, it stands to reason that he would have written the obits over the erased text in the appropriate place. The entries by the scribe suggest that the layout of the manuscript, with its vertical bounding lines providing the extent of the writing grid's edge, was of no concern the scribe either, and it seems rather perverse to squeeze the entry for 1031 into ten, uneven, lines, when the remainder of the leaf is blank. This demonstrates issues of intellectual ownership, if not physical ownership, where the scribe clearly assumes that what he has to say overrides the propriety of the page. This is less the case in the addition he makes to the annal for 1070, where, at the bottom of folio 31v, following the stint of a more aesthetically pleasing hand, he at least maintains the line length of the writing grid, though his writing habitually slips obliquely downwards from the ruled line.

In his desire to fill the gaps in the *Parker Chronicle*, if only partially, this scribe—a generation after the Norman Conquest, records the most relevant facts about Cnut's reign: his grant to Christ Church and his death. All other historical detail remains unsaid. The silence may mean nothing, or one might speculate that it reflects a desire deliberately to say nothing, to permit the past to remain hidden, a desire illustrated at least in the context of this specific English Chronicle, if not more broadly in the scarcity of documents that survive from the period of the first eleventh-century Conquest, *c*.1010 to 1040.

---

[59] This scribe's interest in Cnut's reign is also illustrated in the two forged charters, both of which concern land given originally to Christ Church in the reign of Cnut. One might speculate that the contemporary evidence had been lost or had never been fully committed to written form to account for these two forged rewritings. David Bates (ed.), *Regesta Regum Anglo-Normannorum, The Acta of William I, 1066 to 1087* (Oxford: Oxford University Press, 1998), p. 4, makes the notable comment in this context that 'The Norman Conquest of England is a unique event for many reasons...not least because of the scale of forgery which resulted from it.'

From a Distance

Sociologists and anthropologists suggest that 'distance' is a fundamental prerequisite of the formation of the collective narrative of events—a distance that would explain the inability of many to negotiate with conquest as it happens—and which might well *also* explain the fragments of those texts produced in English in the years during Cnut's reign and after. One sees something of the same fragmentation in English manuscript and diplomatic manufacture in the years after the Norman Conquest, from *c*. 1070 to 1100, but with some notable localized, regional exceptions. It is through this detritus that one might usefully sift to determine the impact of conquest in the eleventh and earlier twelfth century.

There are multiple collective memories and multiple silences in this long period of conquest: and many distinct traceable responses to the cataclysmic events of 1066, just as there are in relation to 1016, though the predominant response there seems to be silence. Even though what is produced following 1016 seems uncontroversial, it is conservative and suggestive of a desire to restore order after cultural trauma; yet through the texts that do exist, it is possible to apprehend the testimony of subjection, even if that testimony in 1030 or 1040 may have been partially erased by the reinstatement of the English line through Edward the Confessor.

There was no such erasure in 1066. Of the well-known reactions to the Conquest, many involving the scurrying around for written evidence to ascertain what belonged to whom in a way that the *F*-Chronicle scribe proved in his work on the *Parker Chronicle*, there is, then, a desire by those in monastic and ecclesiastical institutions (who, to an extent, represent the 'English' because monks, canons and priests are the mediators and regulators, the carers and the punishers) to seek cohesion and a consequent comprehension of events. Complicating this process is the requirement for testimony, the demand by the conquerors that the Anglo-Saxons 'tell'. This 'telling' is heard in the authorized accounts of the Conquest and its aftermath: in the demands of the Domesday Book circuit visits; in the writings of Latin and French historians in the post-Conquest period; in the stitching of the Bayeux Tapestry. Wulfstan II, apparently revered (or feared?) for his knowledge of the law, was called on to give evidence; Ælfwine, Abbot of Ramsey, was also called upon to give evidence in a dispute between Thetford and Bury St Edmunds, and could recall as far back as the days of Cnut;[60] Æthelric, bishop of Chichester, was literally wheeled out of the cloister to utter ancient truths at the Penenden Heath trial, c. 1070.[61] In the accounts, we hear that:

> Ægelricus episcopus de Cicestra, vir antiquissimus et legum terre sapientissimus, qui ex precepto regis advectus fuit ad ipsas antiquas legum consuetudines discutiendas et edocendas in una quadriga.

> Ægelricus bishop of Chichester, a very old man, very learned in the laws of the land, . . . had been brought in a chariot at the king's demand in order to discuss and expound these same old legal customs.[62]

William the Conqueror's demands for truth through oral testimony suggests a distrust of the written like Socrates' in Plato's *Phaedrus*: the real is communicated through eyewitness accounts, first-hand experience of the otherwise lost. At the same time that this testimony is sought, however, it is appropriated by the official recorder and rewritten, simultaneously revealed and erased: we know these senior ecclesiastics, and often less high status witnesses, provided evidence, but we do not know what was said. Indeed, as George Garnett astutely points out in his excellent account of the Conquest and the century beyond, William seemed less interested in acquiring information from the native English in order to learn than in order to overcome.[63] What might appear at first glance to be an accommodation on the part of William and his administrators was thus only part of the strategy of subordination.

And thus we can detect multiple distinct narratives—of the conquerors, the conquered, and the utterly unvoiced—but always through some concerted effort to demonstrate proof materially. This insistence on written proof—not just of what was owned, but what had been lost—is well understood by a number of English in response to the Conquest. It is illustrated most obviously by Wulfstan II of Worcester in his urgency to have his see's cartularies compiled by Hemming and his co-scribes. It is evident too in the compilations of homiliaries and law codes in Worcester, and in the maintenance of that scriptorium's version of the *Chronicle*. This is the noise that responds insistently against the

---

[60] R. C. Van Caenegem (ed.), *English Lawsuits from William I to Richard I*, vol. i: *William I to Stephen (Nos 1–346)* (London, Selden Society, 1990), pp. 27–8, no. 9.

[61] Garnett, *Conquered England*, p. 17.

[62] Van Caenegem, *English Lawsuits*, i. 5b, pp. 8–9.

[63] Garnett, *Conquered England*, pp. 17–18.

Conquest, but also vocalizes, through text, the desperation of the cognizant. These conservative and socially binding manoeuvres are one organized response to crisis, a response that has been described by Francesca Tinti in her work on the Worcester cartularies as a desire 'to preserve the past...to organize and present the past history of that church and its endowment'.[64] More can be said about the motivation for gathering, writing and testifying with such urgency in these years, and the unifying function of making collective memory permanent in this period. In other words—the words of Marc Nichanian—'the witness is not the witness of the historians anymore',[65] and it is, perhaps, through other kinds of written texts than the central historical records that the muted witnesses to conquest can be given voice. That is to say, it is through the continuation of the usual English writings, the homilies and saints' lives, laws and chronicles that the responses to Conquest of the conquered might most easily be heard.

[64] Francesca Tinti, 'Si litterali memori commendaretur: memory and cartularies in eleventh-century Worcester', in Stephen Baxter, Catherine E. Karkov, Janet L. Nelson, and David Pelteret (eds.), Early Medieval Studies in Memory of Patrick Wormald, Studies in Early Medieval Britain (Ashgate, 2009), pp. 475–91, at p. 490.

[65] Nichanian, 'Catastrophic Mourning', pp. 140–1.

| 5 |

'The Saxon is not like us Normans'[1]

The Writing of Conquest

For some, 14 October 1066 represents a political and cultural shift so significant that much of what was Anglo-Saxon was swept away to be replaced not just by a new regime, but by a new social order. No Anglo-Saxon could have known that the events of the Battle of Hastings heralded a permanent loss of their political state. Rather as the twenty-six year reigns of Cnut and his sons ended in the coronation of Edward the Confessor, son of Æthelred II, so many might have forecast that the victory of William, Duke of Normandy, would be similarly transient. It is only hindsight that permits us to know otherwise: there was nothing inevitable about the Conquest's success and the changes brought about by this cultural trauma.

Modern scholarly accounts of the Conquest and its aftermath are plentiful; most rely on the later eleventh- and twelfth-century historiographical writings of authors such as William of Jumièges, Orderic Vitalis, Eadmer of Canterbury, William of Malmesbury, Henry of Huntingdon, John of Worcester, and Gaimar to piece together the events

[1] Rudyard Kipling, 'Norman and Saxon', in *A History of England*, pp. 51–3.

and consequences of the reigns of William I, II, and Henry I.[2] Recent publications have also offered detailed readings of other primary sources, such as the Domesday Book commissioned by William I in 1086, or the *Regesta Regum Anglo-Normannorum*,[3] while the *Anglo-Saxon Chronicle* is usually relied upon to present the alternative view of history of the conquered English. In the recent trenchant and nuanced interpretation of the Conquest by George Garnett, these sources are treated with great care, the better to permit insight into the 'official account' of the events of 1066 and the following century, propagated by William and his officials which sought to authorize and justify William's acquisition of the English throne.[4] Garnett demonstrates, for example, how history was rewritten through the deliberate elision of Harold's short reign, the erasure of the archiepiscopacy of Stigand between 1052 and 1070, and the reconstitution of the Anglo-Saxon state as a tenurial society. Moreover, the manipulated contemporary records testify to an acceptance of the public relations exercise of William as divinely appointed king of the English. For the eleventh century itself, Garnett comments,

> Apart from eloquent silences and rumblings of discontent in the *Anglo-Saxon Chronicle* and the *Vita Ædwardi*'s treatment of the Conquest as divine retribution for the sins of the English in terms very similar to those applied to the Danish invasions of the early eleventh century, the official interpretation of the Conquest was a profoundly successful argument.[5]

So successful was the official interpretation, in fact, that—as was the case with Cnut's conquest of 1016—other perspectives have not yet been fully recovered; the hegemonic party-line is still, to an extent, being followed. In Christopher Harper-Bill's overview of the Anglo-Norman church, in

---

[2] See e.g. Carpenter, *The Struggle for Mastery of Britain*; Crouch, *The Normans*; Ian Short, 'Language and Literature', in Christopher Harper-Bill and Elisabeth van Houts (eds.), *A Companion to the Anglo-Norman World* (Woodbridge: Boydell 2003), pp. 191–213; Hugh M. Thomas, *The English and the Normans: Ethnic Hostility, Assimilation, and Identity, 1066–c.1220* (Oxford: Oxford University Press, 2003). For a set of perceptive readings that focuses on Norman identity, see Laura Ashe, *Fiction and History in England, 1066–1200* (Cambridge: Cambridge University Press, 2007).

[3] Bates, *Regesta Regum Anglo-Normannorum*.

[4] Garnett, *Conquered England*, esp. chapter 1, 'The Justification of Conquest'.

[5] Ibid., p. 42.

one of very few uses of vernacular sources, he reveals that: 'English monastic chronicles complained bitterly of Norman depredation, yet on occasion the diminution of a church's estates can be demonstrated to have pre-dated 1066.'[6] Just as an English note is sounded, then, it is instantly hushed, as if the bitter complaints can be overlooked and silenced. Silence, though, as was revealed in relation to the reign of Cnut, is not always golden; it is not always eloquently indicative of harmonious acceptance. The noiselessness of the Anglo-Saxon in the years after 1066 is, rather, a construct of a modern academy focusing so intensely on sources it self-validates that it obfuscates other voices that have every reason to be considered viable witnesses.

These voices of the English often writing *in* English, which are usually regarded as faint echoes of the dying shouts of an Old English literary heritage, clamour to be heard, both because they survive in such numbers, and partly because of their persistence—a persistence that lasts at least into the thirteenth century. Some of these voices seem to insist on a different testimony—the testimony of those participating in a collective trauma so great that it could not be explicitly articulated for well over a century, a trauma so catastrophic that even mourning could not be fully voiced. And if this interpretation seems to push the boundaries of what might be deemed acceptable,[7] it is salutary to read again the words of Ælfric or of Wulfstan exclaiming the imminent apocalypse and realize that for many Anglo-Saxons during and after October 1066, it must have seemed that day had already come.

The Voice of the English

In the last decade, scholarship has sought to overturn statements previously made bemoaning the lacuna in the English literary tradition between 1066 and 1215, the demise of the language (as if 99 per cent of

---

[6] Christopher Harper-Bill, *The Anglo-Norman Church* (Bangor, 1992), 20; repr. in revised form in Harper-Bill and Van Houts, *A Companion to the Anglo-Norman World*.

[7] And even where there is an insistence on assimilation between the conquerors and conquered, this only ever, at best, extended to freemen, who represented only 50 per cent of the population in the twelfth century. See further, Elaine Treharne, 'Categorization, Periodization: Silence of (the) English', in Rita Copeland, Wendy Scase and David Lawton (eds.), *New Medieval Literatures* 8 (Turnhout: Brepols, 2006), *passim*, and references therein.

the population suddenly stopped speaking English in the latter months of 1066), and the wasteland that characterizes the intellectual capability of the (old) English until the emergence of Middle English texts in the early thirteenth century. Comments on the loss of the English language and its literature abound: as early as 1912, W. P. Ker, suggested that: 'For a long time before and after 1100, there is a great scarcity of English productions...This scantiness is partly due, no doubt, to an actual disuse of English composition.'[8] Even while demonstrating unequivocally the *Continuity of English Prose*, R. W. Chambers cannot resist describing the demise of English in the twelfth century in the following dramatic terms:

> The strangling of English prose was a national disaster, and has much to do with that strange misunderstanding of their own Middle Ages which obsesses so many good Englishmen. There were many gallant English crusaders, and an English king commanded against Saladin. Yet we have nothing in English prose which we can compare with Joinville's *Life of St Louis*...The Norman Conquest robbed us of such possibilities. Of course, the Conqueror did not land at Pevensey with any deliberate intention of destroying the English nationality and the English language; but it was an inevitable consequence of the Conquest that both were nearly destroyed.[9]

This view, evinced too by Freeman in his seminal history of the Norman Conquest ('The Conquest also indirectly affected the language by thrusting it down from the rank of a literary to that of a mere popular language'),[10] seems to have stuck, and is reinforced by the use of the labels 'Old' and 'Middle' English in academe. It reappears across the fundamental studies of the period. The great historian, John Le Patourel, in testifying to the multilingualism of post-Conquest England, reveals that: 'English vernacular literature was not extinguished, though it was driven underground by the requirements of the new Norman aristocracy and the Normanized church; and what was not written in Latin was written in "Anglo-Norman", producing, in the course of the twelfth century, a not undistinguished body of literature.'[11] If the litotic description of the

---

[8] W. P. Ker, *English Literature Medieval* (London: Oxford University Press, 1912), 44.

[9] Chambers, *On the Continuity of English Prose*, pp. lxxxi–lxxxii.

[10] E. A. Freeman, *The History of the Norman Conquest of England* (Oxford: Clarendon Press, 1876), v. 525.

[11] John Le Patourel, *The Norman Empire* (Oxford: Clarendon, 1976), p. 252.

Anglo-Norman literary corpus bespeaks modesty, the underwhelming assessment of English literary output intimates a situation in which determining what 'was not extinguished' seems a hopeless task. Increasing the apparent hopelessness of the situation, John Hudson stated in a popular magazine in 2003 that 'Old English, or Anglo-Saxon as it is also called, largely disappeared as a written language, at least from 1070. It survived and developed as an oral language, used by the lower orders and, importantly, by middling-ranking men and townspeople of English descent...Their language would re-emerge in writing later in the twelfth century, with a considerable infusion of French vocabulary.'[12] Similarly, the loss of written English is mourned by Greenfield and Calder in their classic *New Critical History*, when they note that the best Old English prose of the eleventh century, witnessed in the mid-eleventh-century romance, *Apollonius of Tyre*, 'is a glimpse of a native style that might have developed if English had not been replaced by French after the Norman Conquest'.[13]

It is worth labouring this point: that for most historians or literary scholars, until very recently, literature or *any* writing in English ceased to exist in the post-Conquest period. Why the many dozens of manuscripts produced in English from 1060 to 1200 and beyond are invisible is an interesting and complex question. It seems partly to do with the issue of 'composition': the majority of English texts in this period are not poetic (always the most valued literary genre); and most are not original, since the texts are generally based on pre-existing works, particularly homilies and particularly those of Ælfric. The hierarchizing of literature in this way—venerating the poetic and the original—is at the heart of Christopher Cannon's recent book, *The Grounds of English Literature*, which makes myopic claims in discussing the post-Conquest period:

> Even in the twelfth century most of the survivals in English that we have been willing to call literary are fragments, snippets of poetry which sneak into texts in other languages...No work of literature of any length has been identified until the middle of the twelfth century (perhaps the earliest is the 700-line *Proverbs of Alfred* (c.1150)), but

[12] John Hudson, 'Essential Histories: The Norman Conquest', *History Magazine* 4.1 (January 2003), pp. 17–23.
[13] Stanley B. Greenfield and Daniel G. Calder, *A New Critical History of Old English Literature* (New York: New York University Press, 1986), 97.

even such length provides no evidence that a significant vernacular impulse has taken hold.[14]

Then, as if to remedy this lacuna, Cannon pulls the poem, *The First Worcester Fragment,* from its present physical and temporal context of *c.*1215 to a hypothesized context of origin sometime in Cnut's reign, claiming—without convincing evidence—that, 'If the poem is about any cataclysm, it is certainly not the Norman Conquest, but what we would surely call the Scandinavian (or Danish) Conquest had this earlier event been permanent enough to generate its own abundant history.'[15] This poem, lamenting the loss of English culture, particularly through the depletion of teachers of English,[16] was copied by the scribe known to scholars as the Tremulous Hand of Worcester.[17] It is contained in a fragmentary manuscript, Worcester Cathedral Library F. 174. Its lexis is early Middle English, its cadence contemporary with its manuscript, its content that of an Old English enthusiast, who glossed many manuscripts with a Worcester provenance or origin, and who clearly valued the past with both pragmatism and a sense of the aesthetic.[18] To consider this text in isolation from its context is to perform a disservice to the few able to articulate a perspective that differs from the 'official' in the post-Conquest period, those who testify—even at the distance of 150 years—to the trauma effected by William's victory. To fracture the poem's articulation of suffering by displacing it to an earlier eleventh-century milieu, and then argue that this previous conquest was impermanent and produced no testimony of its own, is to miss the point, to ignore the evidence, even of those texts skimmed over in the earlier chapters of this book.

Highlighting gaps in the literary record instead of looking at what *does* exist means writing-off the one hundred and more surviving codices,

---

[14] Cannon, *Grounds of English Literature*, p. 19. This kind of claim also informs his more recent work, *Middle English Literature: A Cultural History* (Cambridge: Polity, 2008), p. 76.

[15] Cannon, *Grounds of English Literature*, p. 37, although at p. 36, Cannon states the poem 'was almost certainly written after 1066'.

[16] Ed. and trans. Treharne, *Old and Middle English*. I have discussed this extensively, and shown its late date of composition, in 'Making their Presence Felt: Readers of Ælfric, *c.* 1050–1350', in H. Magennis and M. Swan (eds.), *A Companion to Ælfric*, Brill's Companion to the Christian Tradition 18 (Leiden: Brill, 2009), pp. 399–422.

[17] On whom, see Christine Franzen, *The Tremulous Hand of Worcester: A Study of Old English in the Thirteenth Century* (Oxford: Clarendon Press, 1991).

[18] Treharne, 'Making their Presence Felt', pp. 399–404.

many with extensive numbers of vernacular texts.[19] A significant number of prose texts and a small amount of verse survive from the period 1066 to 1215 (unless we regard much of Ælric's corpus as essentially poetic[20]); every genre of literature is represented; and multiple resources are given over to the compilation of the manuscripts, though *de luxe* books containing vernacular materials are exceptionally rare, as was always the case. Scribal expertise demonstrated through this century-and-a-half varies as much as it did in the pre-Conquest period, despite Ker's summary statement that 'much writing of the twelfth century is not good'.[21] What is most notable, perhaps, is the longevity and similarity of both the form and the content of English manuscript production from the second half of the eleventh century until the beginning of the thirteenth. It should be noted, too, that these similarities are much less to do with the lack of creativity of the manuscript compilers than they are with the essential functionalism and adaptability of the vernacular for a wide variety of contemporary purposes, few of which included production for presentation purposes or, as far as one can tell, for the use of lay patrons.

Despite the clear usefulness of English for teaching, preaching, prognosticating, chronicling, and carrying out all ecclesiastical and pastoral duties, there is also a significant trend in the modern scholarship that does recognize vernacular textual production to view the English manuscripts created in the post-Conquest period as principally motivated by 'nostalgia' or 'antiquarianism'.[22] I have addressed this a number of times elsewhere,[23] but the issue is valid here, because regarding the writing of English in the later eleventh and twelfth centuries as the activity of some backward-looking impetus is to seriously undervalue the obvious efforts

[19] See now Orietta Da Rold, Takako Kato, Mary Swan and Elaine Treharne, *The Production and Use of English, 1060 to 1220* (University of Leicester, 2010): http://www.le.ac.uk/ee/em1060to1220/

[20] See Bredehoft, *Authors, Audiences and Old English Verse.*

[21] Ker, *Catalogue*, p. xxvii.

[22] M. T. Clanchy, *From Memory to Written Record*, 2nd edn. (Oxford: Blackwell, 1992), p. 212; Seth Lerer, 'The Afterlife of Old English', in David Wallace (ed.), *Cambridge History of Medieval Literature* (Cambridge: Cambridge University Press, 1999), pp. 7–34.

[23] In 'The Life and Times of Old English Homilies for the First Sunday in Lent', in H. Magennis and J. Wilcox (ed.), *The Power of Words: Anglo-Saxon Studies Presented to Donald G. Scragg on His Seventieth Birthday* (Morgantown: West Virginia University Press, 2006), pp. 205–42; and 'The Life of English in the Mid-Twelfth Century: Ralph D'Escures's Homily on the Virgin Mary', in Ruth Kennedy and Simon Meecham-Jones (eds.), *Literature of the Reign of Henry II* (London: Routledge, 2006), pp. 169–86.

of the manuscript makers, the expense incurred, and the usefulness of the texts to their multiple users. This desire to label texts written in the language used by the majority of the population, even within some post-Conquest ecclesiastical institutions, as nostalgic or perhaps even eulogistic may stem from the lack of obvious originality in textual composition.[24] It may also be a conclusion derived from the judgement of notable modern historians, who, following the laments of Lanfranc and William of Malmesbury, adjudge the Anglo-Saxon church in the mid-eleventh century to have been substantially in decline. Both of these misapprehensions about English texts and the English church can be addressed and disproved.

'In Vetere Novum latet; Vetus in Novo patet'[25]

The following table lists the manuscripts whose main texts in English are datable to the period from c.1050 or 1060 to approximately 1100. It is quite clear from the most cursory glance that English did not suffer a wholesale decline; neither can it possibly have been considered defunct or even archival, given the financial expenditure and human resources and skills required to produce this number of works.[26]

[24] These comments are many, and are discussed in Mary Swan, 'Old English Made New: One Catholic Homily and its Reuses', Leeds Studies in English n.s. 28 (1997): 1–18, and in Treharne, 'The Life of English in the Mid-Twelfth Century'. One example will show the pattern: Thomas Hahn's 'Early Middle English' chapter in Wallace (ed.), Cambridge History, pp. 61–91, is negative about English writings in the century after the Conquest, calling the language an 'obsolete literary standard' (p. 72), which suffered an 'abrupt decline' (p. 71), and was characterized by 'disabililty and disembodiment' personified by the Tremulous Hand and his activities (p. 73), or a conservatism and archival nature, as in the Bodley Homilies (p. 83), by which Hahn means Oxford, Bodleian Library, Bodley 343.

[25] 'The New lies hidden in the Old; the Old is made accessible in the New', St Augustine on the New Testament and its relationship to the Old, in his Quaestiones in Heptateuchum 2, 73 (commenting on Exodus 20:19). See I. Fraipoint and D. de Bruyne (eds.), Sancti Aureli Augustini Quaestionum in Heptateuchum libri VII; De octo quaestionibus ex veteri testamento, CCSL 33 (Turnhout: Brepols, 1958), pp. 1–377.

[26] Published handlists are very useful for this material too. See especially Gneuss, Handlist of Anglo-Saxon Manuscripts; Margaret Laing, Catalogue of Sources for a Linguistic Atlas of Early Medieval English (Cambridge: D. S. Brewer, 1993); and David A. E. Pelteret, Catalogue of English Post-Conquest Vernacular Documents (Woodbridge: Boydell and Brewer, 1992).

Manuscripts[27]

Shelf-Number	Ker	Contents in Brief	Origin	Date
BL, Cotton Otho C. i	[182]	Gregory *Dialogues*		s. xi^{in-2}
Oxford, Bodley 579	[315]	Legal texts	Exeter	s. xi^{in-ex}
CCCC 173	[39]	Parker Chronicle	Winchester	s. xi^{in-2}
CCCC 198	[48]	Homilies		s. xi$^{1-2}$
CCCC 419 + 421	[68+69]	Homilies	C'bury-Exeter	s. xi$^{1-3/4}$
BL, Cotton Tiberius B. i	[191]	Orosius; *Chronicle*		s. xi$^{1-2}$
Gloucester 35	[117]	Homilies (fragment)		s. xi$^{1-2}$
CUL Ff. 1. 23	[13]	Gloss to Psalter	Winchcombe?	s. xi^{med}
CUL Ii. 4. 6	[21]	Homilies + glosses		s. xi^{med}
CCCC 201	[49B]	Homilies, laws		s. xi^{med}
CCCC 265	[53]	Directions confessor	Worcester	s. xi^{med}
CCCC 557	[73]	Homily (fragment)	Worcester	s. xi^{med}
Camb, Pembroke 312	[79]	Psalter (fragment)		s. xi^{med}
Trinity B. 15. 34	[86]	Homilies	Canterbury?	s. xi^{med}
BL, Arundel 155	[135]	Gloss to prayers	Christ Church	s. xi^{med}
BL, Cotton Caligula A. xiv	[138]	Lives of Saints		s. xi^{med}
BL, Cotton Julius A. ii	[158]	Ælfric's *Grammar*		s. xi^{med}
BL, Cotton Julius A. vi	[160]	Gloss to Hymnal	Durham?	s. xi^{med}
BL, Cotton Nero A. i	[163]	Laws	C'bury?	s. xi^{med}
BL, Cotton Otho B. x	[178]	Homilies		s. xi^{med}
BL, Cotton Tiberius A. iii	[186]	Homilies, *RB*	Christ Church	s. xi^{med}
BL, Cotton Tiberius B. iv	[192]	*Chronicle*	Worcester?	s. xi^{med-2}
BL, Cotton Tiberius C. vi	[199]	Gloss to psalter		s. xi^{med}
CCCC 190	[45B]	Ecclesiastical Inst.	Exeter	s. xi^{med-2}

(Continued)

[27] This list is comprised of manuscripts dated to the middle of the eleventh century and later, up to the very end of the century. It excludes solely Latin and French manuscripts, and it excludes single-leaf diplomata. Hyphenated dates illustrate the chronological range of a manuscript's contents, and dating follows the system in Ker's *Catalogue*. Abbreviations are listed at the front of this volume; a list of manuscripts with the full shelf-number appears at the first Index at the back of this volume. 'Ker' refers to Ker, *Catalogue*; BL is London, British Library; Bod. is Oxford, Bodleian Library; CCCC is Cambridge, Corpus Christi College; CUL is Cambridge University Library; St Aug's = St Augustine's, Canterbury; Christ Church = Christ Church, Canterbury. See Da Rold et al., *The Production and Use of English, 1060 to 1220* < http://www.le.ac.uk/ee/em1060to1220/>

Shelf-Number	Ker	Contents in Brief	Origin	Date
BL, Cotton Titus A. iv	[200]	*Rule of Benedict*		s. xi^{med}
BL, Cotton Vespasian D. xii	[208]	Hymnal Gloss		s. xi^{med}
BL, Cotton Vitellius D. xvii	[222]	Homilies		s. xi^{med}
BL, Cotton Vitellius E. xviii	[224]	Psalter Gloss	Winchester	s. xi^{med}
BL, Harley 107	[227]	Ælfric's *Grammar*	Kentish?	s. xi^{med}
BL, Harley 2961	[236]	Inscription	Exeter	s. xi$^{med?}$
BL, Royal 7 C. iv	[256]	Gloss	Christ Church	s. xi^{med}
BL, Royal 12 G. xii	[265]	Ælfric's *Grammar*		s. xi^{med}
BL, Stowe 2	[271]	Psalter Gloss		s. xi^{med}
Bod. Ashmole 328	[288]	Byrthferth Handbook	Ramsey?	s. xi^{med}
Bod. Digby 146	[320]	Aldhelm glosses	Abingdon?	s. xi^{med}
Bod. Hatton 76	[328B]	Herbal	Worcester	s. xi^{med}
Bod. Junius 85, 86	[336]	Homilies		s. xi^{med}
Bod. Laud misc. 482	[343]	Penitential	Worcester	s. xi^{med}
Paris, Lat 8824	[367]	Psalter		s. xi^{med}
Taunton Fragments		Homilies		s. xi^{med}
Wells Manuscript	[395]	*Rule of St Benedict*		s. xi^{med}
CUL Ii. 2. 4	[19]	*Pastoral Care*	Exeter	s. xi$^{3/4}$
CUL Ii. 2. 11	[20]	Gospels	Exeter	s. xi$^{3/4}$
CCCC 191	[46]	*Rule of Chrodegang*	Exeter	s. xi$^{3/4}$
CCCC 196	[47]	Martyrology	Exeter	s. xi$^{3/4}$
CCCC 201	[50]	*Capitula* of Theodulf	Exeter	s. xi$^{3/4}$
Exeter Cathedral 3501		Legal docs	Exeter	s. xi$^{3/4}$–xii^{1}
BL, Cotton Cleopatra B. xiii	[144]	Homilies, etc.	Exeter	s. xi$^{3/4}$
BL, Harley 863	[232]	Continuous gloss	Exeter	s. xi$^{3/4}$
London, Lambeth 489	[283]	Homilies	Exeter	s. xi$^{3/4}$
Bod, Auct. D. 2. 16	[291]	Donation list	Exeter	s. xi$^{3/4}$
Bod, Auct. F. 1. 15	[294]	Donation list	Exeter	s. xi$^{3/4}$
Bod, Auct. F. 3. 6	[296]	Donation list	Exeter	s. xi$^{3/4}$
Bod, Bodley 579	[315]	OE in Leofric Missal	Exeter	s. xi$^{3/4}$
Bod, Bodley 708	[316]	Donation list	Exeter	s. xi$^{3/4}$
Bod, Hatton 113, 114	[331]	Homilies	Worcester	s. xi$^{3/4}$
Bod, Junius 121	[338]	Institutes, laws	Worcester	s. xi^{2}
Camb, Add. 3206	[11]	Church laws		s. xi^{2}
CUL Hh. 1. 10	[17]	Ælfric's *Grammar*	Christ Church	s. xi^{2}

Shelf-Number	Ker	Contents in Brief	Origin	Date
CUL Kk. 3. 18	[23]	Bede, *Hist. Eccles.*	Worcester	s. xi²
CCCC 183	[42]	Land lease	Durham	s. xi²
CCCC 322	[60]	Gregory *Dialogues*		s. xi²
CCCC 391	[67]	Prayers, etc.	Worcester	s. xi²
C'bury, Box CCC	[97]	*Chrodegang* (frag.)	Christ Church	s. xi²
Durham, B. IV. 24	[109]	*Rule of St Benedict*		s. xi²
Lincoln 298	[125]	*Hexateuch* (frag.)		s. xi²
BL, Add. 34652	[128]	*Chrodegang* (frag.)		s. xi²
BL, Add 15350		Codex Wintoniensis	Winchester	s. xi²
BL, Arundel 60	[134]	Psalter Gloss	Winchester	s. xi²⁻ᵉˣ
BL, Burney 277	[136]	Laws (fragment)	Kentish	s. xi²
BL, Cotton Caligula A. xv	[139A]	Computistica	Christ Church	s. xi²
BL, Cotton Faustina A. x	[154A]	Ælfric's *Grammar*		s. xi²
BL, Cotton Tiberius C. i	[197]	Homilies, prayers	Sherborne?	c. 1070
BL, Royal 6 B. vii	[255]	Glosses to Aldhelm	Exeter	s. xi²
BL, Royal 15 B. xxii	[269]	Ælfric's *Grammar*		s. xi²
London, Lambeth 427	[281]	Royal Saints (frag.)	Exeter?	s. xi²
W. Merton	[285]	Homily (frag.)		s. xi²
Bod, Auct D. 2. 14	[290]	Booklist	Bury StEd	s. xi²
Bod, Auct. F. 2. 14	[295]	Wordlist, Glosses	Winchester	s. xi²⁺
Bod, Auct. F. 4. 32	[297]	Homily	Glastonbury?	s. xi²
Bod, Hatton 115	[332]	Homilies	Worcester	s. xi²
Bod, Laud misc. 509	[344]	*Pentateuch*		s. xi²
BL, Tiberius A. xiii		Hemming's Cartulary	Worcester	s. xiᵉˣ

This list of some eighty-five manuscripts and manuscript fragments is the most optimistic calendar of the extant codices containing English. Some are extensive books, like Cambridge, Corpus Christi 322, or London, BL Cotton Tiberius A. iii, or Oxford, Bodleian Library, 113 + 114. Other witnesses to English usage are notes, glosses, and copies of writs and manumissions—traces in predominantly Latin books of a vernacular literate textual culture. These manuscripts, then, represent many different kinds of genre and form, as many, in fact, as Anglo-Saxon England in any of its previous centuries could muster. Homilies, hagiography, lawcodes, medical and scientific works, liturgical and biblical material, pastoral commentary and guides, romance (*Apollonius of Tyre* in CCCC 201), and poetry (*The Death of King Edward,* the *Chronicle*'s Poem on Margaret, and *The Rime of King William*[28]) are all included in this list of works. How could it be plausibly claimed that any part of this period from *c.*1050 or 1060 to 1100 saw the demise of English, a hiatus, a bleak wasteland in English literature's lengthy history? Armed with this information about what survives, such assumptions are untenable.

Emerging from these manuscripts is a polyphony of English voices performing many different functions, sometimes simultaneously; different kinds of texts, produced in differing circumstances, proscribe the interpretation of a univocal response to the Conquest by the people of England. After 1066, as a politically charged linguistic choice, English was used to respond the Conquest by those who had always taken charge of its production—the monks and canons of the regular orders, and by the king and his scribes. For these articulate, elite groups, employing English indicated separate aims, and resulted in quite distinct consequences.

The Demise of English?

Rather than reflecting the decline of the English church post-1050, the production of manuscripts in both the vernacular and Latin in the mid- and second half of the eleventh century illustrates the flourishing of the late Anglo-Saxon church. Claims of a decline prior to the arrival of the Normans were propagated by historians, such as Orderic Vitalis, Henry of Huntingdon and William of Malmesbury, the latter of whom asserts that the Norman Conquest effectively saved the English church from an assured deterioration. In a famous and often-quoted passage, he justifies the events of the Conquest as divine punishment for a nation so wilfully wasting its own talents and resources:

> But zeal both for learning and for religion cooled as time went on, not many years before the coming of the Normans. The clergy, content with a mere smattering of knowledge, scarce mumbled the words of

[28] On all of these, see Thomas A. Bredehoft, *Textual Histories: Readings in the Anglo-Saxon Chronicle* (Toronto: University of Toronto Press, 2001), esp. pp. 111–15.

the sacraments; a man who knew any grammar was a marvel and a portent to his colleagues. Monks, with their finely-woven garments and their undiscriminating diet, made nonsense of their Rule. The nobles, abandoned to gluttony and lechery, never went to church of a morning, as a Christian should...[29]

Citing William of Malmesbury, Christopher Harper-Bill debates the extent of the English church's decline, focusing on Stigand's pluralism and 'the failure of the English church... to keep pace with the remarkable transformation of the Roman see'.[30] Similarly, Frank Barlow, contextualizing the post-Conquest claims of pre-Conquest decline as typical of 'Medieval man [who] was obsessed with the idea of deterioration', nevertheless condones the imagined view of 'the monastic writers of the early eleventh century... They lived in communities which owed their re-establishment, their Rule, and their ideals to the great figures of the tenth-century reformation... The severe check to the movement which developed in Æthelred's reign with the death of the monastic leaders, the fighting in England, and the exorbitant taxation and tributes which fell especially heavily on the monasteries, was therefore to be lamented. And nothing, they considered, occurred between then and 1066 which entirely restored the position'.[31] More recent work has begun to re-evaluate these assertions of a decline in the English church; thus, for example, Mary Frances Giandrea is careful to sift propaganda from substance, ideological bias from extant evidence, and to demonstrate how the repeated use of particular primary sources skews modern scholarship.[32]

Still, the trickling down of prevailing views ultimately has a deep impact, and this is particularly true in the responses by historians to the parlous state of the English church not in some abstract sense, but with regard to its cultural and intellectual legacy. The consequences of this for an appreciation of the vibrancy of vernacular literary production are seen in the remarks of many modern-day scholars. In *Books and Learning in Twelfth-Century England*, R. M. Thomson concentrates his attention on the extant collections

---

[29] *Gesta Regum Anglorum*, i. 459. For an argument countering this propaganda, see my 'The Silence of (the) English'.

[30] Harper-Bill, *Anglo-Norman Church*, pp. 6–8.

[31] Barlow, *The English Church*, pp. 26–7. At no point is it really clear here who Barlow's 'they' might be here.

[32] Mary Frances Giandrea, *Episcopal Culture in Late Anglo-Saxon England* (Woodbridge: Boydell, 2008).

of Latin books from post-Conquest England, collections he has catalogued and analysed over a long and productive career.[33] There is no doubt, of course, as Thomson points out, that the numbers and variety of Latin books produced in England are far greater than their vernacular contemporaries, and that continued to be true throughout the medieval period and into the Early Modern era. More Latin books were produced than French books, and by the end of the twelfth century more French books were made than English. This does not mean, however, that the extant English books we have are easily dismissed; or, rather, *should* be easily dismissed.[34]

Let me be absolutely clear here: all of the English manuscripts and documents that have survived from England to *c.*1200 and beyond are remarkable testimony to a vernacular textual tradition that is rarely paralleled elsewhere in the medieval world.[35] This may be limited in relation to Latin book production; indeed, copying English may yet turn out to have been a specialized activity, but nonetheless it is a notable textual achievement, about which it seems easy to be rather dismissive. Moreover, those manuscripts that survive are the tip of an obvious iceberg, since each of these is dependent on an exemplar, and in some cases, multiple exemplars, necessarily illustrating that there were many other extensive manuscript compilations circulating in eleventh- and twelfth-century England.[36] Ian Short, for example, is compelled to toss out the Old English in order to make room for the new Anglo-Norman literary vernacular; he calls works written in English in the twelfth century (in comparison with Anglo-Norman and French) 'disappointingly undistinguished', lamenting 'the meagre production of literary texts in English', which was essentially a 'native literary vacuum', were it not for a couple of poems and 'a handful of predominantly religious texts'.[37] In relation to book production in the entire

---

[33] R. M. Thomson, *Books and Learning in Twelfth-Century England: The Ending of 'Alter Orbis'?* (Stevenage: Red Gull Press, 2007).

[34] As they sometimes are with sweeping statements like that of Christopher Daniell, *From Norman Conquest to Magna Carta, England 1066–1215* (London: Routledge, 2003), p. 191: 'One estimate is that over 800 manuscripts were copied or acquired by the English churches between *c.*1066 and *c.* 1125—this is a greater number than all the Anglo-Saxon manuscripts of the previous four and a half centuries.' It is not clear what 'Anglo-Saxon' might refer specifically to here—Old-English, Anglo-Latin, or both.

[35] Perhaps the same claim can be made of the Welsh and Irish vernacular survivals in their post-Conquest periods.

[36] As Aaron Kleist reminds us in 'Assembling Ælfric: Reconstructing the Rationale behind Eleventh- and Twelfth-Century Compilations', in Magennis and Swan (eds.), *Companion to Ælfric*, pp. 369–98.

[37] Short, 'Language and Literature', pp. 194–5.

late Anglo-Saxon period from *c.*890 to the Conquest, Thomson damns with faint praise in his summary that: 'I would not want to underestimate the recovery begun by Alfred and continued by the great reformers of the tenth century, but the fact remains that English books and collections on the eve of the Conquest, on the evidence that we have, still look pre-Carolingian: poor in mainstream patristic or classical texts, and of course with a high percentage of their contents in the vernacular.'[38] Fortunately, the claim that book collections in the decades surrounding the Conquest were 'poor' or antiquated can be easily corrected, and the value of the vernacular can be illustrated, particularly with reference to two major English sees in the second half of the eleventh century.

English Polyphony, 1050 to 1100

It is clear that for bishops, such as St Wulfstan of Worcester (*c.*1008–95) or Leofric of Exeter (died 1072),[39] their pastoral work and the desire to consolidate the strength and vitality of their sees prompted the collection, production and use of key Latin and English manuscripts. With the exception of Canterbury, no other centres of manuscript production in England can equal the respective vernacular output of these western sees in the years *c.*1050–1100. In reviewing the manuscripts and texts created for these bishops and their circles, it becomes clear that not only were the pastoral and political roles of these senior prelates of significance in the maintenance of the high standards established in the tenth-century Benedictine reforming movement, but also that these bishops were actively involved in promulgating continental European reforms, particularly those emerging from Lotharingian institutions.[40] Thus, claims

---

[38] Thomson, *Books and Learning*, p. 3.

[39] Emma Mason, 'Wulfstan [St Wulfstan] (c.1008–1095)', *ODNB* [http://www.oxforddnb. com.proxy.lib.fsu.edu/view/article/30099, accessed 26 July 2010]; Frank Barlow, 'Leofric (*d.* 1072)', *ODNB* [http://www.oxforddnb.com.proxy.lib.fsu.edu/view/article/ 16471, accessed 26 July 2010]

[40] Of great importance here is the recent work by Erika Corradini in her doctoral dissertation, 'Leofric of Exeter and his Lotharingian Connections: A Bishop's Books, *c.* 1050–1072' (unpub. PhD University of Leicester, 2008). She shows that Leofric is intimately connected with papal reforms in the 1050s and 1060s, and that he is concerned to address and implement the major aspects of continental reform in his own diocese. See also Joyce Hill, 'Leofric of Exeter and the Practical Politics of Book Collecting', in S. Kelly and J. J. Thompson (eds.), *Imagining the Book* (Turnhout: Brepols, 2005), pp. 77–98.

by post-Conquest historians and Norman prelates, such as Lanfranc, archbishop of Canterbury from 1070, or Maurice, bishop of London from 1086 to 1107,[41] that the English church had decayed and was in urgent need of reform can be shown to be propagandistic, masquerading as justification for the actions of the conquerors in the decades following October 1066, and bolstering the reputation of the Anglo-Norman church itself.

If the words of the Norman prelates and Anglo-Norman writers were just words that would be one thing, but the actions of the colonizers had a real and devastating effect on the English church. Most senior Anglo-Saxon prelates were replaced, including Stigand, archbishop of Canterbury, Godric, abbot of Winchcombe, and Æthelnoth of Glastonbury, leaving few to negotiate the cultural consequences of the Conquest.[42] The most prominent of the survivors is Wulfstan II of Worcester, and he—in parallel with Leofric of Exeter, Wulfketel of Crowland (who was deposed in the mid-1080s),[43] and the few remaining English ecclesiastics—was responsible for maintaining the energetic work of the Anglo-Saxon church in caring for the souls of the majority of the population. This majority spoke English, understood English, and had for a century or so probably been accustomed on a few special occasions to hearing English sermons, and participating in liturgical ceremonies, some parts of which may well have been conducted in the vernacular.

It is not difficult to find evidence for the kind of pastoral, doctrinal and educational work that required the production of homiliaries, hagiographies, Psalters, confessional, legal, educational and regulatory materials, together with other texts, such as medical and encyclopaedic works, prognostications, debates, and patristic writings. Manuscripts of such works in English and Latin were compiled in the eleventh century in the major scriptoria of the Benedictine and secular cathedrals, and in many of the Anglo-Saxon monasteries. These testify to active intellectual and religious cultures

---

[41] For Lanfranc, Maurice and other Norman prelates initially hostile to Anglo-Saxon saints and their churches, see Paul Hayward, 'Translation Narratives in Post-Conquest Hagiography and English Resistance to the Norman Conquest', ANS 21 (1998), pp. 67–93; id., 'Gregory the Great as "Apostle of the English" in Post-Conquest Canterbury', Journal of Ecclesiastical History 55 (2004), pp. 19–39.

[42] Dom David Knowles, The Monastic Order in England 940–1216, 2nd edn. (Oxford: Oxford University Press, 1963), pp. 103–27.

[43] See Hayward, 'Translation Narratives', p. 93.

there. In some cases, and as dictated by the *Regularis Concordia*, following the *Rule of St Benedict*, the books will have been accessible to all the monks.[44] In other cases, it is likely that the books belonged, in the first instance, to the most senior officers of the institution, including the abbots or priors of monasteries, and the bishops of the cathedrals. One is tempted, indeed, to suggest that the majority of *English* books, as well as many Latin manuscripts, that survive from the end of the tenth to the end of the eleventh century belonged originally to those responsible for overseeing the provision for pastoral care; namely, the bishop or the abbot, or their own appointed delegate. Certainly, it seems the libraries of Leofric at Exeter and Ealdred and Wulfstan II at Worcester functioned partly as specifically episcopal collections, and in this they share a great deal of textual material in common.[45]

As is well known from a famous donation list, Leofric was an avid book collector of both Latin and English manuscripts, and he was careful to leave a significant collection to his cathedral on his death in 1072.[46] Apart from this list of books donated to Exeter, there is also a group of manuscripts that seems to sit outside the collection bequeathed to the canons: a set of pastoral, educational and liturgical materials that may have been retained as a specifically episcopal library.[47] In this period, the

---

[44] As must be assumed, for example, from the *Regularis Concordia*'s stipulation that during the Summer weekdays, monks should read between Matins and the bell for Prime: Thomas Symons (ed.), *Regularis Concordia: Anglicae Nationis Monachorum Sanctimonialiumque* (New York: Oxford University Press, 1953), pp. 53–4.

[45] On Leofric's library see Elaine Treharne, 'Producing a Library in Late Anglo-Saxon England: Exeter, 1050–72', *Review of English Studies* n.s. 54 (2003), pp. 155–72, and 'A Bishop's Book: Leofric's Homiliary and Eleventh-Century Exeter', in *Early Medieval Studies in Memory of Patrick Wormald* (Farnham: Ashgate, 2009), pp. 521–37; on the Worcester library in general, see Richard Gameson, 'St Wulfstan, the Library of Worcester and the Spirituality of the Medieval Book', in Julia Barrow and Nicholas Brooks (eds.), *St Wulfstan and his World*, Studies in Early Medieval Britain (Aldershot: Ashgate, 2005), pp. 59–104.

[46] Patrick W. Conner, *Anglo-Saxon Exeter: A Tenth-Century Cultural History* (Woodbridge: Boydell, 1993), and 'Exeter's Relics, Exeter's Books', in Jane Roberts and Janet Nelson (eds.), *Essays on Anglo-Saxon and Related Themes in Memory of Lynne Grundy*, King's College London Medieval Studies (London: King's College, Centre for Late Antique and Medieval Studies, 2000), pp. 117–56. Of fundamental importance for any study of Exeter in the eleventh century are T. A. M. Bishop, 'Notes on Cambridge Manuscripts Part III: MSS. Connected with Exeter', *TCBS* 2/2 (1955), 192–9; and Elaine M. Drage, 'Bishop Leofric and the Exeter Cathedral Chapter, 1050–1072: A Reassessment of the Manuscript Evidence' (unpub. D.Phil. dissertation, University of Oxford, 1978).

[47] Treharne, 'Producing a Library in Late Anglo-Saxon England' and 'The Bishop's Book'.

bishop's duties to his diocese and his canons or monks were onerous, especially when coupled with the advisory role undertaken by many prelates on the king's council. An indication of how seriously the bishop's preaching and ministering to the laity was regarded is given by the homily of Wulfstan I copied into manuscripts that can be shown to have belonged in the second-half of the eleventh century specifically to Leofric at Exeter, and to Wulfstan II at Worcester. The homily, *Lectio secundum Lucam*, contained in the Exeter manuscript, London, BL Cotton Cleopatra B. xiii, and the Worcester sermon collection, Oxford, Bodleian Library, Hatton 113 + 114, stipulates that:

> Bisceopas syndon bydelas and Godes lage lareowas, and hy scylon georne oft and gelome clypian to Criste and for eall cristen folc þingian georne; and hy scylan georne Godes riht bodian and æghwylc unriht georne forbeodan.[48]

> Bishops are the heralds and the teachers of God's law, and they should often and frequently call upon Christ eagerly, and readily intercede for all Christian people; and they should enthusiastically preach the true way of God and fervently prohibit every injustice.

Here, as elsewhere, Wulfstan I formulates the essential duties of the bishop, using key responsibilities that he would go on to repeat in his regulatory *Institutes of Polity*.[49] Wulfstan also uses biblical injunction[50] to reinforce his description of the pastoral and legal responsibilities of the bishop: the bishop as 'bydel', or 'herald, minister, messenger' is both the intercessor between God and his people, urging the people to do God's will, but also mediating God's law and the bishop as 'lareow' or 'teacher, preacher' interpreting God's message and exhorting good Christian behaviour. 'Bydel', moreover, also indicates the officer who would summon the attendee into the court of law, reminding the bishop and his congregation of the final great court appearance, as it were, on Doomsday, when the risen will be led by the angels to judgement.

Preaching, teaching, conducting services, understanding and interpreting the law, acting as secular statesmen and advisers, baptising,

---

[48] Homily XVII in Bethurum (ed.), *Homilies of Wulfstan*, pp. 242–5.

[49] *Fontes Anglo-Saxonici*, s.v. Wulfstan 17, by Stephanie Hollis: http://fontes.english.ox.ac.uk/data/content/astexts/title_sources.asp?refer=C.B.2.3.5

[50] From Ezechiel 34 on the evil of the poor pastor and the example of the true pastor caring for his flock.

ministering to the sick, confirming catechumens, excommunicating or reconciling the sinful, ordaining priests, visiting other dioceses, supervising the clergy (and monks), and dedicating churches are all duties of the bishops represented in English homiletic and instructional materials from this period, and in particular, in the vernacular books used by Leofric, Wulfstan II and many other prelates from 1050–1100. Sermons pertinent to the specific tasks of the bishop are found in the texts written by Wulfstan I, circulating in the homiliaries like BL Cotton Cleopatra B. xiii, and its companion volumes, London, Lambeth Palace 489, and Cambridge, Corpus Christi College, 419 + 421. These books, all used by Leofric, and compiled probably during the earlier years of his episcopacy, testify to his efforts to have at his disposal a wide range of vernacular materials to complete his preaching role satisfactorily.[51] Coupled with the other books we know Leofric to have possessed—including gospels, a grammar, all manner of Latin extensive liturgical materials, psalters, regulatory texts, penitentials, and even poetry[52]—it is clear that the vernacular was very much part of a dedicated, literate English churchman's repertoire in the second-half of the eleventh century.

The claims that can be made for Leofric's commitment to his see and his extensive congregation are derived circumstantially from the material remains he has left to us, and particularly his books. If it were left to historians' assessments to determine Leofric's significance, we might assume him to have been, as Barlow, suggests, neither much loved nor important.[53] Leofric's books, and his efforts to obtain books from a variety of sources, though, rather suggest a concerned, earnest, diligent and busy prelate. That Leofric's scribes were so meticulous in recording his donation of volumes to the canons of Exeter intimates a desire to memorialize that act and the

[51] These (now four) volumes between them contain twenty-five homilies (four for the dedication of a church) written at Exeter. Corpus 419 + 421, possibly from Christ Church, Canterbury, was itself an extensive collection when it arrived at Exeter. See further, Treharne, 'Bishop's Book', *passim*.

[52] See Conner, *Anglo-Saxon Exeter*; and Susan Rankin, 'From memory to record: musical notations in manuscripts from Exeter', *Anglo-Saxon England* 13 (1984), pp. 97–112.

[53] Barlow, *The English Church 1000–1066*, p. 84, describes Leofric as: 'the foreign prelate at his best: detached from, but not insensitive to, local tradition; free from dynastic and tenurial ties, so that, instead of ecclesiastical property being used to endow dependants, private fortune could be put to the use of the church; an able administrator and a progressive force. Yet there is no evidence that he was much loved or even, in the widest sense, important.'

donor himself. It may also be, unlike Wulfstan II of Worcester and other leading prelates of the day, that Leofric did *not* much engage in statesmanship in the later years of his episcopacy,[54] particularly in the post-Conquest period; the sources upon which we rely for information in this period are very parsimonious where Leofric is concerned.[55]

Fortunately, in Wulfstan II, we have a figure about whom a great deal is known, thanks to the survival of contemporary records and books at Worcester, numerous accounts of him in post-Conquest histories, and the *Vita Wulfstani* of William of Malmesbury, translated into Latin from Coleman's Old English life of the saint.[56] Despite the institutional differences between Leofric and Wulfstan II—Leofric was bishop of a secular cathedral following the *Rule of Chrodegang* and Wulfstan a monk-bishop, head of a Benedictine monastic cathedral—the similarities in the episcopal books they owned are striking, and illustrate effectively the commitment and diligence of the late Anglo-Saxon bishop in his pastoral and instructional undertakings.[57] Modern scholars know a great deal about Wulfstan's assiduous care of his diocese, and, from his *Vita*, his love of books and his desire to spread the word of God expose his learning and respect for the written word. In his childhood, as William of Malmesbury reveals, Wulfstan was entrusted by his tutor, Earnwig, with an illuminated Sacramentary and Psalter, which Earnwig then presented to Cnut and Emma. Distraught, Wulfstan was granted a vision, in which

---

[54] He did canvass the pope successfully to have his see moved from Crediton to Exeter in 1050, and he did serve Edward the Confessor throughout his reign: see Hill, 'Leofric of Exeter and the Practical Politics of Book Collecting', pp. 77–98.

[55] Thus, for example, when Exeter was besieged by William I in 1068 following threats of a possible rebellion, Leofric is not mentioned by the major sources, though one might imagine he would have a key intermediary role between the king, nobles, and citizens. See J. O. Prestwich, 'Military intelligence under the Norman and Angevin kings', in George Garnett and John Hudson (eds.), *Law and Government in Medieval England and Normandy* (Cambridge: Cambridge University Press, 1994), pp. 1–30, at pp. 4–8.

[56] M. Winterbottom and R. M. Thomson (eds. and trans.), *William of Malmesbury, Saints' Lives: Lives of SS. Wulfstan, Dunstan, Patrick, Benignus and Indract*, Oxford Medieval Texts (Oxford: Clarendon Press, 2002); henceforth, *Vita Wulfstani*. See also Emma Mason, *St Wulfstan* (Oxford: Blackwell, 1990); and the essays in Julia Barrow and Nicholas Brooks (eds.), *St Wulfstan and his World* (Aldershot, Ashgate Press: 2005).

[57] E. M. Treharne, 'Bishops and their Texts in the later Eleventh Century: Worcester and Exeter', in Wendy Scase (ed.), *Essays in Manuscript Geography: Vernacular Manuscripts of the English West Midlands from the Conquest to the Sixteenth Century* (Turnhout: Brepols, 2007), pp. 13–28.

an angel told him the books would be returned to him;[58] this duly happened, when, on his return from a visit to Cologne, Ealdred, bishop of Worcester gave them to Wulfstan 'in view of the merits of his life', and, moreover, since the books were 'suitable for him and him only', it seems that claims of Wulfstan's 'illiteracy' are much exaggerated.[59] Wulfstan therefore appears to have had his own episcopal library, which may also have included the *Lives* of Saints Oswald and Dunstan, which Wulfstan held in his hand, while he awaited judgement from the king in his case against Archbishop Thomas of York in 1072. Wulfstan's victory in this case is attributed to his faith, and to the saints' support of his case against Thomas,[60] his faith here materialized in and through the written word. Not only did Wulfstan possess his own books and carry particular volumes with him, but also he actively researched religious resources for use in his sermons, going 'out of his way to collect material that would enable him always to speak of Christ, always to put Christ before his hearers'.[61] Since such a large part of Wulfstan's extensive congregation were ordinary Christians who flocked to hear him speak, it is unsurprising that a significant amount of Old English material was produced in Worcester during his prelacy.

Contiguous with the vernacular homiletic and penitential material that Wulfstan kept close are texts exemplifying the conciliar responsibilities of the bishop. In the (now three-volume) collection, Oxford, Bodleian Library, Junius 121 + Hatton 113 + 114,[62] the Latin Decrees of the Council of Winchester in 1072 (enjoining celibacy on senior and regular clergy) precede bilingual penitential texts and vernacular regulatory material, which leads into confessional works, pastoral letters and homilies, and a few prayers. This episcopal collection is indicative of Wulfstan's keen interest in maintaining up-to-date textual references for all elements of his work from the role of national statesman to personal confessor and individual supplicant. The three manuscripts comprise an extensive teaching and preaching tool, put together in its initial form

---

[58] *Vita Wulfstani*, i.1.4, pp. 16–17.

[59] Ibid. i.10.1, pp. 40–1. In his *Gesta Regum Anglorum*, William of Malmesbury comments on the 'sancta simplicitas' ('saintly simplicity') of Wulfstan, which was derided by other prelates as 'illiteracy'. See *Gesta Regum Anglorum*, i. 538–9.

[60] *Vita Wulfstani*, ii.1.6, pp. 62–5.

[61] Ibid. i.14.2, pp. 50–1.

[62] Ker, *Catalogue*, items 331 and 338, pp. 391–9, and pp. 412–18.

from a variety of sources[63] by a single scribe. This denotes a scriptorium staffed with sufficient scribes to permit one to be dedicated to a single task over time: indeed, this appears to be a relatively competent and confident scribe, who is something of an editor of the material being copied.[64] Within the volumes is a mixture of what might be considered the best available texts by Wulfstan I and Ælfric, intermingled with composite homilies and other anonymous texts. The nature of this penitential and homiletic collection changed in later years, as additions by a number of hands indicate a rapid (if not vast) expansion of the materials in the anthology that include an Ælfric homily for a Confessor (item 76), and one for a Dedication of a Church (item 77). These *quando volueris* items supplement the many other texts for non-specified occasions in the manuscripts,[65] which might well be considered of greatest use to a bishop required to preach for a multitude of events, as his schedule allowed.[66]

The use of English in these manuscripts is, of course, pastorally and pragmatically motivated. It is also well known that in the West Midlands in the centuries after the Norman Conquest, the use of English was also motivated by a political desire to retain and promote native language and customs, and to protect the interests of the dioceses, their churches and their congregations. Wulfstan II's understanding of the importance and permanence of the written word, its potential as inspiration, motivation, salvation, and as testimony is not in doubt, given the

---

[63] Godden, *CHII*, pp. lii–liii. Godden describes it as being compiled from 'diverse origins', one source for some items being Cambridge, Corpus Christi College 178, an earlier eleventh-century manuscript with a Worcester provenance.

[64] This editorial activity manifests itself in a number of ways, such as syntactic alteration (usually switching the main and auxiliary verbs around), phonological and other orthographical changes (*hy-hie*, for example), inflexional levelling, particularly of dative *–um* to *–an* or *–en*, the omission of the verbal prefix a- (in *arisan* or *acweccan*, for instance), intratextual lexical alteration (so, *wordum* for *spræcum*, *gesucon* for *gesicton*, *getrymde* for *gestrynde*, *drihten* for *god*, *gimmas* for *gymstanas*), and finally, minor rhetorical flourishes are added, such as 'eall toslopen' becomes 'eall toswollen and toslopen'. See, for example, the lists of variants in the apparatus in Clemoes, *CHI*. Many of these features are very common in Old English manuscripts in the later eleventh and twelfth centuries and indicate a conscious linguistic up-dating of the exemplar. See e.g. Elaine Treharne, 'Reading from the Margins: The Uses of Old English Homiletic Manuscripts in the Post-Conquest Period', in A. N. Doane and K. Wolf (eds.), *Beatus Vir: Early English and Norse Manuscript Studies in Memory of Phillip Pulsiano* (Medieval & Renaissance Texts & Studies, Arizona State University, 2006), pp. 329–58.

[65] Such as those at fols. 1–115 in Hatton 113. See Godden, *CHII*, p. li.

[66] I expand on this in 'Bishops and their Texts', pp. 13–28.

episodes in the *Vita Wulfstani* about his own relationship with books and texts.[67] The ability of the ecclesiastical institution to produce written testimony to its ownership of lands was of key importance, particularly in the post-Conquest period, and Wulfstan ensured his diocese's claims, as mentioned above, by instigating the compilation of Hemming's Cartulary, an extensive and detailed volume which Francesca Tinti describes as illustrating 'St Wulfstan's insistence on the importance of *litteralis memoria*' and giving 'voice to the monks' preoccupations'.[68] Moreover, Wulfstan's most senior monks, like Hemming and Coleman, were those given over to the production and use of manuscripts at Worcester, illustrating the considerable significance attached to this programme of vernacular and Latin composition.

Unity through language; alliance through reform

Wulfstan's commitment to providing pastoral care for the English is illustrated by his frequent travels around his diocese and beyond, reaching out to his people in his preaching and charitable work, and supporting his fellow monks and priests in his role as senior prelate. This concern for those around him, and particularly his English monastic brethren, is further enhanced by his leadership in the formation of a confraternity agreement in the 1070s.[69] From the end of the eighth century, confraternity agreements were made between communities of monks and clerics, building on the tradition established earlier to foster alliances between individuals—both religious and lay.[70] Explicitly stated agreements between religious institutions seem to be rare in Anglo-Saxon and early Anglo-Norman England, particularly those surviving in English. The vernacular agreement between Worcester, Evesham, Chertsey, Bath,

---

[67] Thus, for example, when he was a monk, Wulfstan would pray through the night, sleeping little, but resting his head on a book while prostrate in prayer: *Vita Wulfstani*, i.3.4, pp. 24–7.

[68] Francesca Tinti, *Sustaining Belief: The Church of Worcester from c. 870–1100* (Aldershot: Ashgate, 2010), pp. 136–55, esp. pp. 136–7 and, quoted here, p. 149.

[69] Briefly discussed in Mason, *St Wulfstan*, pp. 197–200; the text is in B. Thorpe (ed.), *Diplomatarium Anglicum Aevi Saxonici* (1865), pp. 615–17, and below.

[70] Megan McLaughlin, *Consorting with Saints: Prayer for the Dead in Medieval France* (Ithaca, NY: Cornell University Press, 1994), p. 83.

Pershore, Winchcombe, and Gloucester extant in CCCC 111,[71] pp. 55–6 (see Figure 5), then, is a significant witness to Wulfstan's desire to foster a close alliance between these seven monastic houses:

On Drihtnes naman hælendes Cristes is þæt Wulfstan, b*isceop*, on Drihtnes naman, hæfð gerædd wið his leofan gebroðra þe him getreowe synd for Gode, 7 for worulde: ðæt is þonne ærest Ægelwig, abb*od* on Eofesham; 7 Wulfwold, abb*od* on Ceortesige; 7 Ælfsige, abb*od* on Baðan 7 þa gebroðra; 7 Eadmund, abb*od* on Perscoran; 7 Rawulf, abb*od* on Wincelcumbe; 7 Særle, abb*od* on Gleweceastre; 7 Ælfstan, decanus on Wigraceastre. Ðæt is þæt we willað georne gehyrsume beon Gode 7 S*ancta* Marian, 7 S*ancte* Benedicte. 7 us sylfe gerihtlæcan swa neah swa we nyht magon, þam rihte, 7 beon swa swa hit awriten is: 'Quasi cor unu*m* & anima una', 7 we willað urum woruld hlaforde Willelme cinincge, 7 Mahthilde [*sic*], þære hlæfdian, holde beon for Gode 7 for worulde.

7 habbe we us gerædd betweonan to ure saule þearfe, 7 to ealra þara gebroðra þe us under þeodde synd, þe munuchades synd: þæt is þæt we willað beon on annesse, swylce ealle þas vii mynstras syn an mynster, 7 beon swa hit her beforan awriten is 'Quasi cor unum & anima una'. Ðæt is þæt we ælcere wucan singan ii. mæssan on ælcum mynstre, synderlice for eallum gebroðrum, Monandæge 7 Fridæge 7 wite se broðar þe capitula mæssewuca bið, þæt þas mæssan geforðige, for ða gebroðra þe libbende synd, 7 for ælcan forðfarenan breðer, ælc þæra þinga foredon swylce hig ealle ætgædere on anum mynstre wæron.

7 nu is þara abboda cwydrædene þæt hig willað beon gode gehyrsume, 7 heora bisceope, to heora gemænelicum þearfe, þæt is þæt heora ælc sceal don an c mæssan, 7 of his agenra handa gebycge, 7 an c þearfendra manna gebaðige, 7 þa fedan, 7 ealle þa gescygean, 7 ælc singe himsylf vii mæssan, 7 him fore don xxx nihta his mete beforan him, 7 ænne pænig on uppan þam mete. God us gefultumige þæt we hit þus motan gelæstan, 7 mid suman gode geeacnian. SIC FIAT.

Ðis synd þara gebroðra naman on Eofesham: þæt is ærest Ægelwig abb*od*, 7 Godric abb*od*, 7 Ægelwine decanes, 7 Ordmær, 7 Godefrið, 7

---

[71] At pages 55–6. See Figure 5. CCCC 111 was part of CCCC 140, a copy of the West Saxon Gospels, originating in Bath. This manuscript was bound with the Bath Cartulary. See Ker, *Catalogue*, pp. 47–9, item 35. The text here is re-edited from the manuscript. Expansions are shown in italics; punctuation is modern, though it follows the manuscript closely.

Þeodred, Regnold, 7 Eadric, 7 Ælfwine, 7 Eadwig, Colling, 7 Leofwine, Ælfric, 7 Wulfwine, Sired, 7 Bruning, Ælmær, 7 Ælfwine, Ægelric, 7 Ægelwyrd, Dunning, 7 Sægeat, Vhtred, 7 Eadweard, Eadmund, Vlf, Brihtric, Wulfsige, Sexa, Ælfwine, Wlmær, Ægelwig.

Ðis syndon þara broðra naman on Ceortesige: þæt is ærest Wulfwold abbod, 7 Ælfward, 7 Sælaf, Oter, 7 Godwine, Æþestan, 7 Eadgar, Eadmær, 7 Godwine, Ælfwine, 7 Benedict, Siwine, 7 Alfwold, Brihtnoð, 7 Ælfric, Godric, 7 Ælfric, Oswold, 7 Ælfric, 7 Wulfward, 7 Wulfric.

Ðis syndon þara gebroðra naman on Baðan: þæt is ærest/Ælfsige abbod, 7 Ælfric, Leofwig, 7 Hieðewulf, Ælfwig, 7 Ægelmær, Eadwig, 7 Godwine, Ægelwine, 7 Oswold, Ælmær, 7 Þeodwold, Eadric, Ægelmær, Sæwulf, Þured, Ægelric, 7 Hærbewine, 7 Godric, munuc on Malmesbury, ealswa ure an, 7 ealswa Wulwerd, Pices broðor, on Tantune.[72]

In the name of the Lord our Saviour Christ, it is that, in the Lord's name, Bishop Wulfstan has taken counsel with his dear brothers who are faithful to him before God and before the world. First then, that is Ægelwig, abbot of Evesham; and Wulfwold, abbot of Chertsey; and Ælfsige, abbot of Bath, and the brothers; Eadmund, abbot of Pershore; and Ralph, abbot of Winchcombe; and Særle, abbot of Gloucester; and Ælfstan, dean of Worcester. That is, that we shall eagerly be obedient to God and to Saint Mary and to Saint Benedict, and direct ourselves as much according to right as we possibly can, and be, as it is written, 'as if of one heart and one soul'. And we shall be loyal to our worldly lord, King William, and to the Lady Matilda, before God and before the world.

And we have taken counsel among ourselves for the need of our souls and of all the brothers' who are subject to us, who are in monastic orders: that is, that we shall be in unity, as if all the seven monasteries were one monastery; and be, as it is written here in front of us, 'as if of one heart and one soul'. That is, that we sing two masses every week in each monastery especially for all the brothers, on Monday and Friday. And be it known to the brother who is *capitula mæsse wuca*, that he perform these masses for the brothers who are living; and, for every departed brother, do each of those things as if they were all together in one monastery.

---

[72] These last three names are added in different hands; the first three (including the anonymous) are written over an erasure.

And now it is agreement of the abbots, that they will be obedient to God and to their bishop, for their common need: that is, that each of them shall perform and, for his own account, buy a hundred masses; and bathe a hundred needy men, and feed them, and shoe them. And each will himself sing seven masses, and for thirty days set their meal before them, and a penny upon the food. May God help us that we might carry this out in this way, and with a measure of good make it flourish. Let it be so.[73]

These are the name of the brothers at Evesham; that is, first, Ægelwig abbot and Godric abbot and Ægelwine, the dean, and Ormær and Godefrið and Þeodred and Regnold and Eadric and Ælfwine and Eadwig and Colling and Leofwine and Ælfric and Wulfwine and Sired and Bruning and Ælmær and Ælfwine and Ægelric and Ægel-wyrd and Dunning and Sægeat and Uhtred and Eadweard and Ead-mund and Ulf, Brihtric, Wulfsige, Sexa, Ælfwine, Wlmær, Ægelwig.

These are the names of the brothers in Chertsey: that is, first, Abbot Wulfwold, and Ælfward and Sælaf, Oter and Godwine, Æþestan and Eadgar, Eadmær and Godwine, Ælfwine and Benedict, Siwine and Alfwold, Brihtnoð and Ælfric, Godric and Ælfric, Oswold and Ælfric, and Wulfward and Wulfric.

These are the names of the brothers in Bath: that is, first, Abbot Ælf-sige, and Ælfric, Leofwig and Hieðewulf, Ælfwig and Ægelmær, Ead-wig and Godwine, Ægelwine and Oswold, Ælmær and Þeodwold, Eadric, Ægelmær, Sæwulf, þured, Ægelric and Hærebewine, and Godric, a monk in Malmesbury, also one of us, and also Wulfwerd Pices,[74] a brother from Taunton.

In her discussion of this text, Mason comments on the predominance of English names and the Englishness of the institutional composition of those involved in the agreement. She also suggests that more is owed to the *Regularis Concordia* than to the *Monastic Constitutions* of Lanfranc in the drawing up of the specific details, particularly in relation to the provision of alms, which is not something dwelled on in Lanfranc's rule.[75] Lanfranc's *Constitutions* were not in circulation until at least 1077—the latest date that this alliance can have been drawn up, since

[73] 1 Esdras 10:12, 'so shall it be done', where all the people respond with one voice.

[74] I am grateful to Dr Jayne Carroll for her assistance with this name, which she inter-prets as a by-name, meaning 'of the point'. I wonder if 'Pices' might be translated as an occupational name referring to the preparation of parchment with the 'pic', an awl?

[75] Mason, *St Wulfstan*, pp. 198–200.

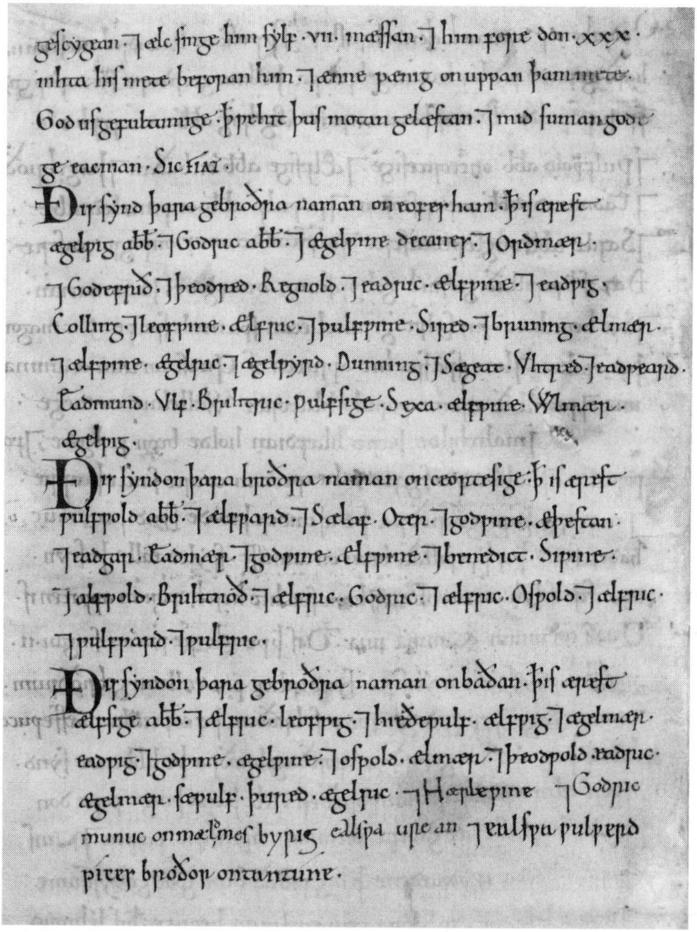

gescygean · 7 ælc singe him sylf · vii · mæssan · 7 him rope don · xxx ·
mhta lis mete beropan him · 7 ænne pænig on uppan þam mmete ·
God us gepuleumnge · þ prhre þus moran gelæstan · 7 mid suman gode
ge tacman · Sic HAI ·

Ðis synd þara gebroðra naman on ropor ham · þis æprst
ægelrig abb · 7 Goðuc abb · 7 ægelrine decaney · 7 Ordmær ·
7 Goðerpuð · 7 þeodred · Regnold · 7 eadrue · ælprue · 7 eadrig ·
Colling · 7 leorpine · ælpruc · 7 pulprine · Sired · 7 bruning · ælmær ·
7 ælprine · ægeluc · 7 ægelþryð · Dunning · 7 Sægeat · Vlrured · 7 eadpeard ·
Eadmund · Vlf · Brulruic · pulfsige · Sæxa · ælprine · Wlmær ·
ægelrig ·

Ðis synðon þara broðra naman on ceoprelige · þ is æprst
pulrpold abb · 7 ælprard · 7 Sælar · Ocer · 7 goðrine · ærescan ·
7 eadrian · Eadmær · 7 goðrine · ælprine · 7 benedict · Sirine ·
7 alrpold · Brulranoð · 7 ælpruc · Goðuc · 7 ælpruc · Osrold · 7 ælpruc ·
7 pulrpard · 7 pulprine ·

Ðis synðon þara gebroðra naman on baðan · þis æprst
ælprig abb · 7 ælpruc · leorprig · 7 hreðepulr · ælprig · 7 ægelmær ·
eadrig · 7 goðrine · ægelrine · 7 osrold · ælmær · 7 þeodpold · eadruc ·
ægelmær · særulr · þured · ægeluc · 7 Harlepine · 7 Goðric
munuc on melmes byrig · ællßa upre an · 7 eulßa pulrerd
prter broðor on ranrune ·

FIG 5   Cambridge, Corpus Christi College, 111, page 56

© Reproduced by permission of the Masters and Fellows, Corpus Christi College Cambridge.

Æthelwig, abbot of Evesham, died early in that year, so perhaps it is not surprising that the spiritual and liturgical motivation was dependent on the *Regularis Concordia*, the foundational document of the English Benedictine movement in the second half of the tenth century.[76] It is surely more than expediency that the *Regularis Concordia* provides the spiritual impetus for this alliance, though, since the agreement—written in the vernacular—indeed seems designed to promote a particularly English sense of Benedictine monastic identity, a decade after the Conquest. This is a complex identity, however, which is Benedictine first, and English second. C. A. Jones, referencing Emma Mason's work, comments that this, and other, contemporary confraternities 'fostered a recusant identity',[77] but the use of 'recusant' is probably inappropriate here, for this alliance includes two French abbots, Serlo of Gloucester and Ralph of Winchcombe, and carefully insists on the loyalty of the allied houses to William and Matilda, albeit in a fashion reminiscent of the very politicized unification of Church and State promulgated by prayers for the monarch in the *Regularis Concordia*. This alliance is thus more about an implicit resistance to perceived Anglo-Norman threats through the closing of ranks than it is about a wilful recusancy, *per se*. The wording of the text does, however, seem deliberately to echo the phrasing of loyalty and lordship, so well elucidated by Alice Sheppard.[78] In her discussion of 'hold hlaford', she shows how closely the ideals of lordship and loyalty are scrutinized in Anglo-Saxon historical and legal materials. William I is seen to fall far below these ideals, which makes the phrase '7 we willað urum woruld hlaforde Willelme cinincge, 7 Mahthilde, þære hlæfdian, holde beon for Gode 7 for worulde' seem rather less positive, for not only is William merely 'urum woruld hlaforde' ('our wordly' (or transient) lord') but his demonstration of loyalty creates very low expectations, and leaves much to be desired.

---

[76] Dom David Knowles and Christopher N. L. Brooke (eds. and trans.), *The Monastic Constitutions of Lanfranc* (Oxford: Oxford University Press, 2002); Symons, *Regularis Concordia Anglicae Nationis Monachorum Sanctimonialiumque*.

[77] *Ælfric's Letter to the Monks of Eynsham*, ed. and trans. C. A. Jones, Cambridge Studies in Anglo-Saxon England 24 (Cambridge: Cambridge University Press, 1998), p. 84.

[78] Sheppard, *Families of the King*, pp. 114–16 (on Cnut), but also see chapter 6, esp. pp. 131–4, where William the Conqueror's lack of lordship skills is examined in relation to his depiction in the *D-Chronicle*.

Notably, in relation to the agreement's insistence of a true loyalty through 'annesse' ('unity'), the core covenant of the participants is the use of the simile through which the monks are to direct themselves *quasi cor unum et anima una*, 'as if of one heart and one soul'. This basic tenet of indivisibility, of shared experience and purpose, describes the apostolic church, in its graceful reception of the Holy Spirit, at Acts 4:32: 'And the multitude of believers had but one heart and one soul (*cor unum et anima una*). Neither did anyone say that aught of the things which he possessed was his own: but all things were common unto them.' It forms the basis of the understanding of the communal Christian life in the 'Northumbrian Priests' Law', where it also occurs as a simile in the opening instruction: 'If anyone offer any wrong to any priest, let all the brethren, with the bishop's succour, zealously see to the remedy; and let it be, in every case of right, as it is written, "quasi cor unum et anima una".'[79] The Northumbrian Priests' Law, until recently thought to be the work of Wulfstan I, but now thought to be that of one of his successors at York,[80] occurs in Cambridge, Corpus Christi College 201, a manuscript with Winchester and Worcester connections. This begs the question of Wulfstan II's familiarity with this manuscript; the shared simile certainly might suggest knowledge of this particular text by the bishop, and a desire to emulate a late Anglo-Saxon quasi-legal concept of unity. Wulfstan II seems, at least, to have had *a* text in front of him, given the emphasis on 'what is written', whether it is Acts 4:32 itself, or the later uses of that motif of a shared heart and soul.

Emerging from this important document is a genuine sense of the regional power and leadership of St Wulfstan at this critical time. Rather like Cluny more than a century earlier, Worcester takes control of a deliberately fostered union of like-minded institutions, eager for reform in their own right, committed to the provision of spiritual guardianship for their own members, living and dead; and dedicated to the sustained

---

[79] Thorpe, *Ancient Laws and Institutes of England*, p. 416. It also occurs as the exact phrase in *Excerptiones pseudo-Ecgberti*, closely associated with Wulfstan I, and contained in the manuscript, Cambridge, Corpus Christi College 265, which has Worcester connections, and seems certainly to have been used by Wulfstan II. Interestingly, the same phrase 'quasi cor unum et anima una' occurs in the late twelfth-century *De Vita Coenobitica, seu communi* (*Treatise on the Common Life*) by Baldwin of Canterbury (bishop of Worcester, 1180–4).

[80] Wormald, *Making of English Law*, pp. 208–9, 396–7.

nourishment of their poor. This alliance, loudly stated in an English sacralized by its position in the manuscript adjacent to Gospels,[81] sanctified
by the holiness of Wulfstan, takes the theory of reform and puts it into
action, thus proving wrong any then-contemporary claims of the decline
of the (old) English church. It is a convincing piece of promotion.

The agreement is more than promotion, however, since it is so determined to demonstrate its concern for living individuals. Rather like the
New Minster *Liber Vitae*—London, BL Stowe 944—with its crowded
lists of confraternity members desiring masses and memorialization
though the inclusion of their names on the folios, the need to be named
is significant. Unlike the *Liber Vitae*, where lists are often necrologies
(obituary notices), these monks at Evesham, Chertsey, and Bath are the
living brothers, whose moment of glory is this snapshot, indicated by
deixis, the demonstrative pronoun 'this' implying the here-and-now of
this historical moment. This determination to enter individuals' names
into the list counters the oblivion and erasure of Conquest, and, as in
many narratives of trauma offers a commemoration, a proof of existence, just as creating Cartularies or forging diplomata offer testimony to
rights and privileges. Even in the copying of the only surviving declaration of the alliance in CCCC 111, though, the moment fragments, as the
monastic communities of Winchcombe, Pershore, Worcester and
Gloucester fail to materialize on the manuscript page. Mason surmises
that 'The text survives only as a copy, in English, and the names of the
brethren of the other houses were probably omitted due to lack of
space';[82] however, not only is the status of this piece in CCCC 111 unclear

---

[81] Note, too, that there are two other Confraternity Agreements from earlier in the
eleventh century: one in *Ælfwine's Prayerbook* (London, BL Cotton Titus D. xxvi and
xxvii, at folios 17v–18r. See Beate Gunzel (ed.), *Ælfwine's Prayerbook*, Henry Bradshaw
Society (London: Boydell, 1993), pp. 157–8); and the other in the Sherborne Pontifical
(Paris, Bibliothèque Nationale, lat. 943, folio 163v). Both are dated to *c*.1030, and both are
included in what are sacred, liturgical books. Both, then, testify to the collective strength
gleaned through confraternity, expressed through the vernacular, at times of trauma (as
identified above in Chapters 3 and 4). Neither of these earlier texts includes the memorialization of individuals. On these two earlier texts, see Benjamin A. Salzman, 'Writing
Friendship, Mourning the Friend in Late Anglo-Saxon Rules of Confraternity', *Journal of
Medieval and Early Modern Studies* 41 (2011), pp. 251–91.

[82] Mason, *St Wulfstan*, p. 198. Mason translates 'ealswa ure an' as 'also another one' and
'Wulwerd Pices broðor' as 'Wulfwerd Pices a *brother*' (p. 198).

(of what is it a copy?), but there also are five lines of blank membrane at p. 56, leaving plenty of space for more names, if those names had survived. As it is, the three after-thoughts—Hærbewine (of Bath, presumably), Godric of Malmesbury, and Wulwerd of Taunton—flesh out the text, adding geographic variation and curious details of Godric's status as 'one of us', despite his coming from Malmesbury, and Wulfwerd's apparent elevation by virtue of being 'Pic's brother'.

The predominance of English monks in these lists of monastic communities contrasts with what we know about the importation of monks from French, and other, institutions in the south and east of England in the aftermath of the Conquest; and what the alliance of monasteries in CCCC 111 demonstrates, unequivocally, is the political importance of English: its ability to create cohesion; to express, both visually[83] and linguistically, independent vision; and to sacralize the vernacular through its association with Wulfstan II, and through its inclusion in a Gospelbook. Like Cnut's *Letter to the English* and Wulfstan I's final words in his stark and hortatory homilies which were written into the Gospels now in York Minster 1, Wulfstan II's monastic alliance was written into a blank folio, originally belonging to CCCC 140. And like York Minster 1, other documents were written into the Bath Gospels in blank folios and at quire ends. These legal, homiletic and historical texts were deliberately entered into the holiest of books in order to preserve them through their association with the word of God. Such actions in Anglo-Norman England, when it is so generally assumed that English met its Doomsday, bear witness to the continuing authority of English. The exclusivity of the vernacular imbued it with the ability to speak political volumes; it upheld its status as a language of the monastery and mediated cultural trauma; and it was the chosen medium of many monks who sought to sustain and improve the best of English religious life, even as they maintained peace through conquest and negotiated the realities of colonization.

---

[83] Through the consistent use here of Anglo-Saxon insular minuscule forms for writing English (with equally appropriate use of Caroline forms for the Latin names).

| 6 |

'A nice little handful it is'[1]

The Remains of Conquest

In around 1070, William I issued the last of his writs in English; he was finished with the pretence that his conquest was a friendly take-over. In late 1066 or early 1067, he had announced to the citizens of London that:

> Willelm kyng gret Willelm bisceop 7 Gosfregð portirefan and ealle þa burhwaru binnan Londone Frencisce and Englisce freondlice. 7 ic kyðe eow þæt ic wylle þæt get beon eallra þæra laga weorðe þe gyt wæran on Eadwerdes dæge kynges. 7 ic wylle þæt ælc cyld beo his fæder yrfnume æfter his fæder dæge. 7 ic nelle geþolian þæt ænig man eow ænig wrang beode. God eow gehealde.

> King William greets Bishop William, and Gosfregð the portreeve and all the citizens in London, French and English, in a friendly manner. And I make it known to you that I desire you to be worthy of all the laws that yet existed in King Edward's day. And I desire that each child be his father's heir after his father's day.

---

[1] Kipling, 'Norman and Saxon', *A History of England*, pp. 51–3.

> And I do not desire that any one among you suffer any wrong. God keep you.'[2]

Within a few years, though, while some of that good will might have remained, the desire to express it in the English vernacular had disappeared.[3] Without the authority of monarchical and senior ecclesiastical validation, English might well have receded completely, were it not so firmly established, and, one might argue, were it not the language in which writers of English could maintain a sense of identity. Once Wulfstan II, the last of the prelates appointed by an Anglo-Saxon king, died in 1095, this might again have seemed a conclusion to the Anglo-Saxon era altogether, never mind the vernacular literary tradition itself. Indeed, Emma Mason, Wulfstan's modern biographer, paints a bleak picture of the future of English written after Coleman's *Life of Wulfstan* (*c.*1100): 'Such further English works as were composed were in one or other of those [regional] dialects, readily intelligible only within a limited radius. There was no great incentive for the younger generation to learn to read or write in English, even though it was the first spoken language of all but the court circle.'[4]

Laments for the death of English in 1066, discussed in the previous chapter, or for the end of English in the 1070s or in 1095,[5] are an inexplicable misrepresentation of the facts. How many manuscripts would it take for us to believe that English survived the Conquest? Why do the many texts that survive somehow not cut the academic mustard? How is it that in order to be counted the hundreds of works composed in English from 1060 to 1220 must be something other—more 'literary', more 'original'—than they already are? That said, there can be no doubt that

---

[2] Bates, *Regesta Regum Anglo-Normannorum*, no. 180, p. 593; discussed in Garnett, *Conquered England*, p. 12. This is similar to Cnut's desire to uphold the Laws of Edgar, for which see Chapter 1 above.

[3] Bates, *Regesta Regum Anglo-Normannorum*, p. 50, tentatively attributes the cessation of the 'large-scale production of Old English writs' to the replacement of English churchmen by French newcomers.

[4] Mason, *St Wulfstan*, p. 270.

[5] Or that unconvincingly ascribes a kind of volition to English itself, as Thomson and Morgan would have us believe ('As a written language, English went into a retreat from which it took a long time to recover') in Nigel Morgan and Rodney M. Thomson (eds.), *The Cambridge History of the Book in Britain: 1100–1400* (Cambridge: Cambridge University Press, 2010), p. 22.

there is a decline in the official production and use of English after the Conquest, if surviving books and diplomata are a realistic reflection of what was originally manufactured. There is also something of a reduction in the range of material written in this vernacular in comparison with a period prior to *c.* 1010, inasmuch as very little poetry survives, in comparison with the four great Anglo-Saxon poetic codices of the tenth and earlier eleventh centuries. In addition, forty years after the Conquest, Anglo-Norman emerges as a major literary language, perhaps influenced by the long and prestigious example set by English, and it becomes the literary (and spoken) vernacular of choice for many aristocrats and nobles, patrons, scholars, and administrators.[6] The French works themselves, to a significant extent, parallel the types of English texts being produced contemporaneously up to *c.* 1180: hagiographies, homilies, Psalter glosses, biblical and para-biblical works, liturgical materials, and histories. Thus, Benedeit's *Voyage de St Brendan*, composed *c.*1106 for Adeliza of Louvain, is one of many saints' lives written in French in the twelfth century; other hagiographies include *La Vie St Alexis* in the St Albans Psalter; Wace's *Vie de ste Marguerite* and *Vie de saint Nicolas*; Guillaume de Berneville's *Vie de saint Gilles*; and Simund de Freine's *La Vie saint Georges*. There are Psalter glosses in Anglo-Norman, a Rule of St Benedict, manuscripts of Canticles, Lapidaries and Bestiaries, the Anglo-Norman *Disticha Catonis*, and a number of significant histories in verse, including Gaimar's *Estoire Des Engleis*, written for Constance Fitzgilbert before 1140, and Wace's *Roman de Rou*. Beyond all of this, Latin continued to dominate manuscript production, and there are thousands of surviving works, covering all genres from the holy to the scurrilous, dramatic and liturgical to historical, contemplative, and scholastic.[7]

Extant English manuscripts from the period *c.*1100–1220 are significantly fewer in number than Latin. Still, as Kipling would have it of Anglo-Saxon England's conquered lands, what survives represents 'a nice little handful':

---

[6] See Ruth J. Dean and Maureen B. M. Boulton, *Anglo-Norman Literature: A Guide to Texts and Manuscripts* (London: Anglo-Norman Text Society, 1999); Ashe, *Fiction and History in England*.

[7] A. G. Rigg, *A History of Anglo-Latin Literature, 1066–1422* (Cambridge: Cambridge University Press, 1992).

Twelfth- and Early Thirteenth-Century Manuscripts containing English[8]

Shelfmark	Ker	Contents in brief	Origin	Date
CCCC 140+111	[35]	Manumissions, etc	Bath	s. xi²-x.ii
CCCC 302	[56]	Homilies		s. xi/xii
CCCC 383	[65]	Laws	St Paul's	s. xi/xii
CCCC 367	[63]	Homilies		s. xii
Trinity R. 9. 17	[89]	Ælfric's *Grammar*		s. xi/xii
BL, Add 9381	[126]	Gospels & docs.	Bodmin	s.xi/xii
BL, Cotton Caligula A. xv	[139B]	*De temporibus*		s. xi/xii
BL, Cotton Domitian viii	[148]	*Chronicle*	Christ Church	s. xi/xii
Oxford, Bodley 155	[303]	List of lands	Barking	s. xi/xii
Salisbury 150	[379]	Psalter Gloss	Salisbury	s. xi/xii
BL, Cotton Tiberius A. xiii	[190]	Hemming's Cartulary	Worcester	c. 1100
Oxford, St John's 17	[360]	Medical, computistica	Thorney	c. 1110
Bod, Ashmole 1431	[289]	Glosses	St Aug's	s.xii
Manchester, JRUL 420		Regulations William I		s.xii
BL, Cotton Domitian ix	[150]	*Chronicle* (fragment)		s. xii¹
BL, Cotton Faustina A. ix	[153]	Homilies		s. xii¹
BL, Cotton Faustina A. x	[154B]	*Rule of Benedict*		s. xii¹
Maidstone, DRc/R1	[373]	*Textus Roffensis*	Rochester	s. xii¹
Bod, Bodley 180	[305]	Boethius		s. xii¹
Bod, Hatton 116	[333]	Homilies	Worcester	s. xii¹
Bod, Laud 636	[346]	*Chronicle*	Peterborough	s. xii¹⁻ᵐᵉᵈ
CCCC 303	[57]	Homilies	Rochester	s. xiiᵐᵉᵈ
Trinity R. 17. 1	[91]	Psalter Gloss	Christ Church	s. xiiᵐᵉᵈ
BL, Add 46487		Cartulary	Sherborne	s. xiiᵐᵉᵈ

(*Continued*)

[8] These are abbreviated titles and shorthand references. Some of the manuscripts are composite, so refer to Ker, *Catalogue*, for precise folios. CCCC = Cambridge, Corpus Christi; BL = British Library; Bod = Oxford, Bodleian Library; St Aug's = St Augustine's, Canterbury; Christ Church = Christ Church, Canterbury; Manchester JRUL = Manchester, John Rylands University Library; Paris BN = Paris, Bibliothèque Nationale. See *The Production and Use of English, 1060 to 1220* <http://www.le.ac.uk/ee/em1060to1220/>

Shelfmark	Ker	Contents in brief	Origin	Date
BL, Cotton Julius A. ii	[159]	*Dicts of Cato*		s. xii^med
BL, Cotton Vespasian D. xiv	[209]	Homilies	Christ Church	s. xii^med
BL, Cotton Vitellius A. xv	[215]	Augustine *Soliloquies*		s. xii^med
BL, Harley 55	[226]	Laws of Cnut	Worcester?	s. xii^med
BL, Royal 7 D. ii	[258]	Glosses	St Aug's	s. xii^med
CUL Ii. 1. 33	[18]	Homilies		s. xii²
CCCC 367	[62]	*De temporibus*		s. xii²
BL, Cotton Claudius B. iv	[142]	Commentary	St Aug's	s. xii²
BL, Cotton Titus D. xxiv	[201]	Formulae	Cistercian	s. xii²
BL, Royal 1 A. xiv	[245]	Gospels		s. xii²
BL, Stowe 57	[272]	Names of letters	Peterborough	s. xii²
Bod, Bodley 343	[310]	Homilies	West England	s. xii²
Bod, Junius 1		*Ormulum*	Bourne	s. xii²
Rawlinson C. 641	[348]	Glosses; proverbs	Rochester?	s. xii²⁺
Christ Church Chp		Cartulary	Eynsham	s.xii²
Trinity B. 14. 52		Trinity Homilies	Middlesex	s. xii^ex
BL, Royal 10 C. v	[262]	Marginalia	(St Paul's?)	s. xii^ex
Paris, BN, lat. 8846		Psalter Glosses	Christ Church	s. xii^ex
Camb, Pembroke 82	[75]	Verses		s.xii/xiii
BL, Cotton Otho A. xiii	[173]	Homilies		
BL, Cotton Vespasian A. xxii		Homilies	Rochester	s. xii/xiii
BL, Royal 7 C. iv	[256]	Scribbles	Christ Church	s.xii/xiii
BL, Royal 10 A. viii	[261]	Names of winds		s.xii/xiii
London, Lambeth Palace 487		Lambeth Homilies	West England	s. xii/xiii
Bod, Bodley 730	[317]	Glossaries	Buildwas	s.xii/xiii
Bod, Hatton 38	[325]	Gospels	Christ Church	s. xii/xiii
BL, Cotton Claudius D. iii	[p. xix]	Rule of Benedict	Witney	s. xiii in.
BL, Harley 6258B		*Medicina de Quadripedibus*		s. xiii in.
Worcester F. 174	[398]	Ælfric's *Grammar*	Worcester	s. xiii in.

Beyond these manuscripts are other cartularies with the vernacular boundary clauses, and the many more codices that include sporadic glosses, a habit of readers that extends throughout the medieval period, and includes Latin and French as well as English. Who these readers might have been is often difficult to detect. In the case of manuscripts written and compiled in the late Anglo-Saxon period, the evidence suggests that many of them belonged, in the first instance, to an individual prelate, before being passed to a successor or the institution to which the prelate belonged. Coleman, Wulfstan's biographer and one-time prior of Westbury-upon-Trym,[9] annotated Wulfstan's homiliary—Hatton 113 + 114—among other manuscripts, and is known to have taken a bishop's role in preaching at Wulfstan's request.[10] His interventions in many Worcester manuscripts bespeak a role that is editorial, critical, and mediatory; that indicates his seniority and authority over the books in which he worked; and that potentially shows the vitality of English preaching at one institution well into the twelfth century. By the end of the eleventh century, though, there were few remaining senior Anglo-Saxon ecclesiastical figures, and it is often tricky to determine who the primary users of these English manuscripts produced throughout the twelfth century were, though most were almost certainly religious—monks, canons, nuns, priests.[11] Secondary users, hearing texts being read or extemporized from earlier reading, seem to have included *conversi* and lay members of religious institutions, and, in relation to hagiographies and homilies, members of congregations in a variety of settings and with a range of understanding. One thing seems certain: there is no single textual community for this diverse English corpus, no monolithic audience of illiterate lay people; rather, users of and audiences for the English texts copied during the twelfth century, and those copied in preceding centuries, varied according to specific historical moments, particular contexts, and multiple places. Thus, for example, many different users of Ælfric's homilies can be detected in one mid-twelfth-century manuscript from

---

[9] Until its closure by Samson, bishop of Worcester.

[10] See, most recently, David Johnson and Winfried Rudolf, 'More Notes by Coleman', *Medium Aevum* 79 (2010), pp. 113–25.

[11] Elaine Treharne, 'The Form and Function of the Old English *Dicts of Cato*', *Journal of English and Germanic Philology* 102.4 (September 2003), pp. 65–85; Susan Irvine, 'Bodley 343' in Swan and Treharne, *Rewriting Old English*.

Kent, CCCC 303.[12] Not only did the three scribes read their respective exemplars as they copied them, but also one of the scribes read *all* the works in the manuscript, correcting the others' mistakes and adding rubrics and *litterae notabiliores* in red minuscule. This scribe, who copied pages pages 226/27–231/28, 231, and 251/10–254/05, uses a more up-to-date form of English, and a more current hand than his two counterparts who stick closely to late West Saxon forms of English and a formal book-hand—a Protogothic minuscule with the insular-shaped letters of *d* (often), *f*, and *g*, but not *r* or *s*. The apparent freedom of the corrector-scribe indicates he has the authority to do his own thing, and is considered to have a superior eye, if he is the corrector. Indeed, his function is enhanced by his role as an occasional glossator, too: at page 23/17, for example, 'sunne' glosses 'leahter'; and at page 23/24, 'blisse' glosses 'wuldor'. These exact glosses are seen in numerous other twelfth-century manuscripts, illustrating the ways in which scribes and readers sought to update the lexis of the pieces that they worked on.[13]

Other contemporary and slightly later hands can be seen glossing the manuscript in English, Latin, and French, and another thirteenth-century reader adopted an early information retrieval system, annotating a homily using a sequence of dots in the margin for rapid identification of the seven deadly sins. This might have been done with a view to the memorization of the sins, and for extemporization of these key parts of the Homily for Rogationtide Tuesday, a significant festival, which seems to have involved the laity in many institutions. The key point here, though, is that the Old English sermon was intelligible to the thirteenth-century reader, as were many of the sermons copied in English from 1000 to 1220, and that these texts were still in use, presumably in a variety of contexts for multiple audiences.

---

[12] See my recent description of this manuscript in *The Use and Production of English Manuscripts, 1060 to 1220* [http://www.le.ac.uk/english/em1060to1220/mss/EM.CCCC .303.htm] and in Timothy Graham, Raymond J. S. Grant, Peter J. Lucas, and Elaine Treharne, *Corpus Christi College, Cambridge I, Anglo-Saxon Manuscripts in Microfiche Facsimile* 11 (Medieval and Renaissance Texts and Studies, Arizona State University, 2004).

[13] Chapter 8 will discuss glossing in more detail. For analogous work on Cambridge, Corpus Christi College, 383, a manuscript from the first quarter of the twelfth century, which contains a list of shipmen and numerous English laws, see Thomas Gobbitt, 'The Production and Use of Cambridge, Corpus Christi College, 383 in the Late Eleventh and First Half of the Twelfth Centuries' (unpub. PhD diss., University of Leeds, 2010).

The English Book, c. 1100–1200

Of all the books listed above, the most extensive group, linked by genre, is the homiletic, or perhaps less restrictively, the religious prose compendium.[14] These books are most extensive both in terms of numbers of survivors, and in terms of range of texts included within the codices. Thirteen such volumes survive from the twelfth and earlier thirteenth centuries. One of these will be set aside for the purposes of this discussion, since it is verse, newly composed, orthographically idiosyncratic, and worth a book-length study in its own right: Oxford, Bodleian Library, Junius 1 (*The Ormulum*). The remaining twelve volumes (Cambridge, University Library, Ii. 1. 33; Cambridge, Trinity College, B. 14. 52; Cambridge, Corpus Christi College, 302, 303, and 367; London, British Library, Cotton Faustina A. ix, Cotton Vespasian A. xxii; Cotton Vespasian D. xiv, Cotton Vitellius A. xv; London, Lambeth Palace, Lambeth 487; Oxford, Bodleian Library, Bodley 343 and Hatton 116) are well known to Anglo-Saxonists as 'later' copies of Old English texts, particularly those by Ælfric and, to a lesser extent, the Vercelli and Blickling homilists, and Wulfstan. Most often employed for their variant texts in the standard editions of pre-Conquest homilies,[15] it has been rare until very recently for these homiliaries to be treated as subjects worthy of sustained study in their own rights.[16] Each is a fascinating portal into the religious and cultural resource of its centre of manufacture; each is indicative of a community response to the pastoral and pedagogic needs of a multitude of users; and each reveals a complex narrative that defies

[14] On the form and function of these codices, see most recently, Aaron Kleist (ed.), *The Old English Homily: Precedent, Practice and Appropriation*, Studies in the Early Middle Ages 17 (Turnhout: Brepols, 2007). See also, Clare Lees, *Tradition and Belief Religious Writing in Late Anglo Saxon England* (Minneapolis, MN: University of Minnesota Press, 1999).

[15] Clemoes, *CHI*; Godden, *CHII*; Pope, *Homilies of Ælfric*; D. G. Scragg (ed.), *The Vercelli Homilies and Related Texts*, EETS o.s. 300 (London: Oxford University Press, 1992); Irvine *Old English Homilies*.

[16] But now, among others, see Aidan Conti, 'Preaching Scripture and Apocrypha: A Previously Unidentified Homiliary in an Old English Manuscript, Oxford, Bodleian Library, MS Bodley 343' (unpub. PhD diss., University of Toronto, 2004); Loredana Teresi, 'Ælfric's or Not? The Making of a Temporale Collection in Late Anglo-Saxon England', in Kleist, *The Old English Homily*, pp. 284–310; George Younge, 'The Compiler of London, BL Cotton Vespasian D. xiv, fols 4–169, and his Audience', in Orietta Da Rold and A. S. G. Edwards (eds.), *English Manuscript Studies 1100–1700* (forthcoming 2012).

any univocal interpretation thus far proposed in scholarship for the production, transmission and reception of this large body of material.

What we know of these homiliaries can be summarized as follows: from what one can glean from the palaeographical, codicological and textual evidence, these are all monastic productions. CCCC 303, Vespasian D. xiv, CUL Ii. 1. 33, and Vespasian A. xxii all hail from Kent, though CUL Ii. 1. 33 seems to have migrated to Ely, where it was completed.[17] On the other side of the country, in the West Midlands, homiletic compilation resulted in Hatton 116, Bodley 343, Lambeth 487, and, possibly, Corpus 367, fols. 3r–6v, 11r–29v.[18] The most likely places of production seem to be Worcester or Hereford, though smaller religious centres are also a possibility.[19] Cambridge, Corpus Christi College 302, Faustina A. ix, and Trinity College, B. 14. 52 are of unknown origin and provenance, but all three seem most likely to be from the eastern side of England, judging by their textual and linguistic affiliations.[20] That said, the scribe of Faustina A. ix demonstrates tentative palaeographical affinities with the hand of the Old English gloss of the earlier Winchester manuscript, the Arundel Psalter (London, BL Arundel 60).[21] Unfortunately, there is very little else

[17] Oliver M. Traxel, *Language Change, Writing and Textual Interference in Post-Conquest Old English Manuscripts: The Evidence of Cambridge, University Library, Ii. 1. 33* (Frankfurt am Main: Peter Lang, 2004); Orietta Da Rold, 'Cambridge, University Library, Ii. 1. 33', Elaine Treharne, 'Making the Book', Mary Swan, 'Writing the Book' and 'Using the Book', in Elaine Treharne, Orietta Da Rold, and Mary Swan (eds.), *Producing and Using English Manuscripts in the Post-Conquest Period, New Medieval Literatures 13* (2012, forthcoming).

[18] Michael Gullick, in a personal communication (2000), suggested that a decorated initial in this part of the manuscript is typical of the West Midlands at this time.

[19] Irvine, *Old English Homilies*; see especially the important article by Peter Kitson, 'Old English Dialects and the Stages of Transition to Middle English', *Folia Linguistica Historica* 11 (1992 for 1990), pp. 27–87.

[20] Elaine Treharne, 'The Dates and Origins of Three Twelfth-Century Manuscripts', in P. Pulsiano and E. M. Treharne (eds.), *Anglo-Saxon Manuscripts and Their Heritage: Tenth to Twelfth Centuries* (Farnham: Ashgate, 1998), pp. 227–52 for Corpus 302 and Faustina A. ix; for Trinity B. 14. 52, see the description in Da Rold, et al., *Production and Use of English Manuscripts, 1060 to 1220* [http://www.le.ac.uk/english/em1060to1220/mss/EM.CTC.B.15.34.htm]

[21] This is one of the manuscripts highlighted selectively in the British Library's Gallery of illuminated manuscripts: *http://www.bl.uk/catalogues/illuminatedmanuscripts/search MSNo.asp* These characteristics do not add up to much individually, but together they make an interesting set of unusual features worth investigating further. For example, distinctive letter-forms include *f* with both the midstroke and headstroke bending down; the *positura* of two dots and a comma occurs in both manuscripts; and the abbreviation for 'drihten' is comprised of a line through the *h*, followed by -*t*; the *litterae notabiliores* are pen-drawn and monochrome, but feature dots and arabesque flourishes.

to confirm this possible localization. Still the homiletic collections are clearly not confined to one particular centre, or one particular region, but they do seem, as far as current knowledge permits, to have emanated from Benedictine houses, where, it is very likely, a sense of English identity, derived from more than a century of intellectual pursuit, was actively maintained by particular members of the community.

Not only are these homiliaries not confined to a particular region, but also they are spread chronologically across at least a century, from *c*.1100 (Corpus 302 and Faustina A. ix) to at least 1200 (Lambeth 487 and Vespasian A. xxii). In itself, this shows that the production of these extensive compilations was an ongoing intellectual and pastoral venture, and that there was some demand for English religious texts throughout the post-Conquest period and into the High Middle Ages. The changing concerns of the homilists, well documented by Kathleen Greenfield more than thirty years ago,[22] can be inferred from the changes that the manuscript compilers made to their earlier Old English exemplars, as represented by manuscripts generally from the eleventh century.[23] The alteration and adaptation of earlier exemplars, the malleability of texts in this period, mean that no two versions of a text are ever identical; even if the content seems identical between different versions, the spelling or punctuation, physical context or layout will differ. In contrast to the superficial sameness of print culture, manuscript culture testifies to the potential variation inherent in textual dissemination. Bernard Cerquiglini and Paul Zumthor's influential works on textual *mouvance* are key to understanding how significant is each manifestation of a manuscript text.[24] With homilies, hagiographies, Psalter and Gospel texts in the post-Conquest period, this major aspect of chirographic culture is yet to be fully explored.[25] Since every text is a specific, historically bound

[22] 'Changing emphases in English vernacular homiletic literature, 960–1225', *Journal of Medieval History* 7 (1981), pp. 283–97. See also, Treharne, *Gluttons for Punishment*; and 'The Life and Times of Old English Homilies'.

[23] See e.g. Mary Swan, 'Preaching Past the Conquest: Lambeth Palace 487 and Cotton Vespasian A. XXII', in Kleist, *The Old English Homily*, pp. 403–23.

[24] Bernard Cerquiglini, *In Praise of the Variant: A Critical History of Philology* (Baltimore: Johns Hopkins University Press, 1999); Paul Zumthor, *Towards a Medieval Poetics* (Minneapolis: University of Minnesota Press, 1992).

[25] See Roy M. Liuzza's important essay, 'Scribal Habit: The Evidence of Old English Gospels', in Swan and Treharne, *Rewriting Old English*, pp. 143–65; see also, Swan, 'Old English Made New'.

instantiation, it would be worth examining each manuscript individually, and, ideally, each text on its own merits. There are trends in the kinds of changes made by manuscript compilers and scribes (sometimes the same person) that evince a number of levels of editorial intervention, and reveal the deliberateness of those editorial acts. Thus, the following passage taken absolutely randomly from the Rogationtide homily in Ælfric's First Series of *Catholic Homilies*, 'In Letania Maiore',[26] shows a typical array of minor alterations:

> …7 biddan þara þreora hlafa: *þæt* is geleafan þære halgan þrynnysse; Sé ælmihtiga fæder is god. 7 his sunu is ælmihtig god. 7 se halga gást is ælmihtig god. na þry gódás. ac hi ealle án ælmihtig god untodæledlic:[27]

Corpus 302, pp. 200/29–201/1

> 7 biddan þæra[28] þreora hlafa *þæt* is geleafan þære halgan þrynnysse. Se ælmihtiga fæder is god. 7 'h'is sunu is ælmihtig god. 7 se halga gast is ælmihtig god. na þry godas. ac hi ealle an ælmihtig god untodæledlic.

Corpus 303, p. 212, lines 3–5

> 7 biddan þære þryre hlafe. *þæt* is geleafan. þæræ halga þrymnesse. Se ealmihti ~~god~~ fæder: is god. 7 is sunu: is ælmihti god. 7 se halga gast: is ælmihtig god. naht þri godes. ac hi ealle an ælmihtig god untod'a'eledlic.

When compared with the 'original' Ælfric text in Royal 7 C. xii, Corpus 302 illustrates only very minor variants, including different punctuation, no accenting, and a probable scribal error in the loss of 'h' at the beginning of 'his'. In contrast, the extract in Corpus 303 shows the ways in which even formal written language, and even language that was being *copied*, reflects more contemporary spellings and inflections. Thus, as is seen widely throughout the twelfth century, there is a levelling of final dative and genitive endings to <e>, and interchangeable

---

[26] Clemoes, *CHI*, xviii, pp. 317–24.

[27] Clemoes, *CHI*, xviii, p. 319, with expansion of abbreviation: 'and pray for the three loaves, that is, faith in the Holy Trinity. The almighty Father is God; and his Son is Almighty God; and the Holy Ghost is Almighty God; not three gods, but they are all one Almighty God, indivisible.' The manuscript used by Clemoes as the base text is London, BL Royal 7 c. xii. Here, the colon represents the *punctus elevatus*.

[28] Corrected from 'þfera'.

variation of <a, e, æ>, <y, i>. The potential syntactic switch of 'god' and 'fæder' in the first line may have been haplographical, but the same text occurs in the eleventh-century Canterbury manuscript, Trinity College, B. 15. 34, where 'Se ælmihtiga "god" is fæder' also occurs.[29] In Corpus 303, too, the punctuation varies, such that there is heavier punctuation in the sequence 'Se ealmihti fæder: is god. 7 is sunu: is ælmihti god. 7 se halga gast: is ælmihtig god'; here, in the manuscript, a simple *punctus* appears to have been altered (in lighter ink) to a *punctus elevatus*, a more marked pause, perhaps increasing the drama of the repetition in public delivery.[30] And finally, a notable emendation that is easy to miss in the Corpus 303 version concerns the noun 'þrymnesse', altered from 'þrynnesse' in other manuscripts, with the exception of the version in the later twelfth-century manuscript, Bodley 343, where 'þrymnesse' also occurs. This may seem like the simple orthographical variation of a medial nasal; however, as Roberta Frank has noted,[31] it appears to be a new calque employed principally in the twelfth century.[32] Small changes such as this are significant, too, particularly as incrementally they can assist scholars in understanding the ways in which English writers and scribes used and understood literary language, especially the West Saxon literary language that they inherited, and which, by the end of the twelfth century, was in terms of its origin, if not its actual form by then, two hundred years old. There is an immense amount of work yet to be done on the language of the English texts copied between 1100 and 1200, and these are under-utilized resources, presumably because the texts are regarded as simply 'copies'. Paralleling the orthographic, phonological, morphological, and syntactic variation in these twelfth-century witnesses to the English homiletic (and legal, biblical, pastoral, educative, prognostic and liturgical) heritage is the considerable lexical alteration within most of the surviving

---

[29] Clemoes, *CHI*, xviii, p. 319, line 66.

[30] Similar emendation of punctuation is found at Corpus 383, folio 42v/19. See Gobbitt, 'The Production and Use of Cambridge, Corpus Christi College, 383', pp. 181–2. The Tremulous Scribe, in the first decades of the thirteenth century, also made very considerable alterations to the punctuation of the English manuscripts upon which he worked.

[31] Roberta Frank, 'Late Old English þrymnys "Trinity": Scribal Nod or Word Waiting to be Born,' in Joan H. Hall, Nick Doane, and Dick Ringler (eds.) *Old English and New: Studies in Language and Linguistics in Honour of Frederic G. Cassidy* (New York: Garland, 1992), pp. 97–110.

[32] See Treharne, 'Dates and Origins of Three Twelfth-Century Manuscripts', p. 242.

manuscripts that supposes a high level of intelligent interaction with the exemplar at hand. This lexical alteration is not consistently done; where it does happen, then, one can assume that the scribe is taking ownership of the process of copying, perhaps because he or she is in a position to validate the work being undertaken, and because the text's intelligibility is forefront in their mind.

Lexical replacement is not the same as glossing, though; on occasion, it might result from the scribe copying a gloss in the exemplar instead of the lemma in the main body of the text. The only way to detect lexical replacement is to read the later version of the work alongside earlier versions.[33] While variation of this kind is particularly interesting since it may indicate idiolectal preference or even conscious modernization on the part of the scribe, it becomes a convincing tool to demonstrate language change when its occurrence is visible in texts across a broad geographical span. Bodley 343, dateable to c.1170 on palaeographical grounds, is a good example here. It is a very extensive Latin and English codex, some of which is in the Homiliary of Angers tradition,[34] and other parts of which contain works by Wulfstan, Ælfric, and Alain de Lille, anonymous homilies, and the Old English poem *The Grave*. In this volume, lexical variants include (in the grammatical form in which they occur) 'sune' for 'bearn', 'inemned' or 'icwæden' for 'geciged', 'pine' for 'susle', '3espæce' for 'gereord', 'time' for 'tide', 'blisse' for 'gefean', 'la3e' for 'æ', 'blissiað' for 'wuldriað', and 'synnen' for 'leahtrum'. This very small sample gives some indication of the lexical alteration, which extends to all verbal and nominal parts of speech, and occurs throughout the English homilies, though not with absolute consistency of application. In one manuscript, like Bodley 343, it is an interesting phenomenon, but given that it occurs throughout the corpus of English writing for 1100–1200, such lexical substitution suggests that some of the scribes—those who make these changes—have a systematic approach to the work they are completing, one which involves the conscious updating of the text. Thus, for example, the contemporary gloss 'blissiað' for 'wuldriað' that

---

[33] Though, of course, the *apparatus criticus* of full scholarly editions (such as Clemoes, *CHI*) provide many of the lexical variants.

[34] Aidan Conti, 'The Circulation of the Old English Homily in the Twelfth Century: New Evidence from Oxford, Bodleian Library, Bodley 343', in Kleist, *Precedent, Practice and Appropriation*, pp. 365–402.

occurs in Corpus 302 in *c.*1100, foreshadows the change embedded in the text of Bodley 343 and other manuscripts, such as Oxford, Bodleian Library, Hatton 38 (the late twelfth-century or early thirteenth-century Gospels from Christ Church),[35] Corpus 303, CUL Ii. 1. 33, and Trinity B. 14. 52.

These kinds of alterations can be witnessed alongside much more comprehensive editorial intervention that again bears witness to the development not only of language, but also of compositional method. In Corpus 303 and Trinity B. 14. 52, for instance, Latin source material is occasionally added to the English explication, presumably to add authority and weight to the text.[36] This is the method of the *Ancrene Wisse* writer, and the London, Lambeth Palace 487 homilist, too; through the appropriation of Latin's gravitas and erudition, their vernacular writings are validated by translation and source appearing together.[37] The manuscript compilers show themselves to be aware of newer developments such as an increased demand, because of scholasticism perhaps, for authoritative pastoral texts. Other indications of thoughtful compilation of pastoral materials come from the manipulation of earlier exemplars. Thus, a twenty-five line excerpt of the homily analysed above, 'In Letania Maiore', occurs in Cotton Vespasian D. xiv,[38] providing the episode of Jonah and the Ninevites in conjunction with other extracts from Ælfric homilies. Extracting from longer works is a typical *modus operandi* of the compiler of Cotton Vespasian D. xiv, as it is, to a lesser extent, of the compiler of CUL Ii. 1. 33. Creating new texts by abbreviating exemplars in this way suggests not only creativity in recomposition, but also an excellent knowledge of the range and detail of the source texts. Close engagement with the Old English homiletic corpus indicates an intellectual and cultural appreciation of the material, and the desire to utilize it effectively for new audiences. This is not, in other words, a mindless process, but one that demonstrates the

[35] Roy Michael Liuzza (ed.), *The Old English Version of the Gospels*, EETS, o.s. 304, 314 (London: Oxford University Press, 1994, 2000).

[36] See e.g. Clemoes, *CHI*, x, 'Dominica in Quinquagessima', p. 263, line 146 (in the apparatus).

[37] Bella Millett (ed.), *Ancrene Wisse: a corrected edition of the text in Cambridge, Corpus Christi College, 402, with variants from other manuscripts*, EETS o.s. 325, 326 (Oxford: Oxford University Press, 2005, 2008).

[38] Clemoes, *CHI*, xviii, pp. 317–18, lines 14–39. See Warner, *Early English Homilies from the Twelfth Century MS. Vesp. D. xiv.*

contemporaneity and currency of the English religious textual tradition right up to the beginning of the thirteenth century, and that unequivocally testifies to a strong commitment to promulgating the inherited Anglo-Saxon past in order to engage with relevance. And even though there is no explicit mention of, or negotiation with, the Norman present in these homiletic texts (as one might expect, indeed, from the articulations of a subordinated nation), there is implicit and important mediation between English and its contemporary milieu, as the work of George Younge demonstrates so proficiently,[39] such that many of these texts both reflect and contribute to innovation in post-Conquest theological and cultural debates.

To a considerable extent, the same can be said about the multiplicity of other English texts copied c.1100 to c.1200 from pre-existing exemplars. It is less easy to make general assertions about the nature of other genres of texts and the manuscripts in which they appear; for example, the surviving legal manuscripts, while sharing a considerable number of texts in common, seem to emerge from different impetuses. The most famous lawbook, the *Textus Roffensis* (Rochester Cathedral A. 3. 5), copied at Rochester in the first quarter of the twelfth century, is a major compilation of Latin and English laws, legalistic liturgical materials (like formulas for excommunication and exorcism and the Coronation charter for Henry I) up to folio 118, and historical records related to Rochester from folios 119 to 235.[40] Copied by a prolific Rochester scribe, probably as a deliberately scholarly compilation, it was possibly 'an impressive weapon for a churchman seeking to defend the position of his English foundation against prowling Norman predators',[41] and its contemporary utility is suggested by the careful updating of the language found in the exemplars (as is the case, in fact, with Corpus 383, possibly from St Paul's Cathedral[42]). Similarly, London, BL Harley 55,

---

[39] Younge, 'The Compiler of London, British Library, Cotton Vespasian D. xiv, fols 4–169', in Orietta Da Rold and A. S. G. Edwards (eds.), *English Manuscript Studies 1100–1700*; and 'The Canterbury Anthology: an Old English Manuscript in its Anglo-Norman Context' (unpub. PhD diss., University of Cambridge, forthcoming 2012).

[40] Ker, *Catalogue*, pp. 443–7; Wormald, *The Making of English Law*, pp. 244–53; Peter Sawyer (ed.), *Textus Roffensis*, Early English Manuscripts in Facsimile XI, 2 vols. (Copenhagen: Rosenkilde and Bagger, 1957–62).

[41] Wormald, *The Making of English Law*, p. 252.

[42] Gobbitt, 'The Production and Use of Cambridge, Corpus Christi College, 383', pp. 184–5.

folios 5–13, is dated to the mid-twelfth century and contains the Laws of Cnut.[43] This booklet, with its modish double-columned *mise-en-page*, is so unremarkable, Wormald comments, it seems clear 'that the day when Anglo-Saxon law was of exclusively antiquarian concern had not yet dawned.'[44]

Resourceful Books

Considering that these manuscripts were produced at different scriptoria and that up to a century separates their production, it is interesting to note the relative uniformity in their physical appearance, particularly in terms of their size.[45] All of the manuscripts are of a broadly similar size (bearing in mind that later binding might have necessitated the trimming of leaves): CCCC 302 is 253 x 168mm; Hatton 116 is 260 x 170mm; Faustina A. ix is 230 x 150mm; Bodley 180 (Boethius' *Consolation of Philosophy*) is 210 mm x 150 mm; CCCC 303 is 260 x 196mm; Vespasian D. xiv is approximately 191 x 122 mm. Corpus 383 is 187 x 115mm; Harley 55 is 270 x 189mm; Cotton Julius A. ii, dated s. xii[med], is 226 x 152mm; Cotton Vitellius A. xv, fols. 4–93, again dated to the middle of the twelfth century, is *c.*200 x 130mm.[46] Into the second half of the twelfth century, books are similar sized (Royal 1 A. xiv, the Gospels from the second half of the twelfth century, measures 218 x 144mm, while Hatton 38, probably copied from Royal A. xiv, is 238 x 158mm), or get smaller: Trinity B. 14. 52 is 136 x 113mm; Lambeth 487 is 176 x 130–133mm. Notably, Bodley 343 is larger (at *c.* 310 x *c.* 205mm), and double-columned in part, presumably because the English texts were copied as part of a larger, Latin codex. What these dimensions show very convincingly is that these codices were conceived of as relatively light and

---

[43] Ker, *Catalogue*, pp. 302–3; Wormald, *The Making of English Law*, pp. 253–5.

[44] Wormald, *The Making of English Law*, p. 255.

[45] In terms of the manuscripts' collation, the standard quiring is eights; the exception is Hatton 116 where the majority of quires are twelves (see Ker, *Catalogue*, p. 406). Interestingly, many of these twelfth-century manuscripts appear to have been produced in separate stints over a period of time. Notable for this method of production are Faustina A. ix, Vespasian D. xiv, and the later manuscript, CUL Ii. 1. 33. All the measurements are those of the individual manuscript descriptions in Ker's *Catalogue*. These have been verified by my own measuring of the manuscripts.

[46] For the latter, see Ker, *Catalogue*, p. 280.

portable, small by the standards of many Latin books in this period,[47] and, by comparison, economical to produce. Each, with the exception of Bodley 343 (and Harley 55, folios 5-13), has the standard single column of writing unlike many Latin manuscripts in the period, which were written in double-column format. This distinction in the page layout between English and Latin manuscripts is interesting, and suggests that rather than follow the new double-column format introduced by the middle of the twelfth century English manuscript compilers followed the traditional single-column layout of pre-Conquest codices. It may be, too, that the single-column format was used to maximize the writing space, which would be particularly important if not a great deal of physical resource was made available for the copying of English. Indeed, in some manuscripts, such as Corpus 303 and Corpus 367, folios 1, 2, 7–10 (Bede's *De Temporibus*), the interlinear space is narrow, and the script is condensed.

The majority of these manuscripts appear to have been pricked prior to folding.[48] CCCC 302 (quires 13 and 14), Faustina A. ix, CCCC 303, Hatton 116, and Vespasian D. xiv have double vertical bounding lines; some of the quires of CUL Ii. 1. 33, all of Hatton 38, and most of Trinity B. 14. 52 have single bounding lines, illustrating newer methods of preparing the page.[49] Generally, ruling is pencil in those manuscripts that date from approximately the middle of the century. These features show that despite the adherence to a single-column format for the production of English books, manuscript compilers and folio preparers adopt newer codicological elements. As such, these books, like the texts they contain, are contemporary and *au fait* with current trends. From the perspective of a politics of text and language, this clearly demonstrates the books are

---

[47] For example, the 'Bury Bible' copied at Bury St Edmunds between 1121 and 1138 measures 520 x 350 mm; Cambridge, University Library, Kk. 4. 6, written at Worcester between *c.*1130 and 1145, and including works of Jerome, measures 339 x 265mm. See P. R. Robinson, *Catalogue of Dated and Datable Manuscripts in Cambridge Libraries*, 2 vols. (Woodbridge: Boydell, 1988), items 119 and 65 respectively.

[48] Some of the manuscripts, such as CCCC 303, have been so tightly bound that it is impossible to see if pricks exist in the inner margin. The exception to this practice in twelfth-century English religious manuscripts is Cambridge University Library Ii. 1. 33 dated to the second half of the twelfth century, where the fifth quire and quires 17–21 are pricked in both margins. See Ker, *Catalogue*, p. 27.

[49] Again, the exception is CUL Ii. 1. 33 where single vertical bounding lines running the length of the page enclose the single column of writing.

created to take their place in the literary and intellectual discourse of the twelfth century; they are, without exception, absolutely functional and relevant to their specific moments of production and transmission.

Contemporary Texts

The fact that the majority of manuscripts written in the post-Conquest period contain versions of earlier texts must not be permitted to preclude the relevance of these vernacular works within their contexts of re-production. The popularity of Ælfric, Wulfstan and the anonymous homilists, of Anglo-Saxon lawcodes, of Alfredian texts, and of vernacular para-liturgical works, for example, is evinced throughout post-Conquest period. Of these genres the sermons, saints' lives and pastoral texts were particularly prolific; these existed in unison with freshly created texts, like the *Ormulum*, given new impetus as a result of the mandates of the Third Lateran Council in 1179.[50]

Those homiliaries and hagiographic collections that preceded Lateran III are bound to have a very great deal in common, both as a specific corpus of post-Conquest religious prose items and as part of the wider corpus of English pastoral texts produced from at least the tenth to thirteenth centuries. Their essentially homogeneous form, *mise-en-page*, and attention to detail of contemporized spelling, lexis, morphology, phonology and syntax—details that vary in consistency within individual manuscripts, but have striking similarities across the corpus—is suggestive of an overarching production agenda, one that I have suggested pertains specifically to a deliberately manufactured collective English Benedictine identity. The promulgation of this identity might, arguably and provocatively, be thought of as volitional literary resistance to the Norman domination of elite religious culture, but which, because of its exclusive vernacularity, was shared not with any hegemony, instead filtering perhaps to the laity in the preaching they heard and teaching they received; or to the priests, nuns,[51] and monks

---

[50] Robert Holt (ed.), *The Ormulum, with the Notes and Glossary of Dr R.M. White*, 2 vols (Oxford: Clarendon, 1878); R. Foreville (ed.), *Latran I, II, III et Latran IV, 1123, 1139, 1179, et 1215*, Histoires des Conciles 6 (Paris: Éditions de l'Orante, 1965).

[51] It seems certain that Cotton Vespasian D. xiv, at least, had a female reader by the end of the twelfth century (see below).

who read and worked on these manuscripts; or to lay brothers and sisters within monastic communities; or even to English-speaking *conversi* (adult converts) such as those identified as entering Christ Church, Canterbury in the twelfth century.[52] This passive resistance is encouraged through English textual production and that set of texts' lack of negotiation, or complicity, with the Conquest: these texts never engage in direct discussion of the Normans in the way that the *Peterborough Chronicle* does. This resistance is passive because it is implicit, emerging overtly and in full force only in the thirteenth century.[53] Resistance, and an assertion of Englishness certainly emerge in the writers who bemoan the catastrophe of the Norman Conquest more than two centuries after its occurrence—writers such as Robert Mannyng in his *Chronicle*, for example, or various *Lives* and *Passions* in the manuscripts of the *South English Legendary*.[54]

However, to talk about 'literary resistance' (as I have done) rising up through the vernacular homilies and hagiographies of pre-Conquest Benedictine writers like Wulfstan and Ælfric oversimplifies a much more complex pattern of multiple narratives that has not been understood precisely. Resistance to Norman hegemony and the displacement of English traditions offers only one avenue of interpretation into some of the many vernacular manuscripts produced in the post-Conquest period. One of the most under-studied codices in this period illustrates, instead, a book that seems to have been produced in a timely fashion precisely to unite Anglo-Norman and Anglo-Saxon as fellow Englishmen celebrating Christian inspiration, and the veneration of an important regional saint.

Oxford, Bodleian Library, Hatton 116 contains twenty-six English sermons and saints' lives, the core coherence of which might be described as evangelising and corrective. All of the texts included in the volume make reference to evangelism, conversion narratives and the correction of

---

[52] Cecily Clark, 'People and Languages in Post-Conquest Canterbury', in Peter Jackson (ed.), *Words, Names and History: Selected Papers Cecily Clark* (Cambridge: D.S. Brewer, 1995), pp. 179–206.

[53] Thorlac Turville-Petre, *England the Nation: Language, Literature, and National Identity, 1290–1340* (Oxford: Oxford University Press, 1996).

[54] Idele Sullens (ed.), *Robert Mannyng of Brune, The Chronicle* (Binghamton, NY: SUNY, 1996). See the explicit and lengthy anti-Anglo-Norman sentiment in the *Life of St Wulfstan* from the late thirteenth-century *South English Legendary* in Elaine Treharne (ed.), *Old and Middle English*, pp. 512–18.

superstitious or heathen practices through Christian intervention.[55] Additional support for this interpretation can be derived from contemporary translingual trends in homiletic dissemination, since *De Auguriis* and *De Falsis Diis* were translated into Old Norse, extant in the early fourteenth-century *Hauksbók*, indicating there, too, this idea of conversion and basic doctrinal education.[56] Conversion, in the broadest sense, includes converting not only those who are not Christian, but also teaching those who are newly Christian, or inspiring those who are less well versed in their faith than is ideal: converting or reaffirming the beginnings of religious devotion into something stronger and more committed. The texts in Hatton 116 seem ideal for these purposes for a congregation affiliated regionally with the West Midlands. The manuscript was glossed by the Tremulous Hand, who worked in or around the Worcester area at the end of the twelfth and beginning of the thirteenth century.[57] Because of this, the manuscript has generally been thought of as a Worcester manuscript, though its unusual quiring in twelves might mitigate against that localization, since Worcester manuscripts of this period are generally quires of eight, and sometimes ten.[58]

Introducing a sequence from Ælfric's First Series of *Catholic Homilies* (John the Baptist to Saint Andrew) is a unique and anonymous *Life of Chad*,[59] the seventh-century 'Apostle of the Mercians', translated principally from Bede's *Ecclesiastical History*, but with sections that borrow from the *Life of St Martin*. Its inclusion at the head of this volume is

---

[55] Ker, *Catalogue*, pp. 403–6. The pieces at the end of the volume (Ælfric's *De Exameron, Interrogationes Sigewulfi, De Duodecim Abusivis, De Auguriis, De Falsis Diis, De Septiformi Spiritu, De Sanguine, De Infantibus*, and *De Cogitatione*) provide a theological guidebook to exemplary Christian practice, warn against witchcraft, idolatory, and superstition and give essential facts about the emergence of Christianity.

[56] *Hauksbók*, ed. F. Jónsson and E. Jónsson from Arnamagnæanske Manuscript 371, 544 and 675 4° (Copenhagen, 1892–96), pp. 156–64, 167–9; see also Arnold Taylor, '*Hauksbók* and Ælfric's *De Falsis Diis*', *Leeds Studies in English* 3 (1969), pp. 1–9; and Thomas N. Hall, 'Old Norse-Icelandic Sermons', in *The Sermon*, ed. Beverly Mayne Kienzle (Turnhout: Brepols, 2000), pp. 661–709.

[57] Franzen, *The Tremulous Hand of Worcester*.

[58] R. M. Thomson, with Michael Gullick, *Catalogue of the Medieval Manuscripts in Worcester Cathedral Library* (Cambridge: D. S. Brewer, 2001). Other manuscripts I have found with quires of twelve at this time point to a Cirencester origin.

[59] R. Vleeskruyer, *The Life of St Chad, An Old English Homily* (Amsterdam: North Holland Publishing Co., 1953). The text is unhelpfully described by Jackson J. Campbell in his review of Vleeskruyer as 'short, insignificant from a literary point of view, and, because of the late date of our copy, [of] only secondary importance as a linguistic document' (*JEGP* 54 (1955): 402–4, at 402).

remarkable: it is chronologically in sequence, since Chad's feast day is March 2nd, but Chad thus effectively heads up a list of vatic and apostolic greats, including John the Baptist and Saints Peter, Paul, and Bartholemew. This is quite a promotion for the saint. Chad became bishop of Lichfield in 667, a see which at its origin incorporated Worcester and Hereford among its vast territory. Notably, in 1148, the new Norman cathedral was consecrated at Lichfield, and the relics of Chad were translated into a superior shrine;[60] the inclusion of the *Life* in this mid, or later, twelfth-century manuscript would seem an obvious correspondence with the celebration that the translation would entail.[61]

The attribution of the *Life of Chad* in Hatton 116 to this precise period when the cult of the saint was being promoted vigorously seems feasible, palaeographically likely, and testifies to the contemporary role played by English texts—politically significant in the context of a saint's translation—within a great cathedral. In previous scholarship, the *Life* has been seen as an archaic nod to the Mercian past, with the text itself being dated to the ninth century by its editor Vleeskruyer in 1953. It seems equally likely, though, that the extant text is a contemporary rendition of an earlier text, and that many of the linguistic forms carefully selected by Vleeskruyer to reinforce his early dating could possibly be attributed to the twelfth century, too, particularly as late West Saxon forms began to modify so evidently by the mid-twelfth century. Vleeskruyer did not have the benefit of research tools we take for granted now: Ker's *Catalogue*, the *Dictionary of Old English*, the *Middle English Dictionary*,

---

[60] D. H. Farmer, 'Ceadda (*d.* 672?)', *Oxford Dictionary of National Biography*, Oxford University Press, 2004; online edn., October 2008 [*http://www.oxforddnb.com.proxy.lib. fsu.edu/view/article/4970*, accessed 24 February 2011]. On the composition of this final form of the *Life of St Chad* being dated to the period of the manuscript's compilation, see Jane Roberts, 'The English Saints Remembered in Old English Anonymous Homilies', in *Old English Prose Basic Readings*, ed. Paul E. Szarmach (New York and London: Garland Publishing Inc., 2000), pp. 433–61.

[61] This would rely on the manuscript being dated to the middle of the twelfth century or later. Ker dates it to the first half, as does Vleeskruyer, and other scholars have followed Ker. The Bodleian Library website *http://bodley30.bodley.ox.ac.uk:8180/luna/servlet/view/ all/when/12th+century%2C+second+half*, however, dates the manuscript as s. xii². I am confident it can be dated to at least the middle of the century, and probably somewhere early in the second half: see Oxford, Bodleian Library, Rawlinson Q. b. 5 (s. xii²) for a close scribal comparison. The blind-ruling of the manuscript should not distract, since this can be offset by the quiring in twelves, which is a new feature in the twelfth century, and, while rare at this time, is seen, as mentioned, in Cirencester manuscripts. I should like to thank Orietta Da Rold for discussing the collation with me.

among others.[62] Some of Vleeskruyer's comments on the *Life of St Chad* in Hatton 116 bear reconsideration, particularly in relation to the vocabulary of the text; thus, for example, he asserts that *andwyrdan* ('to answer') was 'possibly obsolete' even in Old English, but had been completely replaced by *answerian* by the twelfth century.[63] This is not the case, however, and the Lambeth Homilies, datable to the beginning of the thirteenth century, illustrate the use of this verbal form.[64] Similarly, Vleeskruyer states that *carcern* ('prison') was obsolete in Late West Saxon, but it is used in the mid-twelfth-century *Passion of St Margaret* in Corpus 303 (though the text is probably up to a century earlier in origin);[65] *gecigan* ('to call'), apparently rare in Early West Saxon, is, in fact, used in the Vercelli Homilies, and in Ælfric's *Catholic Homilies*, where twelfth-century manuscript copies of individual homilies that use 'gecigan' in a variety of forms, such as Bodley 343, retain it in their versions.[66] Many other instances provided by Vleeskruyer for insisting upon a pre-Alfredian Mercian origin for the *Life of Chad* can be similarly questioned, with uses of lexis that he cites being evinced in late West Saxon or early Middle English (particularly West Midlands texts) into the thirteenth century.[67] In his meticulously detailed, but determinedly

[62] Antonette diPaolo Healey, with John Price Wilkin and Xin Xiang (eds.), *Dictionary of Old English Web Corpus* (Toronto: University of Toronto Press, 2011); S. M. Kuhn and H. Kurath (ed.), *Middle English Dictionary* [http://quod.lib.umich.edu/m/med/]

[63] Vleeskruyer, *Chad*, p. 26.

[64] *Middle English Dictionary*, s.v. 'andwurden'.

[65] Vleeskruyer, *Chad*, p. 26; see now D. G. Scragg and E. Treharne, 'Appendix: The Three Anonymous Lives in Cambridge, Corpus Christi College 303', in Paul E. Szarmach (ed.), *Holy Men and Holy Women: Old English Prose Saints' Lives and Their Contexts* (Binghamton, NY: SUNY, 1996), pp. 180–4.

[66] Vleeskruyer, *Chad*, p. 26; see now Scragg, *Vercelli Homilies*, s.v. 'gecigan' and Godden, *Commentary*, s.v. 'gecigan'. Note in Clemoes, *CHI* II.14, the later twelfth-century Cambridge University Library, Ii. 1. 33 (and other manuscripts, too, occasionally) silently alters 'geciged' to 'geclypod'.

[67] Neither of the labels 'late West Saxon' or 'Early Middle English' is appropriate for any of the material copied from earlier exemplars during the period 1060 to 1200, or so. Other lexical examples that need to be further investigated in the *Life of Chad*, include 'inwit' or 'leornian' (Vleeskruyer, *Chad*, p. 31), the second of which occurs in the Lambeth Homilies and various manuscripts of the *Ancrene Wisse*; and the first in *Ancrene Wisse* (Corpus 402). Likewise, many of his phonological and morphological variants (pp. 72) can be paralleled by other contemporary and later texts, such as Bodley 343 and the Lambeth or Trinity Homilies; for example, *geseh* and *waxan* (p. 74), and the uses of <e> for <ea> or <ae> (pp. 83–6). This is acknowledged at p. 87, but persistently brought back to early Mercian, often on the basis of forms in the Vespasian Psalter.

pro-Mercian, linguistic analysis, Vleeskruyer is certain that the extant *Life of Chad* is directly copied from a pre-Alfredian, ninth-century exemplar,[68] with such signs of 'transitional' English being scribal impositions; I am equally certain that our knowledge of twelfth-century English is nowhere near complete enough to allow for such a statement, and that, rather, the *Life* as it survives, should be regarded as a twelfth-century version of the text that is not deliberately 'archaic', irrespective of the date of its exemplar. Many of the dialectal forms held to be Mercian and ninth-century are common in 'transitional' English of the twelfth century and are attested in the other major homiliaries of the period. Claims of archaism bolster the scholar's desire to reclaim post-Conquest material for Anglo-Saxon England; but this often results in our regarding the text as redundant in its own social and cultural contexts.[69] This rejection of a text's contemporary relevance means scholars fail to see the text as a product of its precise historical moment, when manuscript compilers felt the text had applicability and resonance for an intended audience, and when resources were given over to these texts' composition.[70]

In relation to the *Life of Chad*, when read as a product of its time, its so-called 'archaic' nature (if by 'archaic' we mean always already functionless) quickly dissipates into the imaginary. The 'archaic'—lauding an ancient English saint local to the manuscript's place of production in the Mercian region—is made to do significant cultural work at just the moment of hegemonic appropriation: as the Anglo-Normans, with their new cathedrals dominating the landscape, promote English saints for the advancement of the 'new order',[71] those saints' lives are reproduced in

---

[68] Vleeskruyer, *Chad*, p. 68. His palaeographical evidence for an early exemplar at pp. 69–70 is also suspect, attributing firm dating to the specific positioning of ð and þ that is simply not witnessed in manuscripts from the ninth to the early thirteenth century.

[69] See e.g. Malcolm Godden's recent attempt to reclaim the twelfth-century *Life of St Neot* for early eleventh-century England: 'The Old English Life of St Neot and the legends of King Alfred', *Anglo-Saxon England* 39 (2011), DOI: 10.1017/S0263675110000116. See George Younge's convincing rejection of this argument: '"Those were good days": Representations of the Anglo-Saxon Past in the Old English Homily on Saint Neot', *Review of English Studies* 2012 (forthcoming).

[70] For this common phenomenon of rewriting earlier English texts to fit into new contexts, effectively creating new compositions, see Treharne, 'Life and Times of Old English Homilies for the First Sunday in Lent', and Mary Swan's body of work, including 'Old English Made New'.

[71] The phrase is used by many scholars; see e.g. D. C. Douglas in *William the Conqueror: The Norman Impact upon England* (Berkley: University of California Press, 1964), p. 211.

English, the exclusive language of the subordinated in those first few generations after the Conquest. By 1150, then, when Chad's relics were translated, perhaps this text provided a coming together, a healing for the native and the settler.

Other elements of the English *Life of Chad* link it to vernacular textual events happening elsewhere at the same time; thus, borrowings from Sulpicius Severus' *Vita Martini* in the *Life of Chad* that highlight the saint's ascetic qualities and exemplary life are paralleled by borrowings from Ælfric's *Life of St Martin* in the post-Conquest English *Life of St Giles* in Corpus 303, a mid twelfth-century manuscript probably from Rochester,[72] which like Hatton 116, might have been composed to bridge linguistic and cultural gaps through its inclusion of lives of saints particularly venerated by the Normans (Giles, Nicholas, and Margaret, in particular).

However contemporary a collection Hatton 116 might have been intended to be, though, it was not subject to correction after its initial production, and neither was it the subject of use until the end of the twelfth century, when a collect for St Katherine was added,[73] and after which the Tremulous Hand made his interventions in the manuscript, that are, arguably, more famous than the book itself. At page 396, what appears to be the hand of the Tremulous Hand writes the poetic line 'ic am nout for þisse þinges wo', a line reminiscent of the lyrical poetry beginning to spring up in High Medieval England,[74] and reminding us of the sorrow of the Tremulous Hand so famously inscribed in his lament for a lost England that might have provided

---

[72] Elaine Treharne (ed.), *The Old English Life of St Nicholas with the Old English Life of St Giles*, Leeds Texts and Monographs (Leeds: University of Leeds, 1997). See, for comparison, W. W. Skeat, *Lives of Saints* (ed.), *Ælfric's Lives of Saints*, EETS o.s. 76, 82, 94, 114 (London: Oxford University Press, 1889–1900; repr. as 2 vols., 1966), II. xxxi.302–5.

[73] At p. 395. The antiphon *Ecce crucem domini* was also added to this page. Interestingly, that antiphon appears in Book I of *Ancrene Wisse*, closely related to the *Katherine*-Group of texts, of course.

[74] 'I am nothing because of sorrow of this thing'. This verse line is erroneously transcribed as 'ic am nout for þisse þinges þo' in *IMEV*. Thanks to Chris Jones (St Andrews) and Tom Bredehoft for discussing this line with me. Another updating is the omission of *viii kalendas Septembris* in the title of the homily celebrating St Bartholomew, since the date of Bartholomew's feast-day was changed *c.* 1100 from *viii kalendas Septembris* (25 August) to 24 August: Godden, *Commentary*, p. 258. Note, interestingly, given its date of *c.* 1170, that Bodley 343 has *Passio Apostoli viii kalendas Septembris* (Clemoes, *CHI*, XXXI.1)

the inspiration for his detailed work recuperating earlier English texts for those in his care:[75]

> ... 3et weren þeos biscopes þe bodeden Cristendom:
> Wilfrid of Ripum, Johan of Beoferlai,
> Cuþbert of Dunholme, Oswald of Wireceastre,
> Egwin of Heoueshame, Ældelm of Malmesburi,
> Swiþþun, Æðelwold, Aidan, Biern of Wincæstre,
> Paulin of Rofecæstre, Dunston and Ælfeih of Cantoreburi.
> *Þeos lærden ure leodan on Englisc;*
> næs deorc heore liht, ac hit fæire glod...

> ... Through these men were our people taught in English
> These were the bishops who preached the Christian religion:
> Wilfrid of Ripon, John of Beverly,
> Cuthbert of Durham, Oswald of Worcester,
> Egwin of Evesham, Aldhelm of Malmesbury,
> Swithun, Æthelwold, Aidan, Birinus of Winchester,
> Paulinus of Rochester, Dunstan and Ælfeah of Canterbury.
> These taught our people in English;
> their light was not dim, but glowed beautifully...

[75] Contained in Worcester Cathedral F. 174. On the Tremulous Hand's activities, see Wendy Collier, 'The tremulous Worcester scribe and his milieu: a study of his annotations' (unpub. PhD diss., University of Sheffield, 1992); on the Tremulous Hand's lament for English teachers, see Treharne, 'Making their Presence Felt: Readers of Ælfric, *c.* 1050– 1350', pp. 399–422.

'This isn't fair dealing'[1]

The Unity of Conquest

Englishness Evangelized

Evangelizing is the mission of the preacher and pastor, and ultimately underpins all homiletic and hagiographic composition. But whereas the evangelical, perhaps even missionary, impulse is as the heart of manuscripts like Hatton 116, discussed in Chapter 6, other motives seem to impel the compilers of the mid-twelfth-century manuscripts, Corpus 303 and Cotton Vespasian D. xiv. Particular trends emerge from the close study of later uses of these twelfth-century homiletic manuscripts that can suggest the intentions behind the production of these manuscripts, and the function to which these homilies were subsequently put. In terms of the language of the English texts, particularly in relation to the Anglo-Saxon texts from which they are copied, it is the case that these are sometimes labelled by scholars as exemplifying 'corrupt' or 'late' forms with the implication that they are of little use.[2] The employment of

---

[1] Kipling, 'Norman and Saxon', *A History of England*, p. 52.
[2] For example, Pope *Homilies of Ælfric*, i. 178, states: 'Deviations [from the Late West Saxon Standard] in certain manuscripts of the twelfth century are of course much more numerous [than earlier manuscripts]…'

such terms implicitly suggests that there is a literary and linguistic per-
fection in the pre-Conquest period that is undermined or somehow
destroyed by later textual copies. Literary West Saxon is not, however, an
invariable form of written standard at any point in its history notwithstanding the paradigmatic rigidity of the university Old English Grammar. As Jeremy Smith suggests, late West Saxon is a 'standardized'
language, not a Standard:[3] it is one to which scribes might aspire, but not
necessarily attain. The point here is that late West Saxon with its variant
forms is a living, utilitarian form of written language throughout the
later Anglo-Saxon period, and well into the twelfth century. Its intelligibility is clearly demonstrated by the textual examples cited where by far
the majority of the text remains essentially unaltered. The fact that late
West Saxon was always a formal register of language, one that would not
commonly be a reflection of *parole*, serves to reinforce the argument
about the copying of texts in English in the twelfth century. Adherence
to West Saxon with minor emendations does not imply an antiquarianism or mechanical copying of an archaic language by the scribes responsible; rather, it is an attempt to use the most prestigious register of the
language for the composition of written texts. English in the post-
Conquest period was employed as a living literary language for the writing of formal materials; it was usable, used, and intelligible to native
speakers, excluding those whose languages might have been restricted
to French and Latin. The potential for exclusion, and the ability to
express not simply an evangelizing message through a homily or saint's
life, but a message of continued tradition and the resilience of English
that resonated culturally, means that one might regard some of the books
and texts produced from *c*.1100 to *c*.1200 as politically charged.

Moreover, one can view the extant physical artifact—the manuscript
itself—as well as the language and script of the contents, as representing
passive resistance to Norman hegemony. None of the predominantly

---

[3] Jeremy Smith, *An Historical Study of English: Function, Form and Change* (Routledge:
London, 1996), p. 66. He adds at p. 67: 'Close examination of the written record soon
reveals that "Standard West Saxon" admitted of a good deal more variation than standard
Present-Day English. Not only are there certain lexical habits which are restricted to certain monastic scriptoria, but also there seem to be persistent orthographic distinctions
between the various scriptorial outputs. Codification of these latter features remains an
important task for Anglo-Saxonists'. See also Roger Lass, *Old English: A Historical Linguistic Companion* (Cambridge: Cambridge University Press, 1994), esp. ch. 10, 'The Dissolution of Old English'.

English manuscripts produced from *c.*1060 onwards could be thought of as a *de luxe* or elite volume in contrast to many other comparable volumes made in this period; furthermore, none of the English books, as far as we know, shows any evidence of being manufactured as a result of the kinds of royal and aristocratic patronage seen in numerous cases of Latin and French textual production. They are 'bread-and-butter' books, then. Even so, English texts were clearly considered to be worth producing in a professional and time-consuming manner. While the manuscripts vary in their appearance, in their sustained adherence to Insular Minuscule graphs, and in the level of editorial intervention between exemplar and recontextualized product, one might suspect some of the English books produced in this period are an attempt by an English Benedictine *literati* to create a product that is essentially a refutation of the colonizers' suzerainty. Moreover, a significant number of the texts themselves indicate political concerns that are never in negotiation with Norman hegemony; rather, their focus might demonstrate an awareness of, and attack upon the cultural denigration brought about by the Conquest and its processes, but a refusal to be complicit *in* it by open acknowledgement *of* it.

Indeed, writing English at this time might have been a subversive task, if comments on the status of English as a language are taken seriously. There is derision of English and its sounds in a variety of writings, and not infrequent anti-English sentiment.[4] While there appears to be no extant English text that directly takes on the challenge of refuting racial and linguistic stereotyping, the mere production of manuscripts in English, and the employment of expensive resources to do so, is in itself a refutation of the worthlessness or cacophony of the vernacular. The English manuscripts that survive from the century after the Norman Conquest are testimony to the value of English at a high social and intellectual level, and are self-authenticating evidence against the views that are represented in some contemporary Latin writings. William of Malmesbury

---

[4] For examples of the English as drunkards, as half-beasts with tails, as victims of their own sinfulness, and as voice-bearers of a barbaric language, impenetrable to the Normans, see Paul Meyvaert, ' "Rainaldus est malus scriptor Francigenus"—Voicing National Antipathy in the Middle Ages', *Speculum* 66 (1991), pp. 743–63; and on the sociolinguistic issues involved, for example, see Tim William Machan, 'Language and Society in Twelfth-Century England', in Irma Taavitsainen, Terttu Nevalainen, Päivi Pahta, and Matti Rissanen (eds.), *Placing Middle English in Context* (Berlin: Mouton de Gruyter, 2000), pp. 43–65.

deriding the English at the time of the Norman Conquest reveals that the Battle of Hastings was:

> a day of destiny for England, a fatal disaster for our dear country…

and yet, among the English, learning had deteriorated, morals had declined:

> Drinking in company was a universal practice, and in this passion [the English] made no distinction between night and day. In small, mean houses they wasted their entire substance, unlike the French and the Normans, who in proud great buildings live a life of moderate expense. There followed the vices that keep company with drunkenness, and sap the virility of a man's spirit… In brief, the English of those days wore garments half way to the knee, which left them unimpeded; hair short, chin shaven, arms loaded with gold bracelets, tattooed with coloured patterns, eating till they were sick and drinking till they spewed.[5]

Drunkenness and excess, ironically referred to as the '*largitas incomparabilis Anglicorum*' by Raoul Ardent, a French scholar of the later twelfth century,[6] were the common characteristics of the English according to many writers.[7] The English language itself was, on the odd occasion, the object of derision. William of Malmesbury's *Vita Wulfstani*, comments about Coleman, the author of the Old English Life source, that he was 'a learned man and a master of his native tongue… [who wrote] in a Life that in content was agreeable and serious, and in style simple and unaffected',[8] but that 'I have not always followed Coleman's lead. For example, I have withheld the names of almost all the witnesses, so that barbarous names should not wound the sensibilities of the fastidious reader, and also removed the grand language and little declamations that he borrowed from the Lives of other saints and put in with all too eager piety.'[9]

---

[5] *Gesta Regum Anglorum*, p. 459.

[6] Cited and discussed by Meyvaert, ' "Rainaldus est malus scriptor Francigenus" ', pp. 748–9.

[7] See, most recently, Thomas's relatively sensitive account of stereotyping in *The English and the Normans*, pp. 297–306, espec. pp. 301–2.

[8] *William of Malmesbury: Saints' Lives*, pp. 10–11.

[9] Ibid., pp. 58–9. Andy Orchard, 'Parallel Lives' in Barrow and Brooks (ed.), *St Wulfstan and his World*, pp. 39–57, discusses William of Malmesbury's view of Coleman's writing. Orchard curiously seems to concur with Malmesbury about Coleman's 'overblown comments' (p. 50), and manipulative and sinister writing (pp. 53–5), when such comments on writing by Coleman only exist through Malmesbury's own (potentially derogatory) mediation.

Likewise, in his description of Thorney Abbey in the *Gesta Pontificum*, Malmesbury makes his feelings about the sounds of English quite clear when discussing the saints' relics brought to Thorney 'from all over England': 'I have chosen not to write down their somewhat barbarous names, for they grate on the ear. It is not that I disbelieve or deny their sainthood. What authority have *I* to call into question what holy antiquity has sanctified? But because, as I say, their names sound uncouth and give off a bad smell.'[10] The manipulation of this comment—claiming not to question the authority of the saints, while refusing to name them—is clever rhetoric, but there can be no doubting Malmesbury's distaste for the English language. For him, and other writers, it was associated with rusticity and uncouthness. On one disastrous occasion, at the coronation of William I, this linguistic 'otherness' caused the Normans to panic when the 'harsh [English] accents' of those inside Westminster Abbey brought an attack by the guards outside who 'rashly set fire to some of the buildings'.[11]

The English, then, were characterized as using harsh and barbaric speech, marking themselves off initially from their intellectual and cultural superiors by their monolingualism, their untranslatability.[12] The fact that language was a real social marker absolutely related to status denotes the separateness of the native 'Old' English, at the least of those who did not have access to the prestige of French or the educated *lingua franca* of Latin. Language, intimately associated with status and, in this period, ethnicity, was a source of obvious fracture between the conquerors and the conquered, but also clearly a means of inclusivity among the indigenous English.[13] As well as using English for pastoral and educative

---

[10] *Gesta Pontificum Anglorum*, i. 494–5.

[11] Machan, 'Language and Society in Twelfth-Century England', p. 49.

[12] See Machan's other examples, ibid., pp. 48–50.

[13] See esp. Machan, 'Language and Society in Twelfth-Century England'. But cf. Ian Short, 'Patrons and Polyglots: French Literature in Twelfth-Century England', *Anglo-Norman Sudies* 14 (1991), pp. 229–49. Note also Thomas, *The English and the Normans*, who discusses language at pp. 377–90. His view is that 'I have argued that language was an important social barrier between the two peoples. But if, as the current consensus argues, by the end of the twelfth century all except real immigrants, and perhaps those aristocrats with extensive Norman holdings, spoke English as their native or "maternal" tongue, then the survival of French as an important language would be no more harmful to assimilation and subsequent national unity than the even greater continuing importance of Latin. The shift to English as a first language by the descendants of immigrants would have been part and parcel of the process of assimilation' (pp. 382–3).

purposes in their copying and compilation of manuscripts, the English writers in this period also propagated the language as a worthy vehicle of teaching and learning, countering the hegemonic claims of the Anglo-Latin and Anglo-Norman elite. Thus, Englishness itself, through the saints' lives, homilies, laws, and encyclopaedic texts, was evangelized by this medium.

Countering Conquest

As well as using English to write, explicit comments in English writings about the unacceptability of the *status quo* in the post-Conquest period can be found in a variety of texts, often without mentioning the Conquest itself. In the often-cited *Peterborough Chronicle*, the denunciation of the behaviour of the aristocracy during the Civil War between Stephen and Matilda from in the 1130s and 1140s is very familiar to all students of the period.[14] The author of these continuations to the *Anglo-Saxon Chronicle* also makes numerous other pointed remarks that indicate a keen awareness of division. In the annal for 1130, for example, the writer recounts the visit of Peter of Cluny to Peterborough, and abbot Henry of Angély's promise to subject Peterborough to Cluny. As an English monk of Peterborough, the writer's objection to this is entirely understandable, but his proverbial wisdom is interesting:

> To Burch he com 7 þær behet se abbot Heanri him þet he scolde beieton him þone mynstre of Burch þet his scolde beon underðed into Clunni; oc man seið to biworde: 'Hæge sitteð þa aceres dæleth.' God ælmihtig adylege iuele ræde! 7 sone þæræfter ferde se abbot of Clunni ham to his ærde.[15]

[14] For which see Susan Irvine (ed.), *The Anglo-Saxon Chronicle, A Collaborative Edition 7: MS E* (Cambridge: D. S. Brewer, 2004), pp. 132–6, the lengthy annal for 1137 lamenting the effects of the Civil War in Stephen's reign, and distinguishing (at p. 134) between the oppressed *carlmen* ('common men'), and the *rice man* ('powerful m[e]n').

[15] Irvine, *MS E*, pp. 131–2; my translation. The word 'biworde' occurs only here with this meaning of 'proverb'. See Sheppard, *Families of the King*, pp. 145–55, for an interesting interpretation of the post-Conquest annals as emphasizing land above all other aspects of identity. See esp. pp. 151–2, where Sheppard analyses the annal for 1130 as indicative of the text itself as a defence of English monastic autonomy and the Benedictine order.

> He [Peter] came to Peterborough and there the abbot Henry prom-
> ised him that he would get him the monastery of Peterborough so
> that it would be subjected to Cluny; but as people say proverbially:
> 'Hedge resides that fields divides.' May God almighty devastate such
> evil conspiracy! And soon after that, the abbot of Cluny went home to
> his native place.

Not only is the monk defending his own patch, as it were, but also he does so through the most exclusive mode of communication—a prov-erb, or colloquial turn-of-phrase understood principally by those in the same speech community.[16] Reinforcing this symbolism of ownership and belonging is the use in the final phrase of *ham* and *ærde*, an almost tautological reminder that Peter (and those like him?) belong some-where else, in another place.

The writer of the *Peterborough Chronicle* is no solitary malcontent, despite often being portrayed as such.[17] The composers of less well-known expansions and adaptations of texts, such as the early English *Dicts of Cato*, also had important observations to make within the con-text of works of wisdom. The extant corpus of proverbs, debates, ency-clopaedic texts, and prognostications forms a varied and prolific category within extant twelfth-century English and French literatures.[18] All three versions of the English *Dicts* were copied in the post-Conquest period.[19]

---

[16] The proverb is reminiscent of the binding vernacular boundary clauses written into Latin charters of the period, defining precisely the limits of land to be given and received. This collocation of English land and legal process is important here. The proverb is also re-contextualised in the later *Proverbs of Hendyng*; see Paul Cavill, 'Proverbs and Wisdom' in *Dragons in the Sky*, ed. Stuart Lee and Patrick Conner, http://users.ox.ac.uk/~stuart/dits/contents_wisdom.html

[17] See e.g. Peter Damian-Grint, *The New Historians of the Twelfth-Century Renaissance: Inventing Vernacular Authority* (Woodbridge: Boydell, 1999), pp. 14–16; Daniell, *From Norman Conquest to Magna Carta*, p. 197

[18] The entertaining debates between *Solomon and Saturn*, between *Adrian and Ritheus*, and in the English excerpts from Honorius of Autun's *Elucidarium* are testimony to the post-Conquest flourishing of the genre. See J. E. Cross and T. D. Hill (eds.), *The Prose 'Solomon and Saturn' and 'Adrian and Ritheus'*, McMaster Old English Studies and Texts 1 (Toronto: Toronto University Press, 1982); Warner (ed.), *Early English Homilies from the Twelfth Century MS Vesp. D. xiv*. There are later twelfth-century French versions by Ever-art (*Disticha Catonis*) and by Elie of Winchester (*Catun*), and at least two sets of twelfth-century French Proverbs too. See the authoritative volume by Dean and Boulton, *Anglo-Norman Literature*.

[19] R. S. Cox (ed.), 'The Old English *Dicts of Cato*', *Anglia* 90 (1972), pp. 1–42. See also Treharne, 'The Form and Function of the Old English *Dicts of Cato*', which suggests a specifically monastic audience.

In the unique, expanded redaction contained in London, British Library, Cotton Vespasian D. xiv, the writer gnomically states:

> Wa þære þeode þe hæfð ælðeodigne cyng—ungemetfæstne, feoh georne, and unmildheortne—for on þære þeode byð his gitsung, and his modes gnornung on his earde.[20]
>
> It will be miserable for the nation that has a foreign king—immoderate, eager for money, and merciless—for his avarice will be on the people, and his mind's discontent on his land.

The obvious pertinence of such admonition at precisely the time when the country suffered Stephen's taxation through the Civil War reflects more than simply mindless and meaningless copying. It is reminiscent of the same complaints made in the *Peterborough Chronicle*, and of the kinds of socially meaningful exhortations seen in Wulfstan's homilies in Chapter 3. One sees such overt political commentary elsewhere too. In the late twelfth-century manuscript, Cambridge, Trinity College, B 14. 52—a homiliary that contains texts very much in the tradition of earlier English homilies, but also the 'new' English poem, *Poema Morale*—the text celebrating St Andrew seems to be explicit in its socio-political engagement, as well as in its obvious didactic impulse. The author uses the image of a sinking ship as a metaphor for a troubled nation, a warning against social inequality that seems to have obvious contemporary resonances:

> And gif he [se storm] ship findeð, he fondeð to drenchen hit ȝif he mai. Swo doð in þis woreld þe oreguil and þe wraððe of kinges and of barones þe senden here sergantes to bringen iuele tiðinges, and þermide dreuen þat lond, þat is to water nemned, and bringen on þe folkes heorte grete stormes of nið and of onde and of hatienge, and on here muðe curses and werginges and wurreð uppe chirches, oðer wanieð hire rihtes oðer letteð oðer mid alle binimeð ȝif his mugen, alse þe storm bisinkeð þe ship gif he mai.
>
> And if it finds the ship, it will try to sink it if it can. So too in this world do the pride and wrath of kings and of barons, who send their officers to bring evil tidings, and therewith trouble the land (which is

---

[20] Cox, 'The Old English *Dicts of Cato*', p.15, E, with my own translation.

called the water) and bring upon the hearts of the people great storms
of malice and of envy and of hatred, and of curses in their mouths and
miseries; and war upon churches, or lessen their rights or hinder
them, or withal deprive them of them, if they can, just as the storm
sinks the ship if it is able.[21]

Of particular note in this extract is the distinction to be drawn between
the storm, comprised of kings, barons, and their sergeants[22] and *þe folke*
who are the victims of malice. This unified, English *folke*, the ship upon
the sea (which is life, and paralleled here with the rightful inhabitants of
the land), is allied with the church, upon which attacks are made; and
intimately linked with the people in their subjection is the oppression
of *hire rihtes* 'their rights'. Integrated within a homily on St Andrew, this
is an extraordinarily current sequence of politicized commentary, utilizing for the first time in written records a borrowed lexis for the king's
oppressors and their *oreguil* ('pride') and the English vernacular to the
people and their rights. Given that the *Trinity Homilies* were probably
copied in the last decade of the twelfth century, and that this excerpt is
not untypical of the content and style of the homilies, it is clear that for
this rhetorically adept author at least, obvious unjust divisions in society caused the oppression of the folk, particularly with regard to rights
and to the law. Such strategic observations emerging from the long
period of Angevin legal reforms and of conflict between king and lords
give a rather different perspective than is usually cited by historians.[23]
The homilist provides a voice seldom heard, a carefully constructed
voice, which is yet as close to the 'ordinary person' as we are likely to
detect, and it unequivocally silences claims of assimilation between *þe
riche* and *þe wrecche*, and highlights the responses of the trauma caused
by ill-governance.[24]

---

[21] Morris, *Old English Homilies of the Twelfth Century*, p. 174–6.

[22] These occurrences of the French loanwords, 'baron' and 'sergeant', are the earliest
recorded instances. See the *Oxford English Dictionary*, s.v. baron; s.v.sergeant.

[23] See, for instance, M. T. Clanchy's account in *England and its Rulers, 1066–1272*, 2nd
edn. (Oxford: Blackwell, 1998), pp. 99–112.

[24] Morris, *Old English Homilies of the Twelfth Century*, pp. 178–9: 'the powerful' and
'the wretched', the former being 'lords', the latter 'underlings'. It is worth pointing out, in
terms of vocabulary to express unequal power relations, that 'underling' is first record in
the twelfth-century manuscript, Cotton Vespasian D. xiv (Warner, *Early English Homilies*,
p. 89), where it refers to the Jews.

The Cultural Capital of English

Homilies for the *sanctorale*, like the *Trinity Homilies*' text for St Andrew's Day, can reveal a surprisingly incisive content, evoking contemporary events and presumably, often striking a chord with their various audiences.[25] To an extent, the same stimuli of truth-telling, propaganda, identity-formation and didacticism can be seen to inform many of the English religious texts in the twelfth century. London, BL Cotton Vespasian D. xiv is of particular importance for this discussion. Its localization has been debated by scholars a number of times in the past, the major links being with Rochester and Christ Church, Canterbury, though its date has always been assigned to the mid-twelfth century.[26] Recent research demonstrates with some certainty that the manuscript was copied at Christ Church over a period of time, extending from the middle to the second-half of the twelfth century.[27] One of the hands that adds material at the beginning and end of the core manuscript, uses 'biting' letter forms (*p* and *de*), together with other scribal characteristics not seen earlier than the second half of the twelfth century, and provides a relatively secure *terminus post quem* for the manuscript's completion.[28] It seems most likely that the manuscript was put together over a period of time, as exemplars and the materials required became available. As such, it may be more of an individual or small group's effort at gathering relevant English texts and excerpts of texts, rather than a more institutionally sanctioned production (if such a distinction can be permitted). Other more tentative evidence suggesting a Christ Church origin is palaeographical and artistic. Some similarities are witnessed between the hands of the Vespasian D. xiv scribe who wrote folios 4v–6v/14, 67v, 165r/14–22, 166r/13–168 (and who may be the same scribe as the main hand of the

[25] An example of similar detailed textual investigation is Catherine Cubitt's 'Virginity and Misogyny in Tenth- and Eleventh-Century England', *Gender and History* 12 (2000), pp. 1–32. See also Felice Lifshitz, 'Beyond Positivism and Genre: "Hagiographical Texts" as Historical Narrative', *Viator* 25 (1994), pp. 95–113.

[26] Rima Handley, 'British Museum MS Cotton Vespasian D. xiv', *Notes and Queries* 21 (1974), pp. 243–50; and Mary P. Richards, 'On the Date and Provenance of MS Cotton Vespasian D. xiv, fols. 4–169', *Manuscripta* 17 (1973), 31–5.

[27] See *The Production and Use of English Manuscripts* [http://www.le.ac.uk/english/em1060to1220/mss/EM.BL.Vesp.D.xiv.htm]

[28] For a detailed analysis, see Ker, *Catalogue*, pp. 271–7; see also Treharne, 'The Production and Script of Manuscripts containing English Religious Texts', pp. 31–4.

manuscript, but at a later stage in his career) and the main scribe of London, British Library, Campbell Charter xxii. 2, a Christ Church, Canterbury cyrograph, dated to 1152.[29] Yet further evidence is offered by the style of *litterae notabiliores* and runovers: the large initials of Vespasian D. xiv, which are quite plain, usually have a small roundel inside the frame, and these are very similar to the large initials of London, British Library, Burney 31; runovers similar to those in Vespasian D. xiv are seen in London, British Library, Arundel 55, folio 147. The latter is a Christ Church manuscript; the former is English, but unlocalized.[30]

In terms of content, four pieces in particular point to Canterbury: the anonymous *Life of St Neot*, Ralph D'Escures' *Homily on the Assumption of the Virgin Mary*, Honorius Augustodunensis' *Elucidarium* extracts, and the prayer added to the very beginning of the manuscript in the late twelfth century concerning Thomas Becket. This last item, the prayer, occurs after a prayer to Mary by an 'ancilla' ('a maidservant') at folio 4r:[31]

Deus qui beatum Thomam archipresulem ab exilio reuocatum in ecclesia propria gladiis occumbere uoluisti: praesta quaesumus ut fidei constantia roborati superatis 'hostium' uisibilium 'minis' & inuisibilium eius meritis 7 precibus periculum anime deuitemus. Per dominum nostrum Iesum Christum.

God, who wished blessed Thomas, archbishop, having been recalled from exile, to succumb to swords in his own church, grant, we pray, that we, strengthened by constancy of faith, having overcome the dangers of enemies visible and invisible, may avoid danger to the soul by his merits and prayers. Through our Lord Jesus Christ.[32]

---

[29] George F. Warner and Henry J. Ellis (eds.), *Facsimiles of Royal and Other Charters in the British Museum, Vol I: William I—Richard I* (London: Longmans, 1903), Pl. 19, no. 29. These are not likely to be the same scribe; yet, notwithstanding the different nibs being used, the form of Caroline *g* with its sharply angled final tail-stroke, the round-backed *d*, the *z*-shaped Tironian *nota* on the line, the low *punctus*, and sloping hyphen are interesting comparanda, and I am tempted to suggest these hands might be the same.

[30] Both manuscripts are partially illustrated in the online *British Library Catalogue of Illuminated Manuscripts* [http://www.bl.uk/catalogues/illuminatedmanuscripts/searchMSNo.asp]

[31] See Ker, *Catalogue*, p. 276.

[32] I am grateful for advice from Andrew Prescott, Orietta Da Rold, Richard W. Pfaff, Rebecca Stephenson, and George Younge on the transcription and translation.

A number of the new texts, then, have direct links with Canterbury: Anselm, Archbishop of Canterbury, visited the shrine of St Neot in 1078 or 1079, and sent monks from Bec when it was refounded;[33] Ralph D'Escures was Archbishop of Canterbury;[34] Honorius was known to have visited Canterbury and studied with Anselm in the last years of the eleventh century. He also knew Ralph D'Escures and his work, he was aware of St Wulfstan of Worcester's sermons, and he had connections with Rochester.[35] Anselm, Ralph and Honorius are intellectual stars of the post-Conquest period, and seem to be very important within the context of Vespasian D. xiv. An English writer at Christ Church was clearly aware of the significance of their devotional preferences, and their pastoral and homiletic work, and sought to bring these to a larger audience. He clearly recognized the literary and linguistic merits of English as a medium for up-to-date theological writings.

The new translation into English of extracts from Books I and II of the *Elucidarium* provides, in question and answer format between a master and a pupil, some basic information on Christianity that might be thought supplementary to the exhortation and example of the more homiletic materials in the manuscript. It forms one of the additions to the original core of the book, occurring at folios 159 to 165, and written by two hands, both later than the hand of the main body of the manuscript (though the hand at folio 165/14–22 may be the main scribe, later in his career). The extracts represent a considerable abbreviation of Honorius's text,[36] and in selecting these, the compiler of Vespasian D. xiv omits most of Book II, with its extensive discussion on the sacraments, and concentrated on sin and the differences between good people and evil people, free will and predestination. Book I of the *Elucidarium* (the

[33] See the excellent discussion in David Dumville and Michael Lapidge (eds.), *The Anglo-Saxon Chronicle: A Collaborative Edition 17: The Annals of St Neot with Vita Prima Sancti Neoti* (Cambridge: D. S. Brewer, 1985), pp. xcii–xcvi.

[34] On the Ralph d'Escures homily in this manuscript, see most recently, Aidan Conti, 'The Old Norse Afterlife of Ralph d'Escures's *Homilia de Assumptione Mariae*', *Journal of English and Germanic Philology* 107 (2008), pp. 75–98; and Treharne, "The Life of English in the Mid-Twelfth Century', esp. pp. 100–7.

[35] On Honorius Augustodunensis or Honorius of Autun, see V. J. Flint, 'Honorius Augustodunensis', in Patrick J. Geary (ed.), *Authors of the Middle Ages: Historical and Religious Writers of the Latin West*, ii. 5–6 (Aldershot: Ashgate, 1995), pp. 89–183, and the many citations therein.

[36] For which see Yves Lefèvre (ed.), *L'Elucidarium et Les Lucidaires* (Paris, 1954).

second extract) concerns God, creation and the incarnation and passion of Christ, and the translator focuses here on Christ's resurrection, appearance to the disciples and Mary Magdalene, and ascension. These questions seem principally meant to attest to the proof of God, even though parts of Christ's story, and God allowing evil to prosper in this world, seem designed to perplex and confuse. These are intelligent questions and answers, presupposing a good knowledge of the Bible—Q: 'Why did Jesus appear to Mary Magdalene first?' A: 'Because this is what it says in the Gospel and nothing was written, other than what was known.' Q: 'What did Jesus look like when he ascended?' A: 'He looked as he was before his crucifixion, and when he got above the clouds, he appeared as he did on Mount Thabor.' These are not questions designed for the ill-informed, but rather, for those who have already been educated in the main doctrine of Christianity, but still have issues requiring clarification; in other words, *conversi* or lay brothers, or interested members of a close congregation—adults, and, one might argue, those who have known the outside world, who are not, at this point, long-time members of the monastic institution.

The Homily on St Neot, contained in Cotton Vespasian D. xiv, is most likely to have been translated from a Latin *Vita* in the mid-eleventh century or, perhaps, post-Conquest period though Godden imagines that the English text and its Latin source are much earlier.[37] Up to 1100, Neot is found only infrequently in Kalendars, suggesting his cult became widely established later in the eleventh century, though perhaps somewhat earlier in the west of England.[38] His inclusion in Vespasian D. xiv might be related to the cult of St Neot that was being fostered at Christ Church, and which is illustrated by the inclusion of Neot in the Eadwine Psalter, *c.*1160, and by the possible acquisition of a relic for Christ Church (though only one for Bec, acquired by Anselm, is documented).[39] The

[37] Dumville and Lapidge, *The Annals of St Neots*, pp. lxxv–cxxiv and 110–42, esp. pp. cxvi–cxvii. Godden, 'The Old English Life of St Neot'.

[38] For the Kalendars, see now Rebecca Rushworth (ed.), *Saints in English Kalendars Before A.D. 1100* (London: Henry Bradshaw Society, 2008). Neot has two feastdays, 31 July and 20 October, the latter celebrated in the west of England. See Nicholas Orme, *The Saints of Cornwall* (Oxford: Oxford University Press, 2000), pp. 201–3.

[39] Margaret T. Gibson, T. A. Heslop, and Richard William Pfaff, eds, *The Eadwine Psalter: Text, Image, and Monastic Culture in Twelfth-Century Canterbury*, Publications of the Modern Humanities Research Association 14 (University Park, PA: Penn State University Press, 1992), pp. 70, 78.

narrative relates the story of a later ninth-century native hermit saint who is most famous, perhaps, for providing spiritual guidance to King Alfred, and for appearing in a vision to the king before the Battle of Edington in 878.[40] While the inclusion of the homily in Vespasian D. xiv reflects this contemporary growth in the cult,[41] it may also indicate the deliberate reappropriation of a native saint, a transformation occasioned by the process of translation:

> Eala, mæn þa leofe, þa wæron gode dages on þan gode time for cristenes folcas geearnunge, and rihtwisra heafodmanna. Nu is æighwanen heof and wop, and orfcwealm mycel for folces synnen, and wæstmes, æigðer gea on wude gea on felde, ne synd swa gode, swa heo iu wæron, ac yfeleð swyðe eall eorðe wæstme, and unrihtwisnysse mycele wexeð wide geond wurlde, and sibbe tolysnysse and tælnysse, and se þincð nu wærrest and geapest, þe oðerne mæig beswican, and his æhte him of anymen. Eac man swereð man mare þone he scolde, þy hit is þe wyrse wide on eorðe, and beo þan we mugen understanden, þæt hit is neh domesdæge.[42]

> Oh, dear men, those were good days at that time because of the merits of Christian people and righteous leaders. Now, everywhere, there is weeping and wailing, and great plague because of the people's sins; and crops, both in the grove and in the field, are not as good as they were previously, but the produce of all the land is greatly declining; and unrighteousness is increasing significantly widely throughout the world; and there is dissolution and derogation of peace; and now he who seems most prepared and most cunning can betray someone else, and deprive him of his possessions. Also, more oaths are made than they ought to be, so that it worsens widely through the land, and by this we are able to perceive that it is approaching Doomsday.

The time to which the author abstractly refers, the Golden Age of Alfredian England, directly compares the righteousness of the leaders of the prelapsarian Anglo-Saxon past with those unrighteous leaders

---

[40] See Lapidge, *Vita Prima Sancti Neoti*, pp. lxxv–lxxvii, for an account of the principal Latin *Vita*. See also M. P. Richards, 'The Medieval Hagiography of St Neot', *Analecta Bollandiana* 99 (1981), pp. 259–78.

[41] *Gesta Regum Anglorum* records that 'an old patron at the ear of God', St Neot, had been translated to Crowland during the Danish invasions (i. 486–7).

[42] Warner, *Early English Homilies*, p. 133.

throughout, not just the land, but the whole world. This apocalyptic vision, resonant with images of the imminence of the end, exemplifies post-Conquest English rhetoric at its most forceful, replete with alliteration, intensifiers, end-rhyme, and catalogues of ills reinforcing the pressure to reform. The text reverberates with echoes of Wulfstan's angry admonitions to his countrymen in the *Sermo Lupi ad Anglos*,[43] some century-and-a-half earlier. There, the audience of bishops and *witan* were to spread the urgent message of repentance to assist in rehabilitating the sinful English and in overthrowing the Danes, whose cruel visitations symbolized God's punishment for the repeated vices of the native population.[44]

The Vespasian homilist's gaze touches briefly on his people's sins, but more emphatically focuses on the ills of the world caused by the dissolute nature of the leaders. In his homily, he dwells on St Neot's relationship with King Alfred and, in particular, Alfred's need to atone for his sinful life, a self-redemption that will permit his victorious resolution against Guthrum, and the salvation of his people:

> On þan time wæs Ælfred king, 7 to þan halgen gelomen com emb his sawle þearfe. He hine eac þreade manega worden 7 him to cwæð mid forewitegunge: 'Eala, þu king, mycel scealt þu þoligen on þyssen life...Gewit eallinge fram þinre unrihtwisnysse, 7 þine synnen mid ælmessen ales, 7 mid tearen adi[log]e...'[45]

> At that time, Alfred was king and came often to the saint about his soul's needs. He (Neot) chastized him with many words and prophetically said to him: 'Alas, king, you shall have much suffering in this life...Turn now from your impiety and redeem your sins with almsgiving and blot [them] out with tears...'

Alfred's desire to atone, and his subsequent repentance in this text becomes symbolic of a nation's need to redeem itself of sins effecting Conquest. Alfred's victory over Guthrum, resulting in the peace and prosperity of his nation, creates an heroic exemplum for the post-Conquest English. He is sanctioned by a native English saint, and his heroism is manifested not only through the divine word of God inscribed in

---

[43] For which see Bethurum ,*The Homilies of Wulfstan*, pp. 267–75.
[44] See Wilcox, 'Wulfstan's *Sermo Lupi ad Anglos*'.
[45] Warner, *Early English Homilies*, p. 131.

the English of Alfred's own books, but also through this author's revelatory text. Alfred's repentance and absolution offers a model to resist oppression resulting from defeat. Even as he praises Alfred's achievements, the homilist further signifies Alfred's importance to English literary culture as a symbol of resistance in his attention to Alfred's intellectual mastery of religious texts ('þæt he on godcunden gewriten wel gelæred wæs'[46]) and writing of many books through God's spiritual assistance ('Eac is to wytene, þæt se king Ælfred manega bec þurh Godes gast gedyhte'[47]).

The emphasis on Alfred in this homily on St Neot, as can be clearly seen from these examples, provides the English audience with an English leader who is not the superhuman of the saint's life, but nonetheless represents a heroic, Christian ideal: he is sinful, penitent, pious, educated, touched by God's grace, and, once he has been absolved, the ideal of reformed spiritual leadership. From a cultural perspective, this seemingly mimetic text—replicating a well-established native vernacular tradition of hagiographic writing, and in so doing, resurrecting the greatest king of pre-Conquest England—might seem archaic or antiquarian in impulse. It is neither. Alfred seems to have been of significant importance as the post-Conquest period progressed. One cannot overlook the fact that texts first translated by Alfred and his group of scholars in late ninth-century Wessex are copied in the twelfth century, perhaps for motives much along the lines of those suggested here. The Old English translation of Augustine's *Soliloquies* exists uniquely in London, British Library, Cotton Vitellius A. xv, datable to the mid-twelfth century; and the Old English *Boethius* is extant in Oxford, Bodleian Library, Bodley 180, datable to the first half of the twelfth century. William of Malmesbury himself was keenly aware of Alfred's contribution to the Anglo-Saxon state and its culture. In his *Gesta Regum Anglorum*, Malmesbury provides an estimation of Alfred's merits as a law-giving monarch even through the 'roar of battle'.[48] He comments on Alfred's drawing together of learned advisors, and, focusing on Alfred's absorption of the 'liberal arts' and the king's abilities to translate elegantly, William lists the books

---

[46] Ibid.: 'that he was exceptionally learned about divine writings'.

[47] Ibid.: 'It should also be known that this king Alfred wrote many books by means of God's spirit.'

[48] *Gesta regum Anglorum*, i. 189.

made available in translation by Alfred and his colleagues. The books he specifically mentions are Orosius, Gregory's *Pastoral Care*, Bede's *History of the English*, Boethius' *Consolation of Philosophy*, part of the Psalter, and Alfred's own *Enchiridion*, his *Handbook*.[49] Malmesbury continues:

> In the prologue to the *Pastoral Care* he [Alfred] tells us that he was moved to undertake English versions because the churches in which well-stocked libraries were to be found from early times had, together with their books, been burnt by the Danes; with the results that in the whole island literary studies had been done away with; for everyone had to put fear for his life above zeal for book-learning. And so, he says, he did this for the benefit of his English subjects, that they might now secure a rapid foretaste of something which later on, should peace return, they might learn properly in Latin; and he was proposing to send this book, written on his instructions, to all the principal sees, together with a golden tablet containing a mancus of gold.[50]

This lengthy portrait of Alfred might have helped to consolidate that king's reputation in post-Conquest England, particularly from the perspective of wisdom—a type of English Solomon. Later in the century, the *Proverbs of Alfred*[51] attests to his fame as a gnomic figure, and the casual use of his name in *The Owl and the Nightingale*[52] similarly indicates a king whose reputation was very well established in the vernacular tradition.[53]

The Life of St Neot with its focus on the relationship between the saint and the king is a post-Conquest translation firmly embedded in an Englishness that is 'old' and has a lineage, but explicitly addresses in a divinely ordained language the consequences of incursion and of defeat. In this text, for this hagiographer, the saviour of the ninth-century English is a model for the twelfth-century: his English folk's own,

[49] Ibid., i. 192–3.

[50] Ibid., i. 192–3.

[51] Olaf Arngart (ed.), *The Proverbs of Alfred*, 2 vols. (Lund: University of Lund, 1942–55).

[52] At lines 942–4, for example: 'For hit seide þe King Alfred | "Selde endeð wel þe loþe, | An selde plaideð wel þe wroþe."' ('For as King Alfred put it: "It seldom ends well for a disliked person, and seldom does the angry person plead their case well."')

[53] On this, see Robert Rouse, *The Idea of Anglo-Saxon England in Middle English Romance* (Cambridge: D. S. Brewer, 2005), esp. pp. 42–51.

historical king. In this rhetoric, Alfred is the redeeming monarch, not the re-imagined and idealized king of the 'new', re-branded, English written into the originary myth of Geoffrey of Monmouth and his Arthur.[54]

A clearer vision

The English authors' efforts at social guidance, reform and resistance in the light of the colonization of England indicate that the stereotyping of the native population and, particularly its language, was fallacious. Many of the works written in English in the period subtly challenge and so resist contemporary twelfth-century writers' silencing. They also act to refute those interpretations of modern scholars that deny the existence of twelfth-century English literary texts as worthy of attention, or insist on making them something other than they are: contemporary, relevant, learned. The very act of homiletic, hagiographic and didactic composition and production is a reconfiguration of the cultures of post-Conquest England, countervailing the redundancy of English and the legitimization myth of the Normans as God's retribution and rehabilitation of a moribund nation. These texts reveal an engaged religious community of users of the book, an active and interested readership of English people. For some of the English texts in the twelfth century, there is a much more complex narrative than has been revealed to date, aligning old and new texts in ways that indicate that the vibrancy of the Anglo-Saxon tradition in Ælfric's work functioned at the same interpretative level as material that is, or seems, newer.[55] For literary history, some of these texts offer evidence of an attempt—as much political as it was religious—centring on maintaining a native vernacular that equates

---

[54] There is a vast body of critical material on Geoffrey of Monmouth and on Arthur. A good starting point is Michelle R. Warren, *History on the Edge: Excalibur and the Borders of Britain, 1100–1300*, Medieval Cultures 22 (Minneapolis: University of Minnesota Press, 2000).

[55] The earlier thirteenth-century Rochester manuscript, London, British Library, Cotton Vespasian A. xxii, for example, contains two Ælfric homilies alongside two short, unique English works, one of which discusses God as mother, seen as a twelfth-century theme by Caroline Walker Bynum in *Jesus as Mother: Studies in the Spirituality of the High Middle Ages* (Berkeley: University of California Press, 1982). For these homilies and this motif, see Morris, *Old English Homilies*, pp. 216–45, at pp. 232–3.

to a literature of resistance, even if that resistance is simply a refutation of the stereotype of the English as ignorant *illiteratus*.

These manuscripts clearly demonstrate, in addition, the value placed upon them by preachers, teachers, and casual readers. The thousands of post-Conquest glosses that survive in English books produced throughout the Anglo-Saxon period and beyond testify to the usefulness of the texts within them, and the relationships of the readers with the texts. Glosses exist in English, Latin, and French, alongside longer annotation, *notae* marks, other symbols, and underlinings. For just *twelfth*-century notes, glosses, and marks left in manuscripts collected in Neil Ker's *Catalogue*, an astonishing 138 manuscripts attest to such actions on the part of passers-through of the books.[56] Thus while the Tremulous Hand is the most famous glossator and annotator, he was but one of hundreds of users and perusers of English after the Conquest, and up to the sixteenth century. These annotations and glosses show unambiguously how important these books were felt to be, and how multilingual were the users who wrote in them, perhaps unsurprisingly. It is clear that the English texts were used to read aloud from, if the additions of accents, marks for word-spacing, and different punctuation are anything to go by;[57] they were used to prepare sermons, as the marginal annotation and underlining in Corpus 303 and Faustina A. ix suggest.[58] Readers actively engaged in expanding upon the texts, like the scribe in CUL Ii. 1. 33, who wrote additional material in the margins, much of it related to the English text on that folio, but some of it not clearly so.[59] And many users of the manuscripts wrote material that bore no relationship to the book *per se*, recording their names (frustratingly difficult to trace), or writing snippets of poetry, or practising their penmanship.[60] For some of the books,

[56] This figure is derived by counting every example of twelfth-century, post-production use listed in Ker's *Catalogue*. On glossing in French, Latin and English, see Tony Hunt's remarkable and immeasurably important three-volume work, *Teaching and Learning Latin in Thirteenth-Century England* (Woodbridge: Boydell and Brewer, 1991). Also see Sarah Larratt Keefer and Rolf Bremmer (ed.), *Signs on the Edge: Space, Text and Margin in Medieval Manuscripts* (Paris: Leuven, 2007).

[57] On this phenomenon, see the activities of the Tremulous Hand, as described by David Johnson in his forthcoming work on that reader's punctuation. See also Chapter 6.

[58] Treharne, 'Reading from the Margins', and 'Making their Presence Felt'.

[59] Traxel, *Language Change*; and the description in the *Production and Use of English* database [http://www.le.ac.uk/english/em1060to1220/mss/EM.CUL.Ii.1.33.htm]

[60] In the *Production and Use of English* database, see, among others, Corpus 302, Faustina A. ix, Corpus 383, CUL Ii. 1. 33, and Trinity B. 14. 52.

such as Cotton Vespasian D. xiv with the prayer at folio 4 written by an *ancilla*, the book seems to have moved from its point of origin and become the property of a female reader; the same is true of the Lawbook, Corpus 383, where the thirteenth-century note by *Matildis bery soror magistri Roberti bery de Abbond'* ('Matilda Bery, sister of Master Robert Bery of Abingdon') at folio 24r suggests another female reader, or owner, or curious passer-by. From these brief notes and prayers, the literacy and writing skills of bibliophiles and scribblers becomes apparent, and their attitude to the membrane upon which they so apparently casually inscribe is evident. For these visible ghosts of the past, the English books had a function, and offered opportunities for interaction, education and debate. The same can be said for the greatest product of the twelfth century, the book which more than any other of the period can be said to be a true cultural expression: Cambridge, Trinity College, R. 17. 1, the Eadwine Psalter.

| 8 |

'Say "we", "us", and "ours" when you're talking'[1]

A Truth of Conquest

Cambridge, Trinity College R. 17. 1, the Eadwine or Canterbury Psalter, is a mid-twelfth-century Christ Church, Canterbury production.[2] It is a contemporary of Cambridge, Corpus Christi College, 303, and a close contemporary and stable-mate of Cotton Vespasian D. xiv. The Eadwine Psalter could not be less like these books, themselves good representatives of the average English manuscript produced from 1100 to 1200.

The work is a *psalterium triplex*, a triple Psalter, preceded by a Calendar and followed by the Canticles and Creeds. This three-text Psalter combines the *Gallicanum*, *Romanum*, and *Hebraicum* versions of the Psalms with the *Parva Glosatura*,[3] *tituli*, a sequence of exegetical

---

[1] Rudyard Kipling, 'Norman and Saxon', *A History of England*, p. 53.

[2] The best description of this volume is by Gibson, Heslop and Pfaff, *The Eadwine Psalter*. A half-sized, black and white facsimile was published in the 1930s, for which see M. R. James, *The Canterbury Psalter* (Cambridge: Cambridge University Press, 1935).

[3] The Latin commentary to the Psalms, attributed in the twelfth century to Anselm of Laon. See B. Smalley, *The Study of the Bible in the Middle Ages* (3rd edn., Oxford, 1983), p. 64; and in relation to the Eadwine Psalter specifically, see Margaret Gibson. 'The Latin Apparatus', in Gibson et al., *The Eadwine Psalter*, pp. 108–9.

prologues, Insular French and English complete interlinear glosses, and a full cycle of illustrations. At the end of the volume are two prognosticatory texts (a chiromancy and a onomancy, folio 282); the portrait of the book's designer and participant, Eadwine; followed by an extraordinary colour-wash drawing of the new waterwork system at Christ Church. The whole codex is an important witness to a flourishing multilingual, multivisual, and multimedia culture of literacies, manufactured in a collaborative venture over a period of time by at least ten monastic scribes, plus an additional number of professional miniators and illustrators. It stands in a line of Psalters dating back to the Utrecht Psalter and ending in the slightly later, unfinished Psalter, Paris, Bibliothèque Nationale, Lat. 8846, dated to the end of the twelfth century, which uses the Eadwine Psalter as a source. The latter codex provides further evidence of the interest at Christ Church, Canterbury in this type of monumental scholarly work generally, and both Psalters find their context in glossed Psalters, and other great biblical, liturgical, and scholastic volumes from the post-Conquest period.[4]

In its physical form, the Eadwine manuscript signifies a liminal space, imbricating manifold textual, linguistic and intellectual traditions and practices at a key point in English cultural history as the changes wrought by the Conquest in 1066 became firmly embedded culturally, linguistically, and politically. The volume is a masterpiece of twelfth-century *translatio studii*, commingling the three translations of the Psalms,[5] with additional sets of translations and commentary upon those translations and, as with so many manuscripts from this period, there is a great deal of work required to reveal the implications of these various textual strata and the way that the manuscript functions as a whole. A very good beginning was made in the collaborative volume published in 1992.[6]

---

[4] For the comparable scholarly, glossed volume, see M. B. Parkes, 'Ordinatio and Compilatio', in his Scribes, Scripts and Readers: Studies in the Communication, Presentation and Dissemination of Medieval Texts (London: Hambledon, 2003), pp. 35–70.

[5] The Gallicanum and Hebraicum were Jerome's translations; the Romanum was made in the fourth century and used until the ninth century in continental Europe, when it was superseded (except in Rome) by the Gallicanum, so-called because it was adopted during Charlemagne's reforms. For this, see Andrew Hughes, Medieval Manuscripts for Mass and Office: A Guide to their Organization and Terminology (Toronto: Toronto University Press, 1982), #873, pp. 224–5.

[6] Gibson et al., The Eadwine Psalter.

Widely known, and exhibited as one of the focal pieces of the recent Cambridge Illuminations,[7] lauded for its arguably incomparable opulence, its complexity, its uniqueness even at its moment of production, the Eadwine Psalter has, nevertheless, given rise to expressions of scholarly bafflement at its perceived functions, audiences, and compiler's intentions. In a modern scholarly publication, *The Utrecht Psalter in Medieval Art*, the authors described the Eadwine Psalter thus:

> The Eadwine Psalter may have been designed to contain 'the best of everything', but it seems almost 'good for nothing', at least for nothing practical. It was too large and expensive to be used in the schoolroom, inappropriate for liturgical use, and even its scholarly text was outmoded by the time it was written. Eadwine is a conservative book, a compendium of established knowledge building upon past achievements. This is as true of its decoration as it is of its text.[8]

Frankly, it is inconceivable that this codex could be described as 'good for nothing'. What might prompt such a negative sequence of conclusions? One probable reason might be the manuscript's lack of definability from a linguistic perspective ('its scholarly text was outmoded'), of function ('too large ... to be used in the schoolroom'), and of chronology ('a compendium of ... past achievements'). This book (and other manuscripts in the post-Conquest period, as has been seen) lacks an easily distinguishable label telling us unequivocally of its belonging, since its modishness, its use of English when English is so often thought to have ceased being used for writing, and its apparent indeterminacy of function render it indescribable and thus redundant. This magnificent volume is consigned to the dusty book-box in the attic of the modern scholarly agenda. In relation to its gloss, the great Kenneth Sisam

---

[7] The exhibition, The Cambridge Illuminations, was held at the Fitzwilliam Museum from July to December 2005, attracting many thousands of visitors. The two darkened exhibition rooms contained lit glass cases displaying manuscripts from Cambridge Colleges, including the Eadwine Psalter, placed in a case on the left sidewall of the first room. Even among this distinguished company, the Eadwine Psalter was breathtaking. See the catalogue emerging from the exhibition: Paul Binski and Stella Panayotova (eds.), *The Cambridge Illuminations: Ten Centuries of Book Production in the Medieval West* (London: Harvey Miller, 2005).

[8] Koert van der Horst, William Noel and Wilhelmina C. M. Würstefeld (eds.), *The Utrecht Psalter in Medieval Art* (Universiteit Utrecht: HES Publishers, 1996), p. 236.

comments that the Eadwine Psalter's English gloss 'defies historical analysis', and is 'useless for the analysis of other glosses';[9] and the most recent editor, Phillip Pulsiano, calls it 'a hodgepodge of morphological and phonological features', while fully aware of its linguistic and contextual value.[10] Neither of these scholars' comments is deliberately derogatory, given the focus of Sisam and Pulsiano's extensive work on the corpus of glossed Psalters as a whole. Still, the Eadwine Psalter seems to some to be 'retrospective', and along with the editors of the Utrecht Psalter volume, it might be possible to view as outdated not only the Psalter's illustrations, based on those of the Utrecht Psalter itself, but also every component of its make-up, from its prefatory cycle, text, two sets of vernacular glosses and, indeed, 'in its very script'.[11]

At the hands of the majority of modern scholars the Psalter becomes a memorial—and virtually literally so given its size. Within the context of this received critical reaction, Trinity R. 17. 1 is simply a record to that which has passed, an elegy to the greatness of textual histories now obsolete and functionally discarded.[12] The only validity for much of what is studied and deemed worthwhile, it seems, is contemporaneity, categorizability, and canonicity—each attribute viewed through a modern, anachronistic, and unempathetic lens.

What is redundant is not, of course, the Eadwine Psalter, but among other things, the presentist insistence on the demonstration of codicological and textual newness. And if it is newness that is sought, in every sense, the Eadwine Psalter represents an innovative enterprise, since it is the only complete Psalter of its level of complexity. In terms of human and physical resources alone, it is a stunning feat that will have taken many months, or most probably, a number of years to complete. The manuscript measures 460mm x 230mm (half a metre high); it is 120mm

[9] C. Sisam and K. Sisam (eds.), *The Salisbury Psalter edited from Salisbury Cathedral MS. 150*, EETS o.s. 242 (London, 1959), pp. 56, 58.

[10] Phillip Pulsiano, 'The Old English Gloss of the *Eadwine Psalter*', in Mary Swan and Elaine Treharne (eds.), *Rewriting Old English in the Twelfth Century*, CSASE 30 (Cambridge: Cambridge University Press, 2000), pp. 166–94, at p. 166. Each definition of 'hodgepodge' in the *Oxford English Dictionary* seems somewhat derogatory in relation to morphology (as heterogeneous, a random assemblage, etc.).

[11] Phillip Pulsiano, 'The Old English Gloss', p. 154.

[12] See George Hardin Brown, 'The Dynamics of Literacy in Anglo-Saxon England', The Toller Memorial Lecture 1994, *Bulletin of the John Rylands University Library of Manchester* 77 (1995), pp. 109–42, at p. 138.

thick; and weighs perhaps 28lb.[13] It is impossible to examine the manuscript closely sitting down, even when it is propped up on the cushions used in the Wren Library at Trinity College, Cambridge; one has to stand (and in standing, it is possible to see how top-heavy this manuscript's design is, with [now] very large bottom margins, and a great deal of visual action being in the upper half of the page). Its position within its medieval setting, one might imagine, must surely have been on a lectern, an altar, or other medium of display. Yet despite its immense and impressive dimensions, it is the case that in order to read and interpret any of the glossing hands, or to see the detail in the many illustrations, the viewer has to be no further than half-a-metre or so away.

Appreciating its functionality and its creator's intentionality involve understanding its materiality: these three core aspects of the book make up its architextuality as a holistic artifact, an Edifice of Letters. The size of the volume reflects its material cost: 285 folios in its current state,[14] each bifolium represents the skin of one calf, the spine of the animal running across the page, with immaculate repairs to the few damaged folios in the codex.[15] Most pages have professionally rendered illustrations accompanying the Psalm, and each of the three versions of the Psalms has an elaborately decorated initial introducing the text, every one of which is decorated with gold leaf, lapis lazuli, and other lustrous inks.

The Psalter's expense and its size tells us a good deal about its probable function; this is surely not, despite Margaret Gibson's careful thesis in 1988, a book for the schoolroom or for any reading environment that might involve utilizing the manuscript as a portable object.[16] Moreover, its current condition mitigates against regarding the book as a frequently handled object, for while the lower corners of folios have been made flexible and cloth-like through the turning of the pages, there are no

---

[13] And in size, it is therefore comparable to the Great Bibles of the twelfth century, discussed by Rodney M. Thomson (ed.), *The Bury Bible* (Cambridge: D. S. Brewer, 2002), p. 11 and *passim*.

[14] A number of full-page illustrations, originally prefatory to the text of the Psalms, are in the Pierpont Morgan Library in New York.

[15] Nicholas Pickwoad, 'Codicology', in Gibson et al., *The Eadwine Psalter*, pp. 4–12.

[16] Margaret Gibson, 'Who Designed the Eadwine Psalter?' in Sarah Macready and F. H. Thompson (eds.), *Art and Patronage in the English Romanesque* (London: Society of Antiquaries, 1986), pp. 71–6, at p. 75: 'The Eadwine Psalter is one monastic schoolmaster's response to this crisis [of the "secular" schools' dominance]'.

signs of use indicated by a reader or browser with access to ink and quill.[17] This can therefore only be regarded as the top of the spectrum of *de luxe* books made, as has been discussed by a number of commentators, for some or other patron, a special commission. Gibson's proposal in 1992 that this commission might have been made by Eadwine himself, or by the community of monks at Christ Church seems feasible; Prior Wibert of Christ Church seems an obvious candidate to have ordered the construction of the book, and he, together with other possibilities, such as Thomas Becket, are examined in the Eadwine Psalter collection.[18] The Psalter's function might therefore be perceived to be a cultural and perhaps political statement about the wealth of the community and the resources at its disposal, both in terms of its ecclesiastical and monastic eliteness and its intellectual superiority. In this, the Psalter is part of the twelfth-century trend in England to produce very large, very expensive *de luxe* books, such as the Dover Bible, the Winchester Bible and Psalter, and the Bury Bible. What makes the Eadwine Psalter stand out from these already outstanding marvels is its complexity and its extensive range of scholastic and linguistic material, and its inclusion of English. It is a demonstration of institutional authority and intellectual prowess. Why Christ Church would feel the need to make such a statement in the mid-twelfth century is a question worth pursuing.

If the Eadwine Psalter was indeed designed and used as a politically and culturally charged witness to Christ Church's expansive learning, expertise, and wealth, this would clearly indicate that the volume was not intended to be archival or retrospective, as critics noted above suggest. In fact the methods of production show that this was a Psalter to be used respectfully and without intervention, containing texts that should be understood to be valid and meaningful in their day, not simply as copies or adaptations revisiting archaic exemplars for the sake of a nostalgic nod to the glorious past. And odd as it may seem given the lack of interest in Psalters in contemporary scholarship now, the Psalter was then a key language-teaching tool, even for advanced students as Gretsch

---

[17] Scholastically inclined users, correctors, reference hunters, or casual perusers, witnessed so frequently in other manuscripts—even *de luxe* volumes, like the Bury Bible (Cambridge, Corpus Christi College, 2)—are not present in the Eadwine Psalter. This suggests very strongly that the manuscript was kept somewhere where private reading or any potential for an individual's intervention simply was not possible.

[18] Gibson et al., *Eadwine Psalter*.

has pointed out.[19] Metaphorically teaching 'Language' in mid-twelfth-century Canterbury involved a very visual demonstration of the dynamism of trilingualism, of the practical and theoretical interrelatedness of language: Latin, French, and English, each has its place in the context of this volume, with the Latin dominating, as it would in an ecclesiastical environment, and the two vernaculars being given—*prima facie*—equal weight. A fourth 'language' is created by the illustrations, which form another gloss to the Psalter text.

The functionality and vitality of the manuscript is apparent through its layout, its script, its languages and its comprehensive attention to detail. The whole text—the book and all its parts—is, as Tessa Webber puts it, 'highly complex' and yet completely harmonious. She comments that 'each of the texts is readily identifiable, and the degree of importance accorded each text is immediately obvious',[20] with the Latin *Gallicanum* very clearly taking precedence (and with the English glossed *Romanum* adjacent to it throughout the Psalter; the French being literally marginalized in an interesting visualization of cultural competitiveness). There is, despite what *should* be the competing demand on the eye of each text and illustration, clarity of *mise-en-page* and a unified overarching legibility that signifies each page was meant to be looked at and admired first and foremost, before being read. This is particularly so as no opening of verso and recto is the same as any other; one does not know what to expect as the pages are turned. This emphasis on seeing, the 'ocularcentricity' of the Psalter's design, unequivocally demonstrates the praxis of a multimedia multilingualism, visually striking as well as culturally significant, almost certainly reflecting the monastic politics of Canterbury, *c*.1160. The equal relationship between English and French in this volume reflects its readership, whether it was intended for contemplation and personal study or, as seems more likely, display and public contemplation; here for all to literally see there is unanimity of the three languages operating in England in this period.

---

[19] M. Gretsch, *The Intellectual Foundations of the English Benedictine Reform*, CSASE 25 (Cambridge: Cambridge University Press, 1999), pp. 13–17. Of the twenty-nine Psalters copied in England before 1100, fourteen are provided with a complete or partial interlinear English gloss. Gretsch's analysis, with its unfortunate dismissal of the non-original, later manuscripts, concerns only 'the [pre-Conquest] Old English interlinear versions (in their original form, not in their sometimes garbled and deficient later copies)' (at p. 17).

[20] Teresa Webber, 'The Script', in Gibson et al., *The Eadwine Psalter*, pp. 13–24, at p. 13.

Building the Book

The representation of languages is not the only issue that emerges from studying the Eadwine Psalter. It becomes clear that current common conceptions of 'text' require considerable reassessment in order to interpret the Psalter, particularly because it is not simply the written text (and then, which one of the versions on offer?) that constitutes the full meaning of this artefact; it is the whole book that constitutes TEXT and interpretative potential. That is to say, a complete understanding of the Eadwine Psalter insists on our reading the three-dimensional object as a whole; all component parts, from the (later) binding to the quiring, the vellum, the ink, the versions of the Psalms and the accompanying commentaries contribute to the meaning of the book. As such, no form of reproduction could bring the manuscript and its contents to life,[21] and recognizing *that* is essential to beginning the process of understanding.[22]

How, then, can the Eadwine Psalter be read as TEXT, giving balanced and due attention to the elaborate *mise-en-page* and the material attributes of the manuscript? How can we account for, and provide full testimony to, the 500-plus drawings in the manuscript that accompany the written words, themselves in multiple and multilingual form? The various editions and studies are all immensely valuable and make a major contribution to understanding parts of the manuscript,[23] but each

---

[21] And Psalters, despite their absolute canonical status liturgically and educationally, are, of course, no longer canonical from the literary or historical perspectives, so the audience will always be a select one, and the interest for most publishers in producing any kind of reproduction, is, consequently, limited. Digital reproduction, one could argue, would take us further away from interpreting the text since it is only always two-dimensional, deflated, and each folio is essentially made the same through the standardizing that is integral to digital technology.

[22] I go through some of these points in more detail in my essay, 'The Architextual Editing of Early English', in A.S.G. Edwards and T. Kato (eds.), *Poetica* 71 (2009), pp. 1–13, esp. pp. 7–9.

[23] The Eadwine Psalter exists outside the Wren Library in countless reproductions of selected folios, and especially the Eadwine Portrait; in M. R. James's black and white facsimile of 1930 (*The Canterbury Psalter*); in F. R. Harsley (ed.), *Eadwine's Canterbury Psalter*, EETS os 92 (London, 1889), where the Old English is provided with a Latin source; and Phillip Pulsiano (ed.), *Old English Glossed Psalters, Psalms 1–50* (Toronto, 2001), where the Eadwine Psalter appears lemma by lemma with all the other Old English glossed Psalters in a vertical analysis of each verse; and in dismembered form in Gibson, et al., *The Eadwine Psalter*.

represents loss in the omission or obscuring of crucial and equally-weighted evidence. In James's facsimile of the manuscript, for example, the 'bookness' of the Psalter is retained in the physical form of the fac-simile, but its size is deceptively small, and there is no colour, when the Eadwine Psalter bursts with colour on almost every opening.[24] In the scholarly editions of the English text, the black words on the white page fragment and completely dematerialize the book, as do all textual editions from manuscript. Context and the very visual nature of the book are lost.[25] Moreover, reading cues—the way the manuscript can be genu-inely accessed—are eliminated through the edition or partial publica-tion. Firstly, in those folios where illustrations occur, it is the image that predominates (see Figures 6 and 7). Secondly, the *litterae notabiliores*, which generally, but not always, follow a diminution of size from centre to margin, draw the eye to the three versions of the Psalms, the Latin *Gallicanum* commanding the centre of the page, centre stage, as it would be during the performance of the liturgy. This text, used by the Caroling-ian empire, and adopted by the English church during the latter stages of the Benedictine Reform, is glossed in Latin, and annotated by the com-mentary on either side. Pricking and ruling meticulously guide and con-tain these principal registers creating a *mise-en-page* reminiscent of the great glossed Bibles produced during this period, one of which, now lost, may have been written at Christ Church to accompany this Psalter.

From the majestic late Caroline minuscule or Protogothic script of the *Gallicanum*—a stately and imposing book hand measuring 16mm from ruled line to ruled line—we move to the other two complete ver-sions of the Latin Psalms: the adjacent *Romanum* and the marginal *Hebraicum*. Both of these are written in the same script as the *Gallica-num*, but here each has an x-height of 4mm, with interlinear space meas-uring another 4mm. The relative importance of the three sets of Psalms thus becomes clear from the halving of the space given over to the two versions that lack the currency and status of the *Gallicanum*.

In the case of the *Romanum*, it is interpreted by an English interlinear gloss, while the *Herbraicum* contains an Insular French gloss. The *Romanum* is appropriately and ideologically linked to the English that translates it, for this is the version of the Psalms that was current before

[24] James, *The Canterbury Psalter*.
[25] Harsley, *Eadwine's Canterbury Psalter*; Pulsiano, *Old English Glossed Psalters*.

FIG 6   Cambridge, Trinity College, R. 17. 1, folio 5v

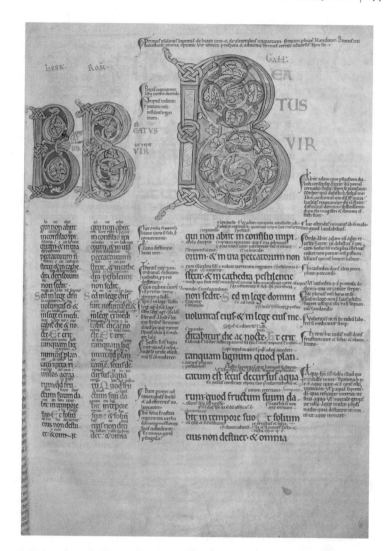

FIG 7   Cambridge, Trinity College, R. 17. 1, folio 6r

and during the Benedictine Reform and, indeed, into the eleventh century in England. It might be regarded as the version that manifests Englishness most clearly during the height of the Anglo-Saxon church. Furthermore, it seems to be specifically linked to Canterbury; the latest manuscript to contain this version as a main text is CUL Ff. 1. 23, the Cambridge or Winchcombe Psalter, copied, as now seems likely, at Canterbury.[26] Analysis of the Psalter manuscripts reveals that Canterbury continued with the use of the *Romanum* decades after Winchester, which seems to have adopted the Gallican version by the end of the tenth century.[27] And, notably, Gretsch comments that 'Ever since the days of St Augustine, the *Romanum* had been the Psalter of the English church'; and its authority as the version of the Psalms used in Rome was well known in Canterbury throughout this period.[28] The incorporation of this version of the Psalms with an English gloss in the Eadwine Psalter plainly cannot be coincidence: its political and ecclesiastical significance is obvious as it performs the role of cultural mediator between the Anglo-Saxon church and its post-Conquest successor, enforcing an essential encounter with collective memories pertaining to the long-standing community at the English primacy.

For its part, the *Hebraicum*—closest to the margins in this tripartite layout—glossed by Insular French, was never used liturgically, and functioned only as a text for scholarly purposes both on the Continent and, more rarely, in England.[29] It is worth considering the possible reasons guiding the inclusion of the French gloss for this version, if the *Hebraicum* were effectively redundant other than for the purpose of study. It suggests that the manuscript is an intellectual bridge between cultures and languages, allowing (if only in theory) intelligibility between the

---

[26] Pulsiano, *Old English Glossed Psalters*, p. xxi. Gneuss, *Handlist of Anglo-Saxon Manuscripts*, no. 4, p. 26, suggests Canterbury or Ramsey. Ker, *Catalogue*, p. 12, suggests the hand of CUL Ff. 1. 23 is similar to that in Cambridge, Trinity College, B. 15. 34 (Ker's item 86), the likeliest origin of which is Canterbury. See, most recently, Binski and Panayotova, *The Cambridge Illuminations*, no. 17, pp. 70–2.

[27] Pulsiano, *Old English Glossed Psalters*.

[28] Gretsch, *Intellectual Foundations*, pp. 289–90. Gretsch links the use of the *Romanum* specifically to Æthelwold, but that makes little sense if Winchester quickly adopted the *Gallicanum*. Might one not think of the *Romanum* being allied instead to Dunstan, especially given his apparent conservatism (Gretsch comments at pp. 284–5 that CUL Ff. 1. 23 is itself 'in a cultural backwater') and his love of Canterbury?

[29] Dominique Markey, 'The Anglo-Norman Version', in Gibson et al., *The Eadwine Psalter*, pp. 139–56.

members of the large and thriving monastic community at Christ Church. Certainly, as Cecily Clark brilliantly documents, there were issues of mutual understanding between the English and the French monks, both representing traditions that seemed to flourish at Christ Church in the twelfth century, but rarely overlap or explicitly work in harmony, apart from in the Eadwine Psalter.[30] It may thus be that Eadwine, the chief designer and a scribe of the volume named after him, was the principal architect of this project intended to bring the community together, to showcase its considerable material resource and intellectual talents. It is little wonder that he was subsequently memorialized in the framed image of him, still one of the best-known icons of a scribe from the medieval period.[31]

Eadwine designed the layout of the entire Psalter, both for the folios containing the Psalms and for those folios upon which the Canticles are copied, which are two-columned in format and incorporate both an Insular French and an English gloss, the former upon the latter, in the interlinear space. As designer, Eadwine was responsible not simply for the *mise-en-page* of the Psalter, but also for the choice and relative size of scripts. For the Latin texts and the Latin glosses, a formal Protogothic book hand of varying size is used. For the Insular French gloss, it is written in more informal hands, but is still recognizably a Caroline minuscule script. For the English, even at this late date, the national vernacular script, English Vernacular Minuscule, predominates throughout, though not always uniformly.[32] Visually, then, the script of the English gloss differentiates it from all surrounding texts and hands. To utilize as many insular forms as appear must be considered a deliberate policy, since at this date, as is well known, distinctions between Insular minuscule and late Caroline minuscule were blurring quite significantly into a hybrid English Vernacular Minuscule, in precisely the same way that the late West Saxon *Schriftsprache* was beginning to illustrate more dialectal

---

[30] Cecily Clark, 'People and Languages in Post-Conquest Canterbury'.

[31] The image might be as late as 1170, according to George Zarnecki, 'The Eadwine Portrait' in Sumner McKnight Crosby, et al., *Études d'art médiéval offertes à Louis Grodecki* (Paris: Ophrys, 1981), pp. 93–8. The image is illustrated on the front jacket of Gibson et al., *The Eadwine Psalter.* He is probably Webber's scribe L1 (p. 14). The following information on scribes is based on my own first-hand study with the manuscript, working with Webber's chapter in Gibson, et al., *The Eadwine Psalter,* pp. 13–24.

[32] As is often the case—but to varying extents—with other manuscripts, like Vespasian D. xiv, and Hatton 116.

features of the scribes who wrote and copied English texts. The different script systems had been put in place during the late tenth century to distinguish the vernacular text from Latin, creating effectively a national script intimately allied to language. Here in the Eadwine Psalter, although not always consistently, the Insular minuscule forms of *f, g, h, r, s* are evinced in the hands of scribes L1 and OE scribes 1–5.[33] Unlike other contemporary manuscripts such as CCCC 303, therefore, which has a predominance of Caroline forms in the writing of its two main scribes, here, all the major scribes write a predominantly insular script (though Caroline forms certainly creep in) reinforcing the impact of English from a visual, as well as linguistic, perspective with its multitude of ascenders and descenders.[34]

Currents of culture

The way in which the Eadwine Psalter has sometimes been described as archaic, 'backward-looking', or obsolete even while it was being produced extends as much to the English vernacular gloss, as it does to any other aspect of the book. The contemporaneity and currency of the volume's texts are very much called into question. Thus, George Hardin Brown comments that the Psalter is 'not so much a text as an encyclopedia';[35] and, according to Patrick O'Neill's detailed analysis, the English gloss is 'a linguistic curiosity', comprised of 'archaic language'.[36] George Hardin Brown further comments:

> the psalter represents a monument of psalmic learning to its creator, the prominently pictured monk, Eadwine. The psalter also exemplifies the end of one civilization, the Anglo-Saxon, and the cultural emergence of the new, Insular French. In this sumptuous volume, the very shabby state of Old English glosses and the evidence in them of

[33] I am using Webber's classification of scribes throughout.

[34] And here I disagree with Patrick O'Neill's evaluation of the Insular French as dominating the vernacular aspect of the folios. See Patrick O'Neill, 'The English Version', in Gibson et al., *The Eadwine Psalter*, pp. 123–38 at p. 137, especially as the French is most marginalized (literally) and the English is placed closer to the *Gallicanum* central text.

[35] George Hardin Brown, 'The Dynamics of Literacy in Anglo-Saxon England', p. 137. How is an 'encyclopaedia' not a 'text'?

[36] Patrick O'Neill, 'The English Version', in Gibson et al., *The Eadwine Psalter*, p. 135.

> the weakening of the Old English inflectional system proclaims the
> end of the age and the development of early Middle English.[37]

One of the main problems here is the use of labels to describe the language: 'shabby', 'archaic', and so forth. This kind of terminology has been applied in many contexts to virtually all manuscripts copied from *c*.1100 to 1200; these include books that contain texts demonstrably associated with pre-existing exemplars, but also those like the *Peterborough Chronicle Continuations* that are extemporized, and, one must assume, comprised of live, contemporary forms of written English. Quite why our superimposed scholarly notions of periodicity have led to such omnipresent criticism of twelfth-century English is particularly curious, given that twelfth-century English has never been accorded a proper trial: it has never been the subject of a full study.[38] Perhaps the lack of a full linguistic analysis makes the dismissal of the evidence essential, for what the evidence suggests is significant instability, making categorization and declension-setting problematic. However, variation is never boundless, for that would make legibility and intelligibility impossible: the variant form is, then, discernible.[39]

Webber identifies five, or possibly six, scribes writing English in this manuscript, and a similar number seem to have provided the Anglo-Norman gloss.[40] Webber's scribe, L[atin]1, as has been noted, is probably Eadwine himself, and he copies folio 6r demonstrating how he wishes to see the manuscript effected—setting the model that is to be followed. Although Webber does not identify him as the scribe of the English gloss on folio 6r, she raises the possibility. Close analysis does indeed support this identification: Psalm 1 at 6r seems to have been copied by Eadwine himself. At the English gloss on folio 6r, apart from another, and somewhat scratchy, hand introducing the psalm with the words 'æði/se were' above the square capitals of *Beatus Vir* (see Figure 7), the gloss seems to give very little to go on, particularly as some of the letter forms are so distinct (Caroline in the Latin, Insular in the English). What evidence can be gleaned, however, does strongly suggest that this is the same

---

[37] Ibid., p. 138.
[38] Scholars, such as Susan Irvine in her edition of *MS E* of the *Anglo-Saxon Chronicle*, give excellent accounts of the forms of their respective texts, and it is from these authoritative introductions that such a full study of post-Conquest English might begin.
[39] The same seems to be true for the Anglo-Norman gloss to the *Hebraicum*.
[40] Webber, 'Script', pp. 17–21.

scribe that wrote the *Gallicanum* and *Hebraicum* on folio 6; namely, Eadwine. This evidence is slight but compelling: it includes the form of the *punctus elevatus*; the one example of the hyphen, which is flattish to the line with a slight flick up; the form of the *c* where the upper stroke is shorter than the lower, so the graph is slightly tilted; the *st* ligature where the crossbar of *t* does not touch the upstroke of the *s*; the feet of the minims also curve up to the right very slightly, again like L1, but not like the *Romanum* hand, where the feet are *praecissa*. Moreover, L1 (Eadwine) writes within the first few illustrations (such as that at folio 6v) and here the wavy-headed Tironian *nota* is identical to the *nota* of the scribe writing the English for Psalm 1. The reason why this matters concerns, again, the role of English in its multilingual context in Christ Church, Canterbury, in the early second half of the twelfth century: for here is an identified scribe and manuscript compiler, and a senior one at that, competent at writing in all three languages *current* at that time, offering institutional validation to both French and English, and thus authorizing the status of both simultaneously and in precisely the same format.

What matters more, perhaps, is this element of cultural currency, for in the relegation of these glosses in English to the category of 'corrupt' and 'archaic', a redundancy is created for the Eadwine Psalter that simply cannot be supported by the size, effort and expense of the volume. I want to look again, briefly, at the interlinear glosses and the method behind their inclusion because they prove more than any other individual component of this manuscript that this book represents a purposeful endeavour with a vitality and utility that have not always been appreciated, though its aesthetic appeal is unquestioned. Indeed, in terms of vitality, the English in this codex may well be the most sustained example of a formal, but contemporary, language in the period of the manuscript's compilation.

The care taken over the presentation of the whole text is immediately obvious: that is, it is expertly written by trained scribes in appropriate grades of script showing an awareness of up-to-date calligraphic trends in the mid-twelfth century and later. Significant care was taken over the main Psalter texts' production, and the glosses, commentary, and paratextual material are meticulously arranged. This is all in a tradition of Psalter copying at Christ Church that suggests an appreciation for this most work-a-day, yet potentially magnificent of liturgical books. The Utrecht Psalter formed the inspiration for the Eadwine Psalter's illustrations,[41] and other exemplars were used for most of the written texts, but the end result is unique, and the English vernacular gloss is unlike any other of the numerous English glosses to Latin Psalters. It contains numerous errors, which might suggest carelessness, but given the scope of the work, error is hardly surprising. Care was taken to ensure a useful and accurate text; heavy corrections to the Old English glosses first entered above the *Romanum* text are made that demonstrate the engagement of the scribes in their work. The level of corrections at many points is very frequent indeed and represents a comprehensive programme of emendation to ensure a 'better' text, such as it was deemed to be. This, then, is not the work of the archivist, or indeed a compiler and his scribes who did not understand the relevance of the text upon which they were working or did not consider these texts to have some immediacy. Indeed, it would be of great interest to analyse the corrections alone to determine what was deemed worth correcting. There are numerous emendations to Psalm 9, for example, in both the French and English versions. In the English, there is such a concerted effort to ensure intelligibility that the corrector gives three alternatives for Latin *refugium*: namely, 'scyld uel rotsung uel frofer'; for *sperent* there is 'wenen uel hyhten'; for *nouerunt* there is 'cuðen uel cniewen'. In this first example, where a triple synonym for *refugium* is provided, the Regius Psalter has only 'rotsung uel frofr' as glosses.[42] The scribe in Eadwine clearly feels compelled to add 'scyld' ('shield'); moreover, in the very same verse, the Eadwine scribe writes 'on gehyþelicnessum uel on gerecum 7 on eærfoðnesse uel swince' where the Regius scribe simply writes 'on gerecum on geswince' for *in oportunitatibus in tribulatione*. This doubling-up of lemmata suggests one or both of two things: either the scribe is immensely assiduous in his work, or he is not sure which form readers might consider more current, so he gives two, or sometimes three alternatives for maximum comprehension.

This corrector is the English Scribe 4 (OE4). One would know this without looking at the folio, because of a distinctive characteristic of his work—the <e> + <æ> combination, where Late West Saxon would have <e> + <a>. This scribe not only corrects the work of other scribes (and is

---

[41] T. A. Heslop, 'Decoration and Illustration', Gibson et al., *The Eadwine Psalter*, pp. 25–61, at p. 25.

[42] *DOE Old English Corpus*, s. v. 'rotsung'.

almost certainly, in fact, the same scribe labelled by Webber as OE1[43]),
but also writes a good portion of the Canticles (Canticles 8, 9 [folios
267v–77v]; Canticles 9.49–50 [folios 278ra/1–5]; Canticles 11, 12–15.24
[folios 278ra/8—280r]; Canticle 15.26–38 [280va/5–280vb/19]), which is
where, if Patrick O'Neill is right,[44] there is a goldmine of contemporary
English language data to be discovered. The Canticles do illustrate an
English that is unlike the Late West Saxon of the pre-Conquest period,
but which is similar to forms of the vernacular found in contemporary
manuscripts, like Corpus 303, Vespasian D. xiv, and the later Trinity B.
14. 52. In these manuscripts, the old and the new rub along together in an
unselfconscious fashion that lays to rest notions of Late West Saxon and
'Early Middle English' as distinct linguistic phenomena. In the Psalter,
the English gloss of verse 19 of the *Canticum Moysi*, for example, reads:

> Forðæn ingeð emlicnesse phæræonis mid feðerfealdum stigendum
> on sie 7 ongeledde ofer hie drihten weter sewe beærn eællengæ
> isræhele eodon þurh drige þurh midde sie.
>
> *Quia introivit equitatus pharaonis cum quadrigis et ascensoribus in*
> *mare et induxit super eos dominus aquas maris filii autem israhel*
> *ambulaverunt per siccum per medium mare.*
>
> (For Pharaoh went in on horseback with his chariots and horsemen
> into the sea: and the Lord brought back upon them the waters of the
> sea: but the children of Israel walked on dry ground in the midst
> thereof.)

O'Neill comments in relation to Psalm 151, which he believes to be an *ex
ingenio* piece of writing, that it is 'consistently Middle English'.[45] The same
could be said of this extract from the *Canticum Moysi*, except to call this
English 'Middle' would suggest it bears little resemblance to the 'Old'. In fact,
these forms of language—the older forms, and the newer ('more middle')
forms—work together in orthographic, phonological and morphological
variation, constrained by flexible boundaries, with the greatest instability
witnessed in the vowels and diphthongs and in the levelling of inflections.

These same characteristics of a language-in-change can be seen in the
opening lines of the non-canonical Psalm 151. This is a contemporary

[43] Webber, 'Script', in p. 19.
[44] Private correspondence, August 2005. See O'Neill, 'The English Version'.
[45] O'Neill, 'The English Version', p. 130.

translation interlineated at folio 281rv. Here the English is accompanied by the French and the Latin:[46]

Ic wes lest	**ic wes sceapheorda mines feader.**
Ieo ere petringneth	ieo peisseie les oveiles min pere
PUSILLUS ERAM	*mei; pascebam oues patris mei.*
Imo[n]g mine broððran 7 alra	**Heo[n]dan mine warhten organan.**
entre mes freres . e	Mes meins firent le orgne.
inter fratres meos.' & ad	*Manus meę fecerunt organum.'*
gugest in mines feader huse	**7 fingras mine gearcaden psalterium.**
plus 'iufres' en la meisun mun pere.	e mi dei a fait erent le saltier.
olescentior in domo patris	*& digiti mei aptauerunt psalterium.*[47]

Features absolutely common to many writings in English in the twelfth century are shown here, and are akin to the work of the English Scribe 4, writing the Canticle above, though this is the English Scribe 2 here (OE2). Again, there is the kaleidoscoping of <a>, <ea>, <e> and <æ> in *feader/fæder* or *wes/wæs*; the replacement of <o> by <a> in the past tense of 'weorcan'; the loss of the medial *n* in words like *heondan* and *imong*, where the macron indicating abbreviation of a nasal has been omitted in the copying process; and, morphologically, the levelling of inflections. Moreover, the use of 'psalterium' here seems to be unique in English, replacing the 'hearpe' of the Anglo-Saxon with the French loanword, 'psalterium'. This is the earliest such occurrence in English, the next recorded case being in Layamon's *Brut* a century later.[48]

This display of contemporary and highly innovative linguistic forms seems less a matter of chance or influence from a particular exemplar, and more attributable to careful and thoughtful scribal intervention in the text, with the key aim of maximizing relevance and intelligibility to a

---

[46] Ibid., pp. 130–1.

[47] 'I was the least among my brothers and a youth in my father's house. I was the shepherd for my father. My hands made an organ and my fingers fashioned a psaltery.'

[48] *Middle English Dictionary*, s.v. 'salteriun'. This occurs in London, British Library, Cotton Caligula A. ix. This first occurrence of a word is by no means confined to a single example; in Psalm 2, verse 9: reges 'rule' is glossed by 'stieren' (where earlier Psalters have 'reces', 'gewissast'). The earliest attested use of 'stiran' ('to rule') in the *MED* is the *Life of St Katherine* from Royal 17. A. 27, *c.* 1225. O'Neill, 'The English Version', p. 130, mentions other loanwords in the English text and notes Anglo-Norman influences on spelling.

contemporary audience. If this were merely for presentation purposes, or simply an exercise in preserving the past, such an effort on the part of the team of scribes—both English and Anglo-Norman—would be inexplicable.[49] There are thousands of examples of what might be regarded as 'updated' features, in addition to the 2,343 independent glosses in the volume, themselves indicating a major contribution to our understanding of the development of English.[50]

Planning the future

Eadwine's portrait at the back of the Psalter (at folio 283v) acts as a personal memorial and as a signature authorizing the validity of the monumental work he oversaw and to which he contributed.[51] The illustration of the buildings and waterworks at Christ Church that follow present a plan *on* a 'planus' (flat surface) of one of the most impressive cathedrals in Europe in the post-Conquest period, but they also leave the reader with a 'plantus', a 'footprint' of how the cathedral and its community of monks worked and lived in *c*.1160–1170, a century after the shock of the Norman Conquest and the trauma that that process brought in its wake. As an art historical object, the Eadwine Psalter has been the focus of much deserved laudation; but as a linguistic tool box for English and Insular French in the mid-twelfth century, it has never received the attention it so obviously demands. This book represents the bringing together of potentially clashing cultures, in a collaborative process fittingly celebrating *opus Dei* and simultaneously promoting the textual histories and traditions fundamental to the English church at its most senior institution. It is an outstanding testament to the truth of a cloistered multilingualism that has yet to be examined in full, but more, it is a

---

[49] The same impetus, though at a reduced level of intervention, is true for the Insular French gloss to the *Hebraicum*, which is not complete, omitting Psalms 125–30 and 149–50. Rather like the English gloss, this other vernacular gloss has been subject to a similar evaluation, demonstrating what Markey has described as 'archaizing forms coexist[ing] with more modern spelling'. See Markey, 'The Anglo-Norman Version', pp. 142–3.

[50] These include poetic vocabulary and words commonly associated with later English, such as *hænde* for *innocentes* at Psalm 25.6. See Pulsiano, *Old English Glossed Psalters*, p. 324.

[51] In the same way as author portraits functioned throughout the late classical and medieval periods.

prime example of the inadequacy of modern definitions of text; of modern understandings of textual culture in the medieval period; and it illustrates perfectly how complex issues of cultural acceptance and mutual respect might be.

Michael Clanchy commented some decades ago that: 'The future of English as a written language was assured not by scribes like the Canterbury monks who attempted to perpetuate Anglo-Saxon, but by less conservative writers who gradually promoted various forms of spoken English to the rank of a literary language.'[52] This is not true. The future of English and the record of voices of *the* English in the twelfth century (as in the eleventh) was in the hands of the literate English elite, those precisely like the Canterbury monks, who preserved linguistic and cultural snapshots of their society and continued the commitment to written language. Through them, through their imagined and real audiences, it is possible to hear the voice of the silenced English. Politics, law, medicine, education, Christian teaching, friendship pacts, and dire warnings were transmitted to multiple audiences—texts that sought to heal cultural trauma, and to ameliorate, perhaps, the loss of status, land, and power. Those to whom sermons were preached, from whom confessions were taken, and who learned from the religious writers of the day through their native tongue took English forward to the more explicitly resistant future. English was, beyond doubt, from the late ninth century onwards, the language of a nation's ideology, its songs, and its history, and in works like Ælfric's homilies, Wulfstan's sermons, and Eadwine's Psalter, English was a language of salvation—at least for those hundreds of thousands who could understand it.

[52] Clanchy, *From Memory to Written Record*, p. 212.

BIBLIOGRAPHY

Where more than one title is listed beneath a single author, the titles are listed alphabetically.

Primary Sources

Arngart, Olaf (ed.), *The Proverbs of Alfred*, 2 vols. (Lund: University of Lund, 1942–55)

Assmann, Bruno (ed.), *Angelsächsischen Homilien und Heiligenleben*, Bibliotek der angelsächsischen Prosa, 13 (Kassel: Wigand, 1889; repr. 1964)

Baker, Peter (ed.), *The Anglo-Saxon Chronicle, A Collaborative Edition MS F* (Cambridge: D.S. Brewer, 2000)

Barker, Nicholas (ed.), *The York Gospels: A facsimile with introductory essays by Jonathan Alexander, Patrick McGurk, Simon Keynes, and Bernard Barr* (London: Roxburghe Club, 1986)

Barlow, Frank (ed.), *Vita Ædwardi Regis*, Oxford Medieval Texts (Oxford: Clarendon Press, 1992)

Bately, Janet (ed.), *The Anglo-Saxon Chronicle, A Collaborative Edition, MS A* (Cambridge: D. S. Brewer, 1986)

Bates, David (ed.), *Regesta Regum Anglo-Normannorum, The Acta of William I, 1066 to 1087* (Oxford: Oxford University Press, 1998)

Belfour, A. O. (ed.), *Twelfth-Century Homilies in MS. Bodley 343*, EETS o.s. 118 (London: Oxford University Press 1909)

Bell, Alexander (ed.), Geffrei Gaimar, *L'Estoire des Engleis* (Oxford: Blackwell, for the Anglo-Norman Text Society, 1960)

Bethurum, Dorothy (ed.), *The Homilies of Wulfstan* (Oxford: Clarendon Press, 1957)

Bishop, T. A. M., and P. Chaplais (eds.), *Facsimiles of English Royal Writs to A.D. 1100 presented to Vivian Hunter Galbraith* (Oxford: Clarendon Press, 1957)

Campbell, Alistair (ed.), *Encomium Emmae Reginae* (Cambridge: Cambridge University Press, 1998)

Clayton, Mary and Hugh Magennis (eds.), *The Old English Lives of St Margaret*, Cambridge Studies in Anglo-Saxon England 9 (Cambridge: Cambridge University Press, 1994)

Clemoes, P. (ed.), *Ælfric's Catholic Homilies: The First Series: Text*, EETS s. s. 17 (London: Oxford University Press, 1997)

Constable, Giles, and B. Smith (eds.), *Libellus de diversis ordinibus et professionibus qui sunt in aecclesia*, Oxford Medieval Texts (Oxford: Clarendon Press, 1972)

Cox, R. S. (ed.), 'The Old English *Dicts of Cato*', *Anglia* 90 (1972), pp. 1–42

Cross, J. E., and T. D. Hill (eds.), *The Prose 'Solomon and Saturn' and 'Adrian and Ritheus'*, McMaster Old English Studies and Texts 1 (Toronto: Toronto University Press, 1982)

Cubbin, G. P. (ed.), *The Anglo-Saxon Chronicle: A Collaborative Edition*, 6: *MS. D* (Cambridge: D. S. Brewer, 1996)

Darlington, R. R., P. McGurk (eds.), Jennifer Bray and P. McGurk (trans.), *The Chronicle of John of Worcester,* vol. ii: *The Annals from 450 to 1066*, Oxford Medieval Texts (Oxford: Clarendon Press, 1995)

Davis, R. H. C., and Marjorie Chibnall (eds. and trans.), *William of Poitiers, Gesta Guillelmi*, Oxford Medieval Texts (Oxford: Clarendon Press, 1998)

Douglas, David C., and George W. Greenaway (eds.), *English Historical Documents 1042–1189* (London: Eyre and Spottiswoode, 1953; repr. 1981)

Dumville, David (ed.), *The Anglo-Saxon Chronicle, A Collaborative Edition, I: MS F, Facsimile Edition* (Cambridge: D.S. Brewer, 1995)

Dumville, D., and M. Lapidge (eds.), *The Annals of St Neots with Vita Prima Sancti Neoti, Anglo-Saxon Chronicle, A Collaborative Edition* 17 (Cambridge: D. S. Brewer, 1985)

Earle, John (ed.), *Gloucester Fragments I: Legends of St Swiðhun and Sancta Maria Ægyptiaca*, (London: Longman, 1861)

Fletcher, C. J., and Rudyard Kipling, *A History of England* (Oxford: Clarendon Press, 1911)

Foreville, R. (ed.), *Latran I, II, III et Latran IV, 1123, 1139, 1179, et 1215*, Histoires des Conciles 6 (Paris: Éditions de l'Orante, 1965)

Fowler, R. (ed.), *Wulfstan's Canons of Edgar*, EETS o.s. 226 (Oxford: Oxford University Press, 1972)

Fraipoint, I., and D. de Bruyne (eds.), *Sancti Aureli Augustini Quaestionum in Heptateuchum libri VII; De octo quaestionibus ex veteri testamento*, CCSL 33 (Turnhout: Brepols, 1958)

Godden, Malcolm (ed.), *Ælfric's Catholic Homilies: The Second Series Text*, EETS s.s. 5 (London: Oxford University Press, 1979)

Godden, Malcolm, *Ælfric's Catholic Homilies: Introduction, Commentary and Glossary*, EETS s.s. 18 (Oxford: Oxford University Press, 2000)

Greenway, Diana (ed. and trans.), *Henry, Archdeacon of Huntingdon, Historia Anglorum: The History of the English People* (Oxford: Clarendon Press, 1996)

Günzel, Beate (ed.), *Ælfwine's Prayerbook*, Henry Bradshaw Society (London: Boydell, 1993)

Harmer, Florence E. (ed.), *Anglo-Saxon Writs*, 2nd edn. (Stamford: Paul Watkins, 1989)

Heslop, T. A., 'Decoration and Illustration', Gibson et al., *The Eadwine Psalter*, pp. 25–61

Hollis, Stephanie, with Bill Barnes, Rebecca Hayward, Kathleen Loncar and Michael Wright (eds.), *Writing the Wilton Women: Goscelin's Legend of Edith and Liber Confortatorius*, Medieval Women Texts and Contexts, 9 (Turnhout: Brepols, 2004)

Holt, Robert (ed.), *The Ormulum, with the Notes and Glossary of Dr. R.M. White*, 2 vols. (Oxford: Clarendon, 1878)

Hunt, Tony, *Teaching and Learning Latin in Thirteenth-Century England*, 3 vols. (Woodbridge: Boydell and Brewer, 1991)

Irvine, Susan (ed.), *Old English Homilies from MS Bodley 343*, EETS o.s. 302 (Oxford: Oxford University Press, 1993)

Irvine, Susan (ed.), *The Anglo-Saxon Chronicle: A Collaborative Edition, 7: MS E* (Cambridge: D. S. Brewer, 2004)

James, M. R., *The Canterbury Psalter* (Cambridge: Cambridge University Press, 1935)

James, M. R., and E. S. Hartland (trans.), *Walter Map's 'De Nugis Curialium'*, Cymmrodorion Record Series 9 (London: Society of Cymmrodorion, 1923)

Johnson, Charles (ed. and trans.), *Dialogus de Scaccario: The Course of the Exchequer and Constitutio Domus Regis* (London: Thomas Nelson, 1950)

Jones, C.A. (ed. and trans.), *Ælfric's Letter to the Monks of Eynsham*, Cambridge Studies in Anglo-Saxon England 24 (Cambridge: Cambridge University Press, 1998)

Jónsson, F., and E. Jónsson (eds.), *Hauksbók* (Copenhagen: Thiele, 1892–6)

Keynes, Simon (ed.), *The Liber Vitae of the New Minster and Hyde Abbey Winchester: British Library Stow 944, together with leaves from British Library Cotton Vespasian A. viii and British Library Titus D. xxvii*, Early English Manuscripts in Facsimile 26 (Copenhagen, 1996)

Knowles, Dom David, and Christopher N. L. Brooke (eds. and trans.), *The Monastic Constitutions of Lanfranc* (Oxford: Oxford University Press, 2002)

Larratt Keefer, Sarah, and Rolf Bremmer (eds.), *Signs on the Edge: Space, Text and Margin in Medieval Manuscripts* (Paris: Leuven, 2007)

Lefèvre, Yves (ed.), *L'Elucidarium et Les Lucidaires* (Paris, 1954)

Liebermann, F. ed., *Die Gesetze der Angelsachsen*, 3 vols. (Halle: Max Niemeyer, 1903–06)

Liuzza, Roy Michael (ed.), *The Old English Version of the Gospels*, EETS, o.s. 304, 314 (London: Oxford University Press, 1994, 2000)

McGurk, P. (ed. and trans.), *The Chronicle of John of Worcester*, vol. iii:: *The Annals from 1067 to 1140 with the Gloucester Interpolations and the Continuation to 1141* (Oxford: Clarendon Press, 1998)

Mellows, W. T. (ed.), *The Peterborough Chronicle of Hugh Candidus*, Peterborough Museum Society (Glossop: Paul Bush, 1941; repr. 1997)

Millett, Bella (ed.), *Ancrene Wisse: A Corrected Edition of the Text in Cambridge, Corpus Christi College, 402, with Variants from Other Manuscripts*, EETS o.s. 325, 326 (Oxford: Oxford University Press, 2005, 2008)

Mommsen, Theodor E., and Karl F. Morrison, trans., *Imperial Lives and Letters of the Eleventh Century* (New York: Columbia University Press, 2000)

Morris, Richard (ed. and trans.), *Old English Homilies of the Twelfth Century*, EETS o.s. 53 (London: Oxford University Press, 1873)

Morris, Richard (ed. and trans.), *Old English Homilies and Homiletic Treatises*, EETS o.s. 29, 34 (London: Oxford University Press; repr. as one vol., 1998)

Mynors, R. A. B., R. M. Thomson, and M. Winterbottom (ed. and trans.), *William of Malmesbury, Gesta Regum Anglorum: The History of the English Kings*, Oxford Medieval Texts, 2 vols. (Oxford: Clarendon Press, 1998)

Napier, A. S. (ed.), *Wulfstan: Sammlung der ihm zugeschriebenen Homilien nebst Untersuchungen über ihre Echtheit*, Sammlung englischer Denkmäler in kritischen Ausgaben, 4 (Berlin: Weidmann, 1883)

O'Brien O'Keeffe, Katherine (ed.), *The Anglo-Saxon Chronicle: A Collaborative Edition 5: MS C* (Cambridge: D. S. Brewer, 2001)

Pope, John C. (ed.), *Homilies of Ælfric: A Supplementary Collection*, EETS o.s. 269, 260 (London: Oxford University Press, 1967–8)

Preest, David, trans., *William of Malmesbury: The Deeds of the Bishops of England [Gesta Pontificum Anglorum]* (Woodbridge: Boydell and Brewer, 2002)

Robertson, A. J. (ed. and trans.), *The Laws of the Kings of England from Edmund to Henry I* (Cambridge: Cambridge University Press, 1925)

Robinson, P. R., *Catalogue of Dated and Datable Manuscripts in Cambridge Libraries*, 2 vols. (Woodbridge: Boydell, 1988)

Rushworth, Rebecca (ed.), *Saints in English Kalendars Before A.D. 1100* (London: Henry Bradshaw Society, 2008)

Sawyer, Peter (ed.), *Textus Roffensis*, Early English Manuscripts in Facsimile XI, 2 vols. (Copenhagen: Rosenkilde and Bagger, 1957–62)

Scragg, D. G. (ed.), *The Vercelli Homilies and Related Texts*, EETS o.s. 300 (London: Oxford University Press, 1992)

Sisam, C., and K. Sisam (eds.), *The Salisbury Psalter edited from Salisbury Cathedral MS. 150*, EETS o.s. 242 (London: Oxford University Press, 1959)

Skeat, W. W., ed. *Ælfric's Lives of Saints*, EETS o.s. 76, 82, 94, 114 (London: Oxford University Press, 1889–1900; repr. as 2 vols., 1966)

Stevenson, W. H., 'Yorkshire Surveys and Other Eleventh-Century Documents in the York Gospels', *English Historical Review* 27 (1912), pp. 1–25

Sullens, Idele (ed.), Robert Mannyng *of Brune, The Chronicle* (Binghamton, NY: SUNY, 1996)

Swanton, Michael (ed. and trans.), *The Anglo-Saxon Chronicle* (London: Dent, 1998)

Symons, Thomas (ed.), *Regularis Concordia Anglicae Nationis Monachorum Sanctimonialiumque: The Monastic Agreement of the Monks and Nuns of the English Nation* (London: Oxford University Press, 1953)

Thomson, Rodney M. (ed.), *The Bury Bible* (Woodbridge: Boydell, 2002)

Thorpe, B. (ed.), *Ancient Laws and Institutes of England* (London: Eyre and Spottiswoode, 1840)

Thorpe, B. (ed.), *Diplomatarium Anglicum Aevi Saxonici* (London: Macmillan, 1865)

Treharne, Elaine, *Old and Middle English, c. 890–1450, An Anthology*, 3rd edn. (Oxford: Blackwell, 2009)

Treharne, Elaine (ed. and trans.), *The Old English Life of St Nicholas with the Old English Life of St Giles*, Leeds Texts and Monographs 15 (Leeds: University of Leeds Press, 1997)

Van Caenegem, R. C. (ed.), *English Lawsuits from William I to Richard I*, vol. i: *William I to Stephen (Nos 1–346)* (London: Selden Society, 1990)

Van Houts, Elisabeth M. C. (ed. and trans.), *The 'Gesta Normannorum Ducum' of William of Jumièges, Orderic Vitalis, and Robert of Torigni*, Oxford Medieval Texts, 2 vols. (Oxford: Clarendon Press, 1992, 1995)

Warner, George F., and Henry J. Ellis (ed.), *Facsimiles of Royal and Other Charters in the British Museum,* vol. i: *William I–Richard I* (London: Longmans, 1903)

Warner, R.-N. ed., *Early English Homilies from the Twelfth-Century MS. Vesp. D. XIV*, EETS o.s. 152 (London: Oxford University Press, 1917 for 1915)

Whitelock, Dorothy (ed.), *English Historical Documents* [*EHD*], vol. i: *c. 500–1042* (London: Eyre and Spottiswoode, 1955)

Whitelock, Dorothy, David C. Douglas, and Susie I. Tucker (eds.), *The Anglo-Saxon Chronicle: A Revised Translation* (London: Eyre and Spottiswoode, 1965)

Whitelock, Dorothy, M. Brett, and C. N. L. Brooke (eds.), *Councils and Synods with other Documents relating to the English Church, I: A. D. 871–1204, Part I: 871–1066* (Oxford: Clarendon Press, 1981)

Wilcox, Jonathan (ed.), *Ælfric's Prefaces*, Durham Medieval Texts 9 (Durham: Department of English, 1994)

Wilmart, Andre, 'La legende de Ste Edith en prose et vers par le moine Goscelin', *Analecta Bollandiana* 56 (1938), pp. 5–101 and 265–307

Winterbottom, M. (ed. and trans.), *William of Malmesbury, Gesta Pontificum Anglorum*, Oxford Medieval Texts, 2 vols. (Oxford: Clarendon Press, 2007)

Winterbottom M., and R. M. Thomson (eds. and trans.), *William of Malmesbury, Saints' Lives: Lives of SS. Wulfstan, Dunstan, Patrick, Benignus and Indract*, Oxford Medieval Texts (Oxford: Clarendon Press, 2002)

Online

Bodleian Library website: [*http://bodley30.bodley.ox.ac.uk:8180/luna/servlet/ view/all*]

British Library Catalogue of Illuminated Manuscripts [http://www.bl.uk/ catalogues/illuminatedmanuscripts/searchMSNo.asp]

The Electronic Sawyer [http://www.trin.cam.ac.uk/chartwww/charthome.html]

Fontes Anglo-Saxonici, *Fontes Anglo-Saxonici* [http://fontes.english.ox.ac.uk]

Antonette diPaolo Healey, with John Price Wilkin and Xin Xiang (eds.), *Dictionary of Old English Web Corpus* (Toronto: University of Toronto Press, 2011) [http://tir.doe.utoronto.ca/index.html]

S. M. Kuhn and H. Kurath (ed.), *Middle English Dictionary* [http://quod.lib. umich.edu/m/med/]

Parker on the Web [http://parkerweb.stanford.edu/parker/actions/page.do? forward=home]

Secondary Sources

Ashe, Laura, Fiction *and History in England, 1066–1200* (Cambridge: Cambridge University Press, 2007)

Bagge, Sverre, 'Warrior, King and Saint: The Medieval Histories about St Óláfr Haroldsson', *Journal of English and Germanic Philology* 109 (2010), pp. 281–321

Barlow, Frank, 'Leofric (d. 1072)', *ODNB* [http://www.oxforddnb.com.proxy.lib. fsu.edu/view/article/16471, accessed 26 July 2010]

Barlow, Frank, *The English Church, 1000–1066* (Hamden, CT: Archon, 1963)

Barlow, Frank, *The Godwins: The Rise and Fall of a Noble Dynasty* (Harlow: Longman, 2002)

Barrow, Julia, 'Wulfstan and Worcester: Bishop and Clergy in the Early Eleventh Century', in Townend, *Wulfstan Archbishop of York*, pp. 141–59

Barrow, Julia, and Nicholas Brooks (eds.), *St Wulfstan and his World* (Aldershot: Ashgate Press: 2005)

Bately, Janet, 'Manuscript Layout', in Donald G. Scragg (ed.), *Textual and Material Culture in Anglo-Saxon England: Thomas Northcote Toller and the Toller Memorial Lectures* (Cambridge: Brewer; 2003), pp. 1–21

Bates, David, *William the Conqueror* (London: Tempus, 1989)

Baxter Stephen, 'Archbishop Wulfstan and the Administration of God's Property', in Townend, *Wulfstan, Archbishop of York*, pp. 161–205

Baxter, S., C. E. Karkov, J. L. Nelson, and D. Pelteret (eds.), *Early Medieval Studies in Memory of Patrick Wormald* (Farnham: Ashgate, 2009)

Binski, Paul, and Stella Panayotova (eds.), *The Cambridge Illuminations: Ten Centuries of Book Production in the Medieval West* (London, Harvey Miller, 2005)

Bishop, T. A. M., 'Notes on Cambridge Manuscripts Part III: MSS. Connected with Exeter,' *Transactions of the Cambridge Bibliographical Society* 2/2 (1955), pp. 192–9

Bolton, Timothy, *The Empire of Cnut the Great: Conquest and the Consolidation of Power in Northern Europe in the Early Eleventh Century* (Leiden: Brill, 2009)

Brand, Paul, *The Making of the Common Law* (London: Hambledon, 1992)

Bredehoft, Thomas A., *Authors, Audiences and Old English Verse* (Toronto: University of Toronto Press, 2009)

Bredehoft, Thomas A., *Textual Histories: Readings in the Anglo-Saxon Chronicle* (Toronto: University of Toronto Press, 2001)

Brooks, Nicholas, 'English Identity from Bede to the Millennium', the Henry Loyn Memorial Lecture, *Haskins Journal* 14 (2005), pp. 33–51

Brown, George Hardin, 'The Dynamics of Literacy in Anglo-Saxon England', The Toller Memorial Lecture, *Bulletin of the John Rylands University Library of Manchester* 77 (1995), pp. 109–42

Brubaker, Leslie, *Dictionary of the Middle Ages* (New York, 1982–9)

Bruce, Alexander M., *Scyld and Scef: Expanding the Analogues* (London, 2002)

Campbell, James, 'The Late Anglo-Saxon State: A Maximum View', in *The Anglo-Saxon State* (London: Hambledon, 2000), pp. 1–30

Cannon, Christopher, *Middle English Literature: A Cultural History* (Cambridge: Polity, 2008)

Cannon, Christopher, *The Grounds of English Literature* (Oxford: Oxford University Press, 2004)

Carpenter, David, *The Struggle for Mastery of Britain, 1066–1284* (London: Penguin, 2003)

Cerquiglini, Bernard, *In Praise of the Variant: A Critical History of Philology* (Baltimore: Johns Hopkins University Press, 1999)

Chambers, R. W. (ed.), *On the Continuity of English Prose from Alfred to More and his School*, EETS o.s. 191A (London: Oxford University Press, 1932)

Clanchy, M. T., *England and its Rulers, 1066–1272*, 2nd edn. (Oxford: Blackwell, 1998)

Clanchy, M. T., *From Memory to Written Record*, 2nd edn. (Oxford, 1992)

Clanchy, Michael, 'Remembering the Past, and the Good Old Law', *History* 55 (1970), pp. 165–76

Clark, Cecily, 'People and Languages in Post-Conquest Canterbury', in Peter Jackson (ed.), *Words, Names and History: Selected Papers Cecily Clark* (Cambridge: D.S. Brewer, 1995), pp. 179–206

Collier, Wendy, 'The Tremulous Worcester Scribe and his Milieu: A Study of his Annotations' (unpub. PhD diss., 1992)

Conner, Patrick W., *Anglo-Saxon Exeter: A Tenth-Century Cultural History* (Woodbridge: Boydell and Brewer, 1993)

Conner, Patrick W., 'Exeter's Relics, Exeter's Books', in Jane Roberts and Janet Nelson (eds.), *Essays on Anglo-Saxon and Related Themes in Memory of Lynne Grundy*, King's College London Medieval Studies (London: King's College, Centre for Late Antique and Medieval Studies, 2000), pp. 117–56

Conti, Aidan, 'Preaching Scripture and Apocrypha: A Previously Unidentified Homilary in an Old English Manuscript, Oxford, Bodleian Library, MS Bodley 343' (unpub. PhD diss., University of Toronto, 2004)

Conti, Aidan, 'The Circulation of the Old English Homily in the Twelfth Century: New Evidence from Oxford, Bodleian Library, Bodley 343', in Kleist, *Precedent, Practice and Appropriation*, pp. 365–402

Conti, Aidan, 'The Old Norse Afterlife of Ralph d'Escures's *Homilia de Assumptione Mariae*', *Journal of English and Germanic Philology* 107 (2008), pp. 75–98

Corradini, Erika, 'Leofric of Exeter and his Lotharingian Connections: A Bishop's Books, c. 1050–1072' (unpub. University of Leicester, 2008)

Crouch, David, *The Normans: The History of a Dynasty* (London: Hambledon, 2002)

Cubit, Catherine, 'Virginity and Misogyny in Tenth- and Eleventh-Century England', *Gender and History* 12 (2000), pp. 1–32

Da Rold, Orietta, 'English Manuscripts 1060 to 1220 and the Making of a Resource', *Literature Compass* 3 (2006), pp. 750–66, DOI: 10.1111/j.1741-4113.2006.00344.x

Da Rold, Orietta, Mary Swan, Takako Kato, and Elaine Treharne, *The Production and Use of English Manuscripts 1060 to 1220* (http://www.le.ac.uk/ee/em1060to1220/) (University of Leicester, 2010)

Damian-Grint, Peter, *The New Historians of the Twelfth-Century Renaissance: Inventing Vernacular Authority* (Woodbridge: Boydell, 1999)

Daniell, Christopher, *From Norman Conquest to Magna Carta, England 1066–1215* (London: Routledge, 2003)

Davies, R. R., *Conquest, Coexistence, and Change: Wales 1063–1415* (Oxford: Clarendon Press, 1987)

Davies, R. R., 'The Peoples of Britain and Ireland, 1100–1400: Identities', *Transactions of the Royal Historical Society* 6th ser., 4 (1994), pp. 1–20

Davis-Secord, Jonathan, 'Rhetoric and Politics in Archbishop Wulfstan's Old English Homilies', *Anglia* 126 (2008), pp. 65–96

Dean, Ruth J., and Maureen B. M. Boulton, *Anglo-Norman Literature: A Guide to Texts and Manuscripts* (London: Anglo-Norman Text Society, 1999)

Doane, A. N., and K. Wolf (eds.), *Beatus Vir: Essays in Memory of Phillip Pulsiano* (Tempe, AZ: MRTS, 2005)

Douglas, D. C., *William the Conqueror: The Norman Impact upon England* (Berkley: University of California Press, 1964)

Drage, Elaine M., 'Bishop Leofric and the Exeter Cathedral Chapter, 1050–1072: A Reassessment of the Manuscript Evidence' (unpub. D.Phil. dissertation, University of Oxford, 1978)

Dumont, Louis, 'A Modified View of our Origins: The Christian Beginnings of Modern Individualism', in M. Carrithers, S. Collins and S. Lukes (ed.), *The Category of the Person: Anthropology, Philosophy, History* (Cambridge: Cambridge University Press, 1985), pp. 93–122

Dumville, David, *Liturgy and the Ecclesiastical History of Late Anglo-Saxon England: Four Studies*, Studies in Anglo-Saxon History 5 (Woodbridge: Boydell, 1992)

Eales, Richard and Richard Sharpe (eds.), *Canterbury and the Norman Conquest: Churches, Saints and Scholars, 1066–1109* (London: Hambledon Press, 1995)

Eyerman, Ron, 'The Past in the Present: Culture and the Transmission of Memory', *Acta Sociologica* 47. 2 (2004), pp. 159–69

Farmer, D. H., 'Ceadda (*d.* 672?)', *Oxford Dictionary of National Biography* (Oxford: Oxford University Press, 2004; online edn, Oct 2008) [*http://www.oxforddnb.com.proxy.lib.fsu.edu/view/article/4970*]

Flint, V. J., 'Honorius Augustodunensis', in Patrick J. Geary (ed.), *Authors of the Middle Ages: Historical and Religious Writers of the Latin West*, II, 5–6 (Aldershot: Ashgate, 1995), pp. 89–183

Foot, Sarah, 'The Making of *Angelcynn*: English Identity before the Norman Conquest', *Transactions of the Royal Historical Society* 6th ser., 6 (1996), pp. 25–49

Frank, Roberta, 'Late Old English *Þrymnys* "Trinity": Scribal Nod or Word Waiting to be Born', in Joan H. Hall, Nick Doane and Dick Ringler (eds.), *Old English and New: Studies in Language and Linguistics in Honour of Frederic G. Cassidy* (New York: Garland, 1992), pp. 97–110

Frantzen, Allen (ed.), *Desire for Origins: New Language, Old English, and Teaching the Tradition* (New Brunswick, NJ: Rutgers University Press, 1991)

Franzen, Christine, *The Tremulous Hand of Worcester: A Study of Old English in the Thirteenth Century* (Oxford: Clarendon Press, 1991)

Franzen, Christine (ed.), *Worcester Manuscripts*, Anglo-Saxon Manuscripts in Microfiche Facsimile 6 (Tempe, AZ: MRTS, 1998)

Freeman, E. A., *The History of the Norman Conquest of England* (Oxford: Clarendon Press, 1876)

Gameson, Richard, 'St Wulfstan, the Library of Worcester and the Spirituality of the Medieval book', in Barrow and Brooks, *St Wulfstan and his World*, pp. 59–104

Gameson, Richard, *The Manuscripts of Early Norman England (c. 1066–1130)* (Oxford: Oxford University Press for the British Academy, 1999)

Garnett, George, *Conquered England: Kingship, Succession, and Tenure, 1066–1166* (Oxford: Oxford University Press, 2007)

Gatch, Milton McC, *Preaching and Theology in Anglo-Saxon England: Ælfric and Wulfstan* (Toronto: Toronto University Press, 1977)

Gerchow, Jan, 'Prayers for King Cnut: The Liturgical Commemoration of a Conqueror', in Carola Hicks (ed.), *England in the Eleventh Century* (Stamford: Paul Watkins, 1992), pp. 219–38

Giandrea, Mary Frances, *Episcopal Culture in Late Anglo-Saxon England* (Woodbridge: Boydell, 2008)

Gibson, Margaret, 'Who Designed the Eadwine Psalter?' in Sarah Macready and F. H. Thompson (eds.), *Art and Patronage in the English Romanesque* (London: Society of Antiquaries, 1986), pp. 71–6

Gibson, Margaret T., T. A. Heslop, and Richard William Pfaff (eds.), *The Eadwine Psalter: Text, Image, and Monastic Culture in Twelfth-Century Canterbury*, Publications of the Modern Humanities Research Association, 14 (University Park: Pennsylvania State University Press, 1992)

Gillingham, John, *The English in the Twelfth Century: Imperialism, National Identity and Political Values* (Woodbridge: The Boydell Press, 2000)

Gneuss, Helmut, *Handlist of Anglo-Saxon Manuscripts: A List of Manuscripts and Manuscript Fragments Written or Owned in England up to 1100* (Tempe, AZ; MRTS, 2001)

Gobbitt, Thomas, 'The Production and Use of Cambridge, Corpus Christi College, 383 in the Late Eleventh and First Half of the Twelfth Centuries' (unpub. PhD diss., University of Leeds, 2010)

Godden, M., 'The Old English Life of St Neot and the legends of King Alfred', *Anglo-Saxon England* 39 (2011), DOI: 10.1017/S0263675110000116

Golding, Brian, *Conquest and Colonisation: The Normans in Britain, 1066–1100*, British History in Perspective (London; Macmillan, 1994)

Graham, Timothy, Raymond J. S. Grant, Peter J. Lucas, and Elaine Treharne, *Corpus Christi College, Cambridge I, Anglo-Saxon Manuscripts in Microfiche Facsimile* 11 (MRTS, Arizona, 2004)

Greenfield, Kathleen, 'Changing emphases in English vernacular homiletic literature, 960–1225', *Journal of Medieval History* 7 (1981), pp. 283–97

Greenfield, Stanley B., and Daniel G. Calder, *A New Critical History of Old English Literature* (New York: New York University Press, 1986)

Gretsch, Mechthild, *The Intellectual Foundations of the English Benedictine Reform*, CSASE 25 (Cambridge: Cambridge University Press, 1999)

Hahn, Thomas, 'Early Middle English' in Wallace (ed.) *Cambridge History of Medieval Literature*, pp. 61–91

Hall, Thomas N., 'Old Norse-Icelandic Sermons', in Beverly Mayne Kienzle (ed.), *The Sermon* (Turnhout: Brepols, 2000), pp. 661–709

Hall, Thomas N., 'Wulfstan's Latin Sermons', in Townend, *Wulfstan, Archbishop of York*, pp. 93–139

Handley, Rima, 'British Museum MS Cotton Vespasian D. xiv', *Notes and Queries* 219 (1974), pp. 243–50

Hare, Michael, 'Cnut and Lotharingia: Two Notes', *Anglo-Saxon England* 33 (2002), pp. 261–78

Harper-Bill, Christopher, *The Anglo-Norman Church* (Bangor, 1992), 20; repr. in revised form in Harper-Bill and Van Houts, *A Companion to the Anglo-Norman World*

Harper-Bill, Christopher, and Elisabeth Van Houts (eds.), *A Companion to the Anglo-Norman World* (Woodbridge: Boydell, 2003), pp. 1–18

Hatfield, J. T., W. Leopold, and A. J. F. Ziegelschmidt (eds.), *Curme volume of linguistic studies*, Language Monographs 7 (Baltimore: Waverley Press, 1930)

Haugen, Einar, *The Scandinavian Languages: An Introduction to their History* (London: Faber & Faber, 1976)

Hayward, P. A., 'Translation Narratives in Post-Conquest Hagiography and English Resistance to the Norman Conquest', *Anglo-Norman Studies* 21 (1998), pp. 67–93

Hayward, Paul, 'Gregory the Great as "Apostle of the English" in Post-Conquest Canterbury', *Journal of Ecclesiastical History* 55 (2004), pp. 19–39

Heslop, T. A., 'Decoration and Illustration', in Gibson et al., *The Eadwine Psalter*, pp. 25–61

Hill, Joyce, 'Ælfric, Authorial Identity and the Changing Text', in Scragg and Szarmach, *The Editing of Old English*, pp. 177–89

Hill, Joyce, 'Leofric of Exeter and the Practical Politics of Book Collecting', in S. Kelly and J. J. Thompson (eds.), *Imagining the Book* (Turnhout: Brepols, 2005), pp. 77–98

Horobin, Simon and Jeremy Smith, *An Introduction to Middle English* (Edinburgh: Edinburgh University Press, 2002)

Hudson, John, 'Essential Histories: The Norman Conquest', *History Magazine* 4.1 (January 2003), pp. 17–23

Hudson, John, *The Formation of the English Common Law: Law and Society in England from the Norman Conquest to Magna Carta* (London: Longman, 1996)

Hughes, Andrew, *Medieval Manuscripts for Mass and Office: A Guide to their Organization and Terminology* (Toronto: Toronto University Press, 1982)

Innes, Matthew, 'Danelaw Identities: Ethnicity, Regionalism, and Political Allegiance', in Dawn Hadley and J. D. Richards (eds.), *Cultures in Contact: Scan-*

dinavian settlement in England in the ninth and tenth centuries (Turnhout: Brepols, 2000), pp. 65–88

Johnson, David, and Winfried Rudolf, 'More Notes by Coleman', *Medium Aevum* 79 (2010), pp. 113–25

Jones, Christopher A., 'Wulfstan's Liturgical Interests', in Townend, *Wulfstan, Archbishop of York*, pp. 325–52

Jurovics, Raachel, '*Sermo Lupi* and the Moral Purpose of Rhetoric', in Paul E. Szarmach and Bernard Huppé (eds.), *The Old English Homily and its Backgrounds* (Albany, NY: SUNY, 1978), pp. 203–20

Karkov, Catherine E., *The Ruler Portraits of Anglo-Saxon England*, Anglo-Saxon Studies 3 (Woodbridge: Boydell & Brewer, 2004)

Kazanjian, David, and Marc Nichanian, 'Beween Genocide and Catastrophe', in David L. Eng and David Kazanjian (eds.), *Loss: The Politics of Mourning* (Berkeley, University of California Press, 2003), pp. 125–47

Kennedy, A. G., 'Cnut's Law Code of 1018', *Anglo-Saxon England* 11 (1983), pp. 57–81

Ker, N. R., *Catalogue of Manuscripts Containing Anglo-Saxon* (Oxford: Clarendon Press, 1957; repr. with supplement, 1991)

Ker, W. P., *English Literature Medieval* (London: Oxford University Press, 1912)

Keynes, Simon, 'Cnut's earls', in Alexander R. Rumble (ed.), *The Reign of Cnut: King of England, Denmark and Norway*, Studies in the Early History of Britain (London: Leicester University Press, 1994) pp. 43–88

Keynes, Simon, 'The Additions in Old English', in Nicholas Barker (ed.), *The York Gospels: A facsimile with introductory essays by Jonathan Alexander, Patrick McGurk, Simon Keynes, and Bernard Barr* (London, Roxburghe Club: 1986), pp. 81–99

Keynes, Simon, 'Wulfsige, bishop of Sherborne', in Katherine Barker, David A. Hinton and Alan Hunt (eds.), *St Wulfsige and Sherborne: Essays to Celebrate the Millennium of the Benedictine Abbey 998–1998* (Oxford: Oxbow, 2005), pp. 53–94

Kitson, Peter, 'Old English dialects and the Stages of Transition to Middle English', *Folia Linguistica Historica* 11 (1992 for 1990), pp. 27–87

Kleist, Aaron, 'Assembling Ælfric: Reconstructing the Rationale behind Eleventh- and Twelfth-Century Compilations', in Magennis and Swan, *Companion to Ælfric*, pp. 369–98

Kleist, Aaron J. (ed.), *The Old English Homily: Precedent, Practice and Appropriation* (Turnhout: Brepols, 2007)

Knowles, Dom David, *The Monastic Order in England 940–1216*, 2nd edn. (Oxford: Oxford University Press, 1963)

Laing, Margaret, *Catalogue of Sources for a Linguistic Atlas of Early Medieval English* (Cambridge: D. S. Brewer, 1993)

Lapidge, Michael, *The Anglo-Saxon Library* (Oxford: Oxford University Press, 2006)

Lapidge, Michael, John Blair, Simon Keynes, and Donald Scragg (eds.), *The Blackwell Encyclopaedia of Anglo-Saxon England* (Oxford: Blackwell, 1999)

Larson, L. M., *Canute the Great, 995–1035* (New York: Putnam, 1912)

Lass, Roger, *Old English: A Historical Linguistic Companion* (Cambridge: Cambridge University Press, 1994)

Lawson, M. K., *Cnut: The Danes in England in the Early Eleventh Century*, The Medieval World (London: Longman, 1993)

Le Patourel, John, *The Norman Empire* (Oxford: Clarendon, 1976)

Lees, Clare A., *Tradition and Belief: Religious Writing in Late Anglo-Saxon England*, Medieval Cultures 19 (Minneapolis: University of Minnesota Press, 1999)

Lees, Clare, 'Whose Text is it Anyway? Contexts for Editing Old English Prose', in Scragg and Szarmach, *The Editing of Old English*, pp. 97–114

Lerer, S., 'The Afterlife of Old English', in Wallace, *Cambridge History of Medieval Literature*, pp. 7–34

Lifshitz, Felice, 'Beyond Positivism and Genre: "Hagiographical Texts" as Historical Narrative', *Viator* 25 (1994), pp. 95–113

Lionarons, Joyce Tally, *The Homiletic Writings of Archbishop Wulfstan* (Woodbridge: Boydell and Brewer, 2010)

Liuzza, Roy M., 'Scribal Habit: The Evidence of Old English Gospels', in Swan and Treharne, *Rewriting Old English*, pp. 143–65

Loyn, Henry, '*De Iure Domini Regis*: A Comment on Royal Authority in Eleventh-century England', in Carola Hicks (ed.), *England in the Eleventh Century* (Stamford: Paul Watkins, 1992), pp. 17–24

Machan, Tim William, *English in the Middle Ages* (Oxford: Oxford University Press, 2003)

Mack, Katherin, 'Changing Thegns: Cnut's Conquest and the English Aristocracy', *Albion* 16, 4 (1984), pp. 375–87

Maddicott, J. R., 'Edward the Confessor's Return to England in 1041', *English Historical Review* 119:482 (2004), pp. 650–66

Magennis, Hugh, and Mary Swan (eds.), *A Companion to Ælfric* (Leiden: Brill, 2010)

Magennis Hugh, and J. Wilcox (eds.), *The Power of Words: Anglo-Saxon Studies Presented to Donald G. Scragg on His Seventieth Birthday* (Morgantown: West Virginia University Press:, 2006)

Markey, Dominique, 'The Anglo-Norman Version', in Gibson et al., *The Eadwine Psalter*, pp. 139–56

Mason, Emma, *St Wulfstan* (Oxford: Blackwell, 1990)

Mason, Emma, 'Wulfstan [St Wulfstan] (c. 1008–1095)', *ODNB* [http://www .oxforddnb.com.proxy.lib.fsu.edu/view/article/30099, accessed 26 July 2010]

McLaughlin, Megan, *Consorting with Saints: Prayer for the Dead in Medieval France* (Ithaca, NY: Cornell University Press, 1994)

Meaney, Audrey L., ' "And we forbeodað eornostlice ælcne hæðenscipe": Wulf-stan and Late Anglo-Saxon and Norse "Heathenism" ', in Townend, *Wulfstan, Archbishop of York*, pp. 460–500

Meyvaert, Paul, ' "Rainaldus est malus scriptor Francigenus"—Voicing National Antipathy in the Middle Ages', *Speculum* 66 (1991), pp. 743–63

Morgan, Nigel, and Rodney M. Thomson (eds.), *The Cambridge History of the Book in Britain: 1100–1400* (Cambridge: Cambridge University Press, 2010)

Nichanian, Marc, 'Catastrophic Mourning', in David L. Eng and David Kazan-jian (eds.), *Loss: The Politics of Mourning* (Berkeley, University of California Press, 2003), pp. 99–124

Oakley, Anne M., 'The Cathedral Priory of St Andrew, Rochester', *Archaeologia Cantiana* 91 (1975), pp. 47–60

Orchard, Andy, *A Critical Companion to Beowulf* (Cambridge: D. S. Brewer, 2003)

Orchard, Andy, 'Parallel Lives', in Barrow and Brooks, *St Wulfstan and his World*, pp. 39–57

Orchard, Andy, 'Re-editing Wulfstan: Where's the Point?' in Townend, *Wulf-stan: Archbishop of York*, pp. 63–91

Orchard, Andy, 'Wulfstan as Reader, Writer, and Rewriter', in Kleist (ed.), *The Old English Homily*, pp. 311–41

Orme, Nicholas, *The Saints of Cornwall* (Oxford: Oxford University Press, 2000)

Owen-Crocker, Gale, 'Pomp, piety, and keeping the woman in her place: the dress of Cnut and Ælfgifu-Emma', *Medieval Clothing and Textiles* 1 (2005), pp. 41–52

Owen-Crocker, Gale (ed.), *Working with Anglo-Saxon Manuscripts* (Exeter: Exeter University Press, 2009)

Parkes, M. B., 'Ordinatio and Compilatio', in his *Scribes, Scripts and Readers: Studies in the Communication, Presentation and Dissemination of Medieval Texts* (London: Hambledon, 2003), pp. 35–70

Parry, Benita, 'Resistance Theory/theorising resistance, or two cheers for nativ-ism', in *Colonial discourse/postcolonial theory*, ed. Francis Barker, Peter Hulme and Margaret Iversen (Manchester: Manchester University Press, 1996), pp. 172–96

Pelteret, David A. E., *Catalogue of English Post-Conquest Vernacular Documents* (Woodbridge: Boydell, 1990)

Pickwoad, Nicholas, 'Codicology', in Gibson et al., *The Eadwine Psalter*, pp. 4–12

Pollock, Frederick, and Frederic William Maitland, *The History of English Law before the time of Edward I*, 2nd edn, with a new introduction and bibliography by S. F. C. Milsom, 2 vols. (Cambridge: Cambridge University Press, 1968; first publ. 1895)

Poole, Russell, 'Skaldic Verse and Anglo-Saxon History: Some Aspects of the Period 1009–1016', *Speculum* 62 (1987), pp. 265–98

Prestwich, J. O., 'Military intelligence under the Norman and Angevin kings', in George Garnett and John Hudson (eds.), *Law and Government in Medieval England and Normandy* (Cambridge: Cambridge University Press, 1994), pp. 1–30

Pulsiano, Phillip (ed.), *Old English Glossed Psalters, Psalms 1–50* (Toronto: Toronto University Press, 2001)

Pulsiano, Phillip, 'The Old English gloss of the *Eadwine Psalter*', in Swan and Treharne, *Rewriting Old English*, pp. 166–94

Pulsiano, Phillip, and E. M. Treharne (eds.), *Anglo-Saxon Manuscripts and Their Heritage* (Aldershot: Ashgate, 1998)

Pulsiano, Phillip, and Elaine Treharne (eds.), *The Blackwell Companion to Anglo-Saxon Literature* (Oxford: Blackwell, 2001)

Rankin, Susan, 'From Memory to Record: Musical Notations in Manuscripts from Exeter', *Anglo-Saxon England* 13 (1984), pp. 97–112

Richards, Mary P., 'On the Date and Provenance of MS Cotton Vespasian D. xiv, ff. 4–169', *Manuscripta* 17 (1973), 31–5

Richards, Mary P., 'The Medieval Hagiography of St Neot', *Analecta Bollandiana* 99 (1981), pp. 259–78

Richards, Mary P., *Texts and Their Traditions in the Medieval Library of Rochester Cathedral Priory*, Transactions of the American Philosophical Society, 78 (Philadelphia: The American Philosophical Society, 1988)

Rigg, A. G., *A History of Anglo-Latin Literature, 1066–1422* (Cambridge: Cambridge University Press, 1992)

Roberts, Jane, 'The English Saints Remembered in Old English Anonymous Homilies', in Paul E. Szarmach (ed.), *Old English Prose Basic Readings* (New York and London: Garland Publishing Inc., 2000), pp. 433–61

Rouse, Robert Allen, *The Idea of Anglo-Saxon England in Middle English Romance* (Cambridge: D. S. Brewer, 2005)

Rumble, A. R. (ed.), *The Reign of Cnut, King of England, Denmark and Norway* (London: Leicester University Press, 1994)

Salzman, Benjamin A., 'Writing Friendship, Mourning the Friend in Late Anglo-Saxon Rules of Confraternity', *Journal of Medieval and Early Modern Studies* 41 (2011), pp. 251–91

Sauer, Hans, 'Knowledge of Old English in the Middle English Period?' in R. Hickey and S. Puppel (eds.), *Language History and Linguistic Modelling: A Festschrift for Jacek Fisiak on his 60th Birthday*, Trends in Linguistics, Studies and Monographs 101 (Berlin, 1997), pp. 791–814

Sayles, W. G., *Ancient Coin Collecting V: the Romaion-Byzantine Culture* (Iola, WI: Octavo, 1998)

Scragg, Donald G., *A Conspectus of Scribal Hands Writing English, 960–1100* (Woodbridge: Boydell & Brewer, 2012)

Scragg, D. G., and P. E. Szarmach (eds.), *The Editing of Old English: Papers from the 1990 Manchester Conference* (Woodbridge: Boydell & Brewer, 1994)

Scragg, D. G., and E. Treharne, 'Appendix: The Three Anonymous Lives in Cambridge, Corpus Christi College 303', in Paul E. Szarmach (ed.), *Holy Men and Holy Women: Old English Prose Saints' Lives and Their Contexts* (Binghamton, NY: SUNY, 1996), pp. 180–4

Sharpe, Richard, 'The prefaces of 'Quadripartitus', in George Garnett and John Hudson (eds.), *Law and Government in Medieval England and Normandy: Essays in honour of Sir James Holt* (Cambridge: Cambridge University Press, 1994), pp. 148–72

Sheppard, Alice, *Families of the King: Writing Identity in the 'Anglo-Saxon Chronicle'* (Toronto: University of Toronto Press, 2004)

Short, Ian, 'Language and Literature', in Harper-Bill and Van Houts, *Companion to the Anglo-Norman World* , pp. 191–213

Short, Ian, 'Patrons and Polyglots: French Literature in Twelfth-Century England', *Anglo-Norman Studies* 14 (1991), pp. 229–49

Short, Ian, '*Tam Angli quam Franci*: Self-Definition in Anglo-Norman England', *Anglo-Norman Studies* 18 (1995), pp. 153–75

Sisam, K., 'Mss. Bodley 340 and 342: Ælfric's *Catholic Homilies*', in K. Sisam, *Studies in the History of Old English Literature* (Oxford: Clarendon Press, 1953), pp. 148–98 [originally published in *Review of English Studies* vii (1931)]

Smalley, B., *The Study of the Bible in the Middle Ages*, 3rd edn. (Oxford: Oxford University Press, 1983)

Smith, Jeremy, *An Historical Study of English: Function, Form and Change* (Routledge: London, 1996)

Stafford, Pauline, *Queen Emma and Queen Edith: Queenship and Women's Power in Eleventh-Century England* (Oxford: Blackwell, 1997)

Stafford, Pauline, 'The laws of Cnut and the history of Anglo-Saxon royal promises', *Anglo-Saxon England* 10 (1982), pp. 173–90

Stafford, Pauline, *Unification and Conquest: A Political and Social History of England in the Tenth and Eleventh Centuries* (London: Hodder Arnold, 1989)

Stenton, Doris M., *English Justice between the Norman Conquest and the Great Charter, 1066–1215* (London: Allen and Unwin, 1965)

Stenton, F. M., *Anglo-Saxon England*, 3rd edn. (Oxford: Oxford University Press, 1971)

Stephenson, Paul, *The Legend of Basil the Bulgar-Slayer* (Cambridge: Cambridge University Press, 2003)

Stokes, Peter A., 'English Vernacular Minuscule, 980–1030', unpub. DPhil dissertation (University of Cambridge, 2005)

Strohm, Paul, *Theory and the Premodern Text*, Medieval Cultures 26 (Minneapolis: University of Minnesota Press, 2000)

Suedfeld, Peter, 'Reactions to Societal Trauma: Distress and/or Eustress', *Political Psychology* 18.4 (1997), pp. 849–61

Swan, Mary, 'Ælfric as Source: The Exploitation of Ælfric's *Catholic Homilies* from the Late Tenth to Twelfth Centuries' (unpub. PhD diss., University of Leeds, 1993)

Swan, Mary, 'Holiness Remodelled: Theme and Technique in Old English Composite Homilies', in Beverly Mayne Kienzle et al. (eds.), *Models of Holiness in Medieval Sermons: Proceedings of the International Symposium (Kalamazoo, 407 May 1995)*, Textes et Études du Moyen Âge. (Louvain-la-Neuve, 1996), pp. 35–46

Swan, Mary, 'Identity and Ideology in Ælfric's Prefaces', in Magennis and Swan, *A Companion to Ælfric*, pp. 247–69

Swan, Mary, 'Old English Made New: One Catholic Homily and its Reuses', *Leeds Studies in English* n.s. 28 (1997), pp. 1–18

Swan, Mary, 'Preaching Past the Conquest: Lambeth Palace 487 and Cotton Vespasian A. XXII', in Kleist, *The Old English Homily*, pp. 403–23

Swan, Mary, and E. M. Treharne (eds.), *Rewriting Old English in the Twelfth Century*, Cambridge Studies in Anglo-Saxon England 30 (Cambridge: Cambridge University Press, 2000)

Szarmach, Paul E. (ed.) *Holy Men and Holy Women: Old English Prose Saints' Lives and Their Contexts* (Albany, NY: SUNY, 1996)

Szarmach, Paul E., and Bernard Huppé (eds.) *The Old English Homily and its Backgrounds* (Albany, NY: SUNY, 1978)

Taavitsainen, Irma, Terttu Nevalainen, Päiva Pahta, and Matti Rissanen (eds.), *Placing Middle English in Context*, Topics in English Linguistics 35 (Berlin: Mouton de Gruyter, 2000)

Taylor, Arnold, '*Hauksbók* and Ælfric's *De Falsis Diis*', *Leeds Studies in English* 3 (1969), pp. 1–9

Teresi, Loredana, 'Ælfric's or Not? The Making of a Temporale Collection in Late Anglo-Saxon England', in Kleist, *The Old English Homily*, pp. 284–310

Thomas, Hugh M., *The English and the Normans: Ethnic Hostility, Assimilation, and Identity, 1066–c.1220* (Oxford: Oxford University Press, 2003)

Thomson, R. M., *Books and Learning in Twelfth-Century England: The Ending of 'Alter Orbis'?* (Stevenage: Red Gull Press, 2007)

Thomson, R. M., *The Bury Bible* (Cambridge: D. S. Brewer, 2002)

Thomson, Rodney M., with Michael Gullick, *Catalogue of the Medieval Manuscripts in Worcester Cathedral Library* (Cambridge: D. S. Brewer, 2001)

Thomson, R. M., 'Malmesbury, William of *(b. c.1090, d.* in or after 1142)', *Oxford Dictionary of National Biography* (Oxford: Oxford University Press, 2004) [http://www.oxforddnb.com/view/article/29461]

Tinti, Francesca, 'From episcopal conception to monastic compilation: Hemming's Cartulary in context', *Early Medieval Europe* 11 (2002), pp. 233–61

Tinti, Francesca, '*Si litterali memorię commendaretur*: memory and cartularies in eleventh-century Worcester', in S. Baxter, et al. (eds.), *Early Medieval Studies in Memory of Patrick Wormald* (Farnham: Ashgate, 2009), pp. 475–97

Tinti, Francesca, *Sustaining Belief: The Church of Worcester from c. 870–1100* (Farnham: Ashgate, 2010)

Townend, Matthew, 'Contextualizing the *Knútsdrápur*: Skaldic Praise-Poetry at the Court of Cnut', *Anglo-Saxon England* 30 (2001), pp. 145–79

Townend, Matthew (ed.), *Knutsdrapur*, in Diana Whaley (ed.), *Skaldic Poetry of the Scandinavian Middle Ages* (forthcoming. See http://skaldic.arts.usyd.edu.au/db.php)

Townend, Matthew, *Language and History in Viking Age England: Linguistic Relations between Speakers of Old Norse and Old English*, Studies in the Early Middle Ages 6 (Turnhout: Brepols, 2002)

Townend, Matthew (ed.), *Wulfstan, Archbishop of York: The Proceedings of the Second Alcuin Conference*, Studies in the Early Middle Ages 10 (Turnhout: Brepols, 2004)

Traxel, Oliver M., *Language Change, Writing and Textual Interference in Post-Conquest Old English Manuscripts: The Evidence of Cambridge, University Library, Ii. 1. 33* (Frankfurt am Main: Peter Lang, 2004)

Treharne, Elaine, 'Bishops and their Texts in the later Eleventh Century: Worcester and Exeter', in Wendy Scase (ed.), *Essays in Manuscript Geography: Vernacular Manuscripts of the English West Midlands from the Conquest to the Sixteenth Century* (Turnhout: Brepols, 2007), pp. 13–28

Treharne, Elaine, 'Cambridge, Corpus Christi College, 303 and the Old English Lives of Saints Margaret, Giles and Nicholas' (unpub. PhD diss., University of Manchester, 1992)

Treharne, Elaine, 'Categorization, Periodization: The Silence of (the) English in the Twelfth Century', in Rita Copeland, Wendy Scase, and David Lawton (ed.), *New Medieval Literatures* 8 (Turnhout: Brepols, 2006), pp. 248–75

Treharne, Elaine, *Gluttons for Punishment: The Drunk and Disorderly in Old English Sermons*, The Annual Brixworth Lecture, 2nd ser., 6 (University of Leicester, 2007)

Treharne, Elaine, 'Introduction', and 'The Production and Script of Manuscripts Containing English Religious Texts in the First-Half of the Twelfth Century', in Treharne and Swan (eds.), *Rewriting Old English*, pp. 1–40

Treharne, Elaine, 'Making their Presence Felt: Readers of Ælfric, c. 1050–1350', in Magennis and Swan (eds.), *A Companion to Ælfric*, pp. 399–422

Treharne, Elaine, 'Manuscript Sources of Old English Poetry', in Gale Owen-Crocker (ed.), *Working with Anglo-Saxon Manuscripts* (Exeter: Exeter University Press, 2009), pp. 88–111

Treharne, Elaine, 'Medieval Manuscripts: The Good, the Bad, the Ugly', in Matt Hussey and Jack Niles (eds.), *The Genesis of Texts: Essays in Honour of A. N. Doane* (Turnhout: Brepols, 2012)

Treharne, Elaine, 'Post-Conquest Old English', in Pulsiano and Treharne, *Blackwell Companion to Anglo-Saxon Literature*, pp. 401–14

Treharne, Elaine, "Producing a Library in Late Anglo-Saxon England: Exeter, 1050–72", *Review of English Studies* n.s. 54 (2003), pp. 155–72

Treharne, Elaine, 'Reading from the Margins: The Uses of Old English Homiletic Manuscripts in the Post-Conquest Period', in A. N. Doane and K. Wolf (eds.), *Beatus Vir: Early English and Norse Manuscript Studies in Memory of Phillip Pulsiano* (MRTS, Arizona, 2006), pp. 329–58

Treharne, Elaine, 'Scribal Connections in late Anglo-Saxon England', in Cate Gunn and Catherine Innes-Parker (ed.), *Texts and Traditions of Medieval Pastoral Care: Essays in Honour of Bella Millett* (Woodbridge: Boydell and Brewer, November 2009), pp. 29–46

Treharne, Elaine, 'The Architextual Editing of Early English', in A.S.G. Edwards and T. Kato (eds.), *Poetica* 71 (2009), pp. 1–13

Treharne, Elaine, 'The Bishop's Book: Leofric's Homiliary and Eleventh-Century Exeter', in Baxter et al., *Early Medieval Studies*, pp. 521–37

Treharne, Elaine, "The Dates and Origins of Three Twelfth-Century Manuscripts', in P. Pulsiano and E. M. Treharne (eds.), *Anglo-Saxon Manuscripts and Their Heritage: Tenth to Twelfth Centuries* (Aldershot: Ashgate, 1998), pp. 227–52

Treharne, Elaine, 'The Form and Function of the Old English *Dicts of Cato*', *Journal of English and Germanic Philology* 102.4 (2003), pp. 65–85

Treharne, Elaine, 'The Life and Times of Old English Homilies for the First Sunday in Lent', in Magennis and Wilcox, *The Power of Words*, pp. 205–42

Treharne, Elaine, 'The Life of English in the Mid-Twelfth Century: Ralph D'Escures's Homily on the Virgin Mary', in Ruth Kennedy and Simon Meecham-Jones (eds.), *Literature of the Reign of Henry II* (London: Routledge, 2006), pp. 169–86

Treharne, Elaine, 'The Politics of Early English', The Toller Memorial Lecture, *Bulletin of the John Rylands University Library of Manchester* (2010 for 2006), 101–22

Treharne, Elaine, 'The Vernaculars of Medieval England, 1170–1350', in Andrew Galloway (ed.), *Cambridge Companion to Medieval Culture* (Cambridge: Cambridge University Press, 2011), pp. 217–36

Treharne, Elaine, 'Writing the Book', in Elaine Treharne, Orietta Da Rold, and Mary Swan (eds.), *Producing and Using English Manuscripts in the Post-Conquest Period*, New Medieval Literatures 13 (special issue, forthcoming, 2012)

Turville-Petre, Thorlac, *England the Nation: Language, Literature, and National Identity, 1290–1340* (Oxford: Oxford University Press, 1996)

Tyler, Elizabeth, 'Talking about History in Eleventh-Century England: the *Encomium Emmae Reginae* and the Court of Harthacnut', *Early Medieval Europe* 13 (2005), pp. 359–83

Upchurch, Robert, 'A Big Dog Barks: Ælfric of Eynsham's Indictment of the English Pastorate and *Witan*', *Speculum* 85 (2010), pp. 505–33

van Caenegem, R. C., *The Birth of the English Common Law*, 2nd edn. (Cambridge: Cambridge University Press, 1988; first publ. 1973)

van der Horst, Koert, William Noel and Wilhelmina C. M. Würstefeld (eds.), *The Utrecht Psalter in Medieval Art* (Universiteit Utrecht: HES Publishers, 1996)

Vleeskruyer, R. (ed.), *The Life of St Chad, An Old English Homily* (Amsterdam: North Holland Publishing Co., 1953)

Walker Bynum, Caroline, *Docere Verbo et Exemplo: An Aspect of Twelfth-Century Spirituality*, (Missoula: UMinnesotaP 1979)

Walker Bynum, Caroline, *Jesus as Mother: Studies in the Spirituality of the High Middle Ages* (Berkeley: University of California Press, 1982)

Wallace, David (ed.), *The Cambridge History of Medieval English Literature* (Cambridge: Cambridge University Press, 1999)

Warren, Michelle R., *History on the Edge: Excalibur and the Borders of Britain, 1100–1300*, Medieval Cultures 22 (Minneapolis: University of Minnesota Press, 2000)

Webber, Teresa, *Scribes and Scholars at Salisbury Cathedral, c. 1075–c. 1125* (Oxford, 1992)

Webber, Teresa, 'Script and Manuscript Production at Christ Church, Canterbury, after the Norman Conquest', in Richard Eales and Richard Sharpe (eds.), *Canterbury and the Norman Conquest: Churches, Saints and Scholars, 1066–1109* (London: Hambledon Press, 1995), pp. 145–58

Webber, Teresa, 'The Script', in Gibson et al., *The Eadwine Psalter*, pp. 13–24

Whitelock, Dorothy, 'Wulfstan and the Laws of Cnut', *English Historical Review* 63 (1948), pp. 433–52

Wilcox, Jonathan, 'Wulfstan's *Sermo Lupi ad Anglos* as Political Performance', in Townend, *Wulfstan of York*, pp. 375–96

Williams, Anne, 'England in the Eleventh Century' in Harper-Bill and Van Houts, *Companion to the Anglo-Norman World*, pp. 1–18

Williams, Anne, 'The Spoliation of Worcester', *Anglo-Norman Studies* 19 (1999), pp. 383–408

Withers, Benjamin, 'Unfulfilled promise: the rubrics of the Old English Prose Genesis', *Anglo-Saxon England* 28 (1999), pp. 111–39

Wormald, Patrick, 'Archbishop Wulfstan: Eleventh-Century State-Builder', in Townend, *Wulfstan, Archbishop of York*, pp. 9–27

Wormald, Patrick, *Legal Culture in the Early Medieval West: Law as Text, Image and Experience* (London: Hambledon, 1999)

Wormald, Patrick, *The Making of English Law: King Alfred to the Twelfth Century. Volume I: Legislation and its Limits* (Oxford: Blackwell, 1999)

Wormald, Patrick, 'Wulfstan (d. 1023)', *Oxford Dictionary of National Biography* (Oxford University Press, 2004) [http://www.oxforddnb.com.proxy.lib.fsu.edu/view/article/30098, accessed 18 July 2010]

Young, Robert C., *Postcolonialism: A very short introduction* (Oxford: Oxford University Press, 2003)

Younge, George, 'The Canterbury Anthology: an Old English Manuscript in its Anglo-Norman Context' (unpub. PhD diss., University of Cambridge, forthcoming 2012)

Younge, George, 'The Compiler of London, British Library, Cotton Vespasian D. xiv, fols 4–169, and his Audience', in Orietta Da Rold and A. S. G. Edwards (eds.), *English Manuscript Studies 1100–1700* (forthcoming 2012)

Zarnecki, George, 'The Eadwine Portrait' in Sumner McKnight Crosby, et al., *Études d'art médiéval offertes à Louis Grodecki* (Paris: Ophrys, 1981), pp. 93–8

Zumthor, Paul, *Towards a Medieval Poetics* (Minneapolis: University of Minnesota Press, 1992)

INDEX OF MANUSCRIPTS

Note: See pages 99–101 and 125–26 for lists of (predominantly) literary manuscripts and fragments written in English from *c.* 1060 to *c.* 1220. The Index below concerns discussion of individual manuscripts.

GENERAL INDEX